Security Challenges and Opportunities of Artificial Intelligence/Big Data Scenarios

Security Challenges and Opportunities of Artificial Intelligence/Big Data Scenarios

Guest Editors

Xiaodan Yan

Ke Yan

Muyi Sun

MDPI

Basel • Beijing • Wuhan • Barcelona • Belgrade • Novi Sad • Cluj • Manchester

Guest Editors
Xiaodan Yan
School of Electronic Engineering
Beijing University of Posts and Telecommunications
Beijing
China

Ke Yan
Department of Mechanical and Electrical Engineering
Hunan University
Changsha
China

Muyi Sun
School of Electronic Engineering
Beijing University of Posts and Telecommunications
Beijing
China

Editorial Office
MDPI AG
Grosspeteranlage 5
4052 Basel, Switzerland

This is a reprint of the Special Issue, published open access by the journal *Electronics* (ISSN 2079-9292), freely accessible at: https://www.mdpi.com/journal/electronics/special_issues/9AK926T3HV.

For citation purposes, cite each article independently as indicated on the article page online and as indicated below:

Lastname, A.A.; Lastname, B.B. Article Title. *Journal Name* **Year**, *Volume Number*, Page Range.

ISBN 978-3-7258-7380-7 (Hbk)
ISBN 978-3-7258-7381-4 (PDF)
https://doi.org/10.3390/books978-3-7258-7381-4

Contents

About the Editors

Xiaodan Yan

Xiaodan Yan is an associate professor at the School of Electronic Engineering, Beijing University of Posts and Telecommunications (BUPT), where he also serves as a master's supervisor and a supported talent of the "Tuoju Talent Program". His research interests focus on satellite laser networking, integrated security of satellite internet, security of optical communication systems and optical networks, multimodal large language models (including multimodal cognitive computing and large model security and governance), as well as artificial intelligence and big data security. He has undertaken a series of key research projects, including national defense vertical research projects, the National Natural Science Foundation of China Youth Fund Project, the China Postdoctoral Science Foundation General Program, the BUPT Introduction Talent Research Start-up Project, and horizontal projects cooperating with Tencent and People's Education Press; in terms of teaching reform, he is responsible for the key construction project of BUPT's "Challenge Course" established in 2024. He serves as a letter review expert for national-level projects, a Guest Editor for the *Electronics* and *Sensors* journals, and a committee member of the Cognitive and Behavioral Special Committee of the Chinese Command and Control Society. Having obtained his doctoral degree from BUPT in 2020, he was selected to be a part of Beihang University's "Outstanding Hundred Postdoctoral Support Program" in the same year, and now conducts his research relying on the State Key Laboratory of Information Photonics and Optical Communications.

Ke Yan

Ke Yan is a professor and doctoral supervisor at the College of Mechanical and Vehicle Engineering, Hunan University, with his academic affiliation in the discipline of Management Science and Engineering. Dr. Yan Ke was ranked in the world's leading 2% scientists selected by Stanford University in 2020, 2021, and 2022 (consecutive single years), and was also recognized for his whole career in 2022. He is an internationally recognized expert in the fields of AI, IoT, smart buildings, and smart environments. Dr. Yan Ke has worked in many overseas universities, institutes, and research groups, gaining research experiences and maintaining long-term cooperative relationships with professors from those universities and institutes. He currently serves on the Editorial Boards of several academic journals, including *IEEE Transactions on Industrial Informatics, IEEE/ACM Transactions on Computational Biology and Bioinformatics, Building and Environment,* and *Frontiers of Engineering Management.* As of January 30, 2023, he has published more than 70 SCI papers, with a total citation count of 3000+ and an H-index of 32. Dr. Yan Ke's main research interests include intelligent buildings, information-based building management systems, the design of automatic fault diagnosis systems for air-conditioning equipment, building total energy management, energy consumption prediction, and photovoltaic (PV) power generation forecasting.

Muyi Sun

Muyi Sun is an Associate Research Fellow at the Vision Perception and Generation Laboratory, School of Artificial Intelligence, Beijing University of Posts and Telecommunications (BUPT), with a Ph.D. in Control Science and Engineering from BUPT. Previously, he was a Postdoctoral Researcher at the Institute of Automation, Chinese Academy of Sciences. His core research focuses on multi-modal medical image analysis and multi-modal human-centric generation, covering technologies like Transformer, GAN, and diffusion models. He has led projects including the National Natural Science Foundation of China Youth Funding Project and the China Postdoctoral Science Foundation Special Funding Project, and served as a System Review Expert for the National Natural Science Foundation of China. As a first or corresponding author, he has published papers in top journals and conferences such as *IJCV*, *TMI*, *TIFS*, *CVPR*, and *ACM MM*, with his work "AnyFace" selected as a *CVPR* 2022 Best Paper Finalist and winning the *IEEE ICAMechS* Best Paper Award. He also acts as a reviewer for over 20 leading journals/conferences, serves as a Guest Editor for *Electronics*, teaches AI-related courses, and has guided students to win national/provincial competitions and secure the Beijing Natural Science Foundation "QiYan" Project.

electronics

MDPI

Article

The Impact of Security Protocols on TCP/UDP Throughput in IEEE 802.11ax Client–Server Network: An Empirical Study

Nurul I. Sarkar [1,*], Nasir Faiz [1] and Md Jahan Ali [2]

1 Department of Computer and Information Sciences, Auckland University of Technology, Auckland 1010, New Zealand; faiz.nasir@outlook.com
2 Department of IT and Electrical Engineering, International College of Auckland, Auckland 1010, New Zealand; jahan.a@ica.ac.nz
* Correspondence: nurul.sarkar@aut.ac.nz; Tel.: +64-211758390

Abstract

IEEE 802.11ax (Wi-Fi 6) technologies provide high capacity, low latency, and increased security. While many network researchers have examined Wi-Fi security issues, the security implications of 802.11ax have not been fully explored yet. Therefore, in this paper, we investigate how security protocols (WPA2, WPA3) affect TCP/UDP throughput in IEEE 802.11ax client–server networks using a testbed approach. Through an extensive performance study, we analyze the effect of security on transport layer protocol (TCP/UDP), internet protocol layer (IPV4/IPV6), and operating systems (MS Windows and Linux) on system performance. The impact of packet length on system performance is also investigated. The obtained results show that WPA3 offers greater security, and its impact on TCP/UDP throughput is insignificant, highlighting the robustness of WPA3 encryption in maintaining throughput even in secure environments. With WPA3, UDP offers higher throughput than TCP and IPv6 consistently outperforms IPv4 in terms of both TCP and UDP throughput. Linux outperforms Windows in all scenarios, especially with larger packet sizes and IPv6 traffic. These results suggest that WPA3 provides optimized throughput performance in both Linux and MS Windows in 802.11ax client–server environments. Our research provides some insights into the security issues in Gigabit Wi-Fi that can help network researchers and engineers to contribute further towards developing greater security for next-generation wireless networks.

Keywords: IEEE 802.11ax; security; Wi-Fi 6; TCP/UDP; WPA3; packet loss; throughput

1. Introduction

The IEEE 802.11ax (Wi-Fi 6) standard, released in 2018, represents a major step toward improving wireless performance by supporting higher capacity, reduced latency, and more efficient spectrum utilization [1]. Unlike its predecessor (802.11ac), 802.11ax operates on both 2.4 GHz and 5 GHz bands, making it well-suited for IoT and dense environments. More recently, Wi-Fi 7 (802.11be) has emerged, but Wi-Fi 6 remains widely deployed in enterprise and residential networks due to its maturity and compatibility [2,3].

While the technical features of Wi-Fi 6, such as OFDMA and MU-MIMO, have been extensively documented in the literature [1,2,4–9], less attention has been paid to the interaction between these features and advanced security protocols. WPA3, introduced in 2018, was designed to replace WPA2 with stronger encryption, resistance to brute-force attacks, and improved protection in public networks. However, the impact of WPA3 on real-world IEEE 802.11ax performance remains underexplored.

 https://doi.org/10.3390/electronics14193890

IEEE 802.11ax client–server networks have become central to evaluating Wi-Fi 6 performance in real-world deployments. Unlike simulation-only environments, client–server testbeds allow for the empirical measurement of throughput, latency, jitter, and packet loss under controlled conditions. Several studies have analyzed Wi-Fi 6 enhancements such as MU-MIMO, OFDMA, and higher-order modulation in client–server setups, but most of these works have focused on baseline MAC/PHY performance or secured connections [10,11]. Very few have examined the effect of WPA3 in such environments, despite its growing importance as the default security protocol for modern networks. This study builds on client–server methodologies to investigate how WPA2 and WPA3 influence TCP/UDP throughput in IEEE 802.11ax networks, thereby extending the scope of prior research to address both performance and security dimensions.

Most prior studies have focused on WPA2 or older standards (e.g., IEEE 802.11ac), often using simulation environments with limited validation in practical testbeds [3,12–14]. Few have examined WPA3 empirically in Wi-Fi 6 networks, particularly across transport protocols (TCP/UDP), network protocols (IPv4/IPv6), and different operating systems.

This study addresses that gap by conducting a testbed-based evaluation of WPA2 and WPA3 in IEEE 802.11ax client–server networks. Specifically, we analyze throughput, jitter, and packet loss under varying packet sizes, transport protocols, and operating systems (Windows and Linux). The findings provide practical insights into the performance–security trade-offs in Wi-Fi 6 and demonstrate that WPA3 can deliver strong security while maintaining optimized throughput.

1.1. Research Challenges

In this study, we address the following three research questions/challenges:

Research Question 1: What impact does WPA3 have on throughput performance of 802.11ax client–server networks?

To address Research Question 1, we identify and discuss the key factors influencing security protocols affecting the performance of 802.11ax networks. These factors include encryption overhead, key management, and protocol negotiation times. The proposed solution involves analyzing WPA3 protocols in both personal and enterprise settings using a RADIUS server for enterprise-level authentication. WPA3 introduces small overheads due to its advanced encryption, but it ensures greater security and maintains high throughput in 802.11ax networks due to the efficiency of the protocol in high-density environments.

Research Question 2: What impact do transport layer protocols (TCP and UDP) have on throughput performance of IEEE 802.11ax client–server network across both IPv4 and IPv6 for varying packet sizes?

The selection of transport protocols (TCP or UDP) can significantly influence network performance, particularly when combined with IP protocols (IPv4 vs. IPv6) and varying packet sizes. The connection-oriented nature of TCP contrasts with the connectionless approach of UDP, leading to differences in overhead, which in turn affects throughput and latency.

To explore Research Question 2, we examine the specific factors that distinguish the impact of TCP and UDP on network performance in both IPv4 and IPv6 environments. The key factors include protocol overhead, packet loss, and throughput efficiency. In our methodology, both TCP and UDP protocols were implemented and tested across IPv4 and IPv6 networks using different packet sizes. The findings revealed that UDP, being connectionless, delivered lower latency but experienced higher packet loss compared to TCP. Conversely, TCP, due to its connection-oriented design, achieved higher throughput, particularly with larger packet sizes. Additionally, IPv6 demonstrated slightly improved performance with large packets, attributed to its more efficient header structure.

Research Question 3: What impact does multi-user MIMO (MU-MIMO) have on the performance of 802.11ax networks, and how can security protocols (WPA3) be optimized to support this?

The IEEE 802.11ax introduces uplink and downlink MU-MIMO, allowing for multiple devices to communicate simultaneously. However, managing multiple simultaneous connections in high-density environments (e.g., public places or large offices) poses challenges for maintaining high throughput and low latency, especially when security protocols like WPA3 are applied. The complexity of securing these parallel connections without degrading performance needs to be explored.

To address Research Question 3, we assess the various dynamics that influence the performance of MU-MIMO in high-density environments, including channel interference, device synchronization, and security overhead. The proposed solution implements uplink and downlink MU-MIMO in IEEE 802.11ax networks with WPA3 encryption and tests performance in crowded scenarios. Our results show that MU-MIMO significantly improves throughput by allowing for multiple devices to communicate simultaneously. However, the additional encryption overhead from WPA3 introduces minimal delays in device synchronization. To mitigate this, we propose optimizing WPA3 key management and encryption algorithms, ensuring that security does not negatively impact MU-MIMO performance.

1.2. Research Scope and Contribution

The main contributions of this paper are outlined as follows:

- We provide an in-depth evaluation of 802.11ax security protocols (WPA2 and WPA3) in client–server networks. To this end, we thoroughly investigated the impact of WPA2 and WPA3 on system performance in both personal and enterprise networking environments.
- We optimize WPA3 performance in high-density environments by reducing the overhead introduced by advanced encryption processes, ensuring both security and efficiency in wireless communication. To this end, we demonstrate the effect of these security protocols on network throughput.
- We provide a comparative analysis of the impact of transport layer protocols (TCP and UDP) on system performance for IPv6 network layer protocol. To this end, we provide a detailed comparison of TCP and UDP protocols, analyzing their performance across both IPv4 and IPv6 802.11ax networks. By varying packet lengths, we examined protocol efficiency, packet loss, and latency. This contribution provides an insight into the optimal transport protocols and packet lengths for achieving higher throughput and reliability in both legacy and modern IP networks Wi-Fi 6 standards.
- We study the performance optimization of Multi-User Multiple-Input Multiple-Output (MU-MIMO) in high-density 802.11ax networks. To this end, we investigate the impact of uplink and downlink MU-MIMO in 802.11ax in high-density environments, focusing on the synchronization and management of multiple devices. We also explored the methods of security protocols like WPA3 that could be optimized to maintain high throughput and low latency in such settings. Our study demonstrates practical methods to improve MU-MIMO performance, enabling efficient multi-user communication in dense networks while ensuring robust security.

1.3. Structure of the Paper

The related works on 802.11ax Wi-Fi security protocols and network performance are presented in Section 2. The research methodology is discussed in Section 3. The system evaluation, test results, and analysis of the impact of security protocols (WPA2, WPA3), transport protocols (TCP, UDP), and IP versions (IPv4, IPv6) on system performance are presented in Section 4. The benefits and practical implications are discussed in Section 5. Finally, the paper is concluded in Section 6.

2. Background and Related Work

IEEE 802.11ax, also known as Wi-Fi 6, represents a significant evolution in wireless networking technology. It addresses growing demands for high-speed, high-capacity wireless communication, especially in dense environments such as offices, stadiums, and urban areas. While Wi-Fi 6 promises substantial improvements over its predecessor (IEEE 802.11ac), particularly in terms of throughput, latency, and capacity, several factors influence its real-world performance, including security protocols, transport layers (TCP/UDP), and network layers (IPv4/IPv6). These factors are crucial when assessing the practical application of Wi-Fi 6 in diverse environments [3,11–13,15–17].

Wi-Fi 6 introduces several key features that distinguish it from previous Wi-Fi standards. Orthogonal Frequency Division Multiple Access (OFDMA) and MU-MIMO significantly enhance the efficiency and capacity of the network by enabling simultaneous data transmission from multiple devices. The enhanced Basic Service Set (BSS) coloring feature reduces interference in high-density environments, further improving throughput [11].

The work by Khorov et al. [13] provides an in-depth analysis of the enhancements brought by 802.11ax, particularly in crowded environments. Their study shows that the standard is well-suited to handle the increasing proliferation of IoT devices, smart appliances, and other connected devices, which require stable and high-capacity wireless networks. However, while Wi-Fi 6 offers numerous advancements, its performance is subject to various external factors, especially in relation to the security protocols that protect data integrity and user privacy [13]. Security protocols are vital for safeguarding wireless networks, particularly in enterprise and public environments. The WPA3 protocol, introduced to replace WPA2, provides enhanced encryption and better protection against brute-force attacks. However, the trade-off is the additional computational overhead introduced by WPA3, which can degrade network performance, especially in bandwidth-intensive applications.

Wi-Fi PPDU begins with a Short Training Field (STF) for coarse synchronization and AGC convergence, followed by a Long Training Field (LTF) for channel estimation and fine timing/frequency offset correction; the data field then carries the encoded payload. This legacy framing remains foundational across modern amendments, including IEEE 802.11ax, and is orthogonal to higher-layer security (WPA2/WPA3), which operates above the PHY [18].

Alghamdi [17] conducted a comparative analysis of WPA2, and WPA3 security protocols on Wi-Fi networks and found that WPA3's advanced encryption mechanisms introduced significant latency and reduced throughput compared to WPA2. However, the existing literature has focused primarily on isolated environments, and there is limited research on the interaction between security protocols and other network layers, such as the transport and internet layers. This research addresses this gap by critically examining the effect of WPA2 and WPA3 on Wi-Fi 6 performance in different transport (TCP/UDP) and network layers (IPv4/IPv6) to provide a more holistic understanding of how security protocols influence network performance in real-world applications. The transition from IPv4 to IPv6 has been a major focus in recent networking literature, driven by the growing demand for IP addresses due to the proliferation of IoT devices and mobile technology. IPv6 offers a larger address space, better routing efficiency, and enhanced support for mobile networks, making it more suitable for modern networking needs. It also eliminates the need for Network Address Translation (NAT), reducing overhead and improving performance [19]. Deng et al. [20] demonstrated that IPv6 generally outperforms IPv4 in Wi-Fi networks, particularly in terms of latency and throughput. However, these studies focused primarily on earlier Wi-Fi standards such as IEEE 802.11ac, and there is limited research on how IPv6 performs in Wi-Fi 6 environments, particularly in combination with advanced security protocols like WPA3. WPA3 was introduced in 2018 as a successor to WPA2 to strengthen wireless security against emerging attacks. Its main motivations include stronger protection against brute-force dictionary attacks, forward secrecy, and improved usability in open networks. WPA3-Personal employs the Simultaneous Authentication of Equals (SAE) key exchange, which is resistant to offline password-guessing attacks, while WPA3-Enterprise supports 192-bit minimum security. Encryption is achieved using AES-256-GCMP and, in some configurations, ChaCha20-Poly1305. Additionally, WPA3 introduces Opportunistic Wireless Encryption (OWE) for encrypting open networks without requiring credentials. Our empirical findings—minimal throughput degradation (<4%)—are consistent with WPA3's intended design of balancing robust security with high performance.

MU-MIMO is one of the most important features of Wi-Fi 6, allowing multiple devices to communicate simultaneously with the access point. This significantly enhances network capacity and reduces latency in high-density environments. However, managing multiple connections poses challenges, particularly when security protocols like WPA3 are in place. Hoefel [11] explored the impact of MU-MIMO on network performance in Wi-Fi 6 networks and found that while MU-MIMO improves throughput, it also increases the complexity of device synchronization, especially when encryption is enabled. Additionally, packet size plays a significant role in determining network performance. Larger packets generally lead to higher throughput but can cause more packet loss in congested networks. Tsetse et al. [3] showed that packet size optimization is crucial for balancing throughput and latency in Wi-Fi networks.

The literature highlights significant advancements in Wi-Fi 6 technology, particularly in terms of throughput, latency, and efficiency. However, the interaction between security protocols, transport layers, and network layers remains underexplored. While WPA3 offers enhanced security, its impact on network performance is substantial, particularly when combined with TCP/UDP protocols and IPv4/IPv6 configurations. By critically analyzing these interactions, this research contributes to the optimization of Wi-Fi 6 networks for both performance and security, addressing the gaps identified in the existing literature. Deng et al. [9] provide a comprehensive evaluation of IEEE 802.11ax WLANs, emphasizing its ability to enhance throughput and spectral efficiency. The study highlights the role of OFDMA in enabling simultaneous transmission to multiple users, thereby reducing contention and improving network efficiency. Similarly, Weller et al. [15] focus on the performance measurement of 1024-QAM and downlink OFDMA, demonstrating significant improvements in data rates and spectral efficiency. Their findings indicate that these features are particularly effective in environments with high user density, such as stadiums and urban areas. However, the performance gains of Wi-Fi 6 are not without challenges. Qu et al. [7] note that the efficient deployment of Wi-Fi 6 requires careful configuration and management of network resources. For instance, the dynamic allocation of OFDMA subcarriers and the optimization of MU-MIMO transmissions are critical for maximizing throughput. The study also highlights the need for robust interference management techniques to mitigate the impact of co-channel interference in dense deployments.

Alghamdi [5] examines the impact of security protocols on the performance of WLANs, focusing on IEEE 802.11ac. The study highlights the trade-offs between security and performance, noting that encryption and authentication mechanisms can introduce significant overhead, thereby reduce throughput and increase latency. While the study predates Wi-Fi 6, its findings are relevant for understanding the security-performance trade-offs in modern WLANs. Tsetse et al. [3] extend this analysis to IEEE 802.11ac networks, demonstrating that the overhead associated with security protocols can have a pronounced impact on network performance. Their findings suggest that the implementation of advanced security mechanisms in Wi-Fi 6 must be carefully balanced against the need for high throughput and low latency.

The studies provide valuable insights into the performance and security of Wi-Fi 6 networks. However, several gaps remain in the literature. First, there is limited research on the interaction between advanced security mechanisms and the performance of Wi-Fi 6 in high-density environments. Second, the impact of Wi-Fi 6E on network security requires further investigation, particularly in the context of emerging threats and vulnerabilities. Finally, more work is needed to address the challenges of deploying Wi-Fi 6 in real-world scenarios, including interference management, resource allocation, and the optimization of security protocols. The summary of related work is presented in Table 1.

Table 1. Summary of related work on impact of security protocols on Wi-Fi client–server network.

Reference	Scope	Transport Layer (TCP/UDP)?	IP Layer (IPv4/v6)?	Gigabit Wi-Fi Security?	Testbed Approach?
[12]	Overview of 802.11	×	×	×	×
[9]	Performance evaluation of 802.11ax	√	×	×	√
[19]	802.11ax performance for Infrastructure	√	√	×	√
[15]	Wi-Fi 6 performance of 1024-QAM and DL OFDMA	√	×	√	√
[16]	Wireless security in Wi-Fi 6e networks	×	×	√	×
[7]	Survey and performance evaluation of 802.11ax	√	√	√	√
[5]	Throughput analysis of 802.11ac security	√	×	√	√
[4]	Impact of security on 802.11ac networks	√	×	√	√
[13]	Tutorial on 802.11ax high efficiency WLANs	√	√	×	√
	Exploring Wi-Fi 6 security	√	√	√	√
Our work	Investigated the effect of Wi-Fi 6 Security on TCP/UDP throughput and packet losses in client–server networks using a testbed approach.				

3. Methods

3.1. *Research Methodology Adopted*

We employ a test-bed measurement approach to study the system performance. Research methodologies are typically categorized into three main types: qualitative analysis, quantitative analysis, and a mixed-method approach that combines both. For this study, a quantitative approach was adopted (testbed) to evaluate the network's performance.

In this study we focus on system throughput performance. We also measure jitter and packet losses empirically. The network performance metrics that we considered are briefly discussed next.

- Throughput: Throughput is the quantity of application layer data transferred across the network. It is the rate at which messages are transmitted from source to the destination node. For instance, a network throughput is the average data rate (measured in bits per second) across the network. For maximum performance, all packets must be able to get to the right destination without any errors. If an excessive number of packets are losing their way during transmission, the network's performance is likely to be dropped. Therefore, it is crucial to keep track of network traffic speed. It can help gain the visibility of network performance in real-time and provide better understanding of the rate of delivery of packets. The network's throughput average is generally believed to reflect the network's overall performance accurately. The fact that if network throughput performance is not optimal indicating an issue with packet loss or network congestion on the network.
- Packet Loss: Packet losses occur when some or all the data packets moving over a network do not reach their destination. Loss of packets in the TCP connection can also

prevent congestion and deliberately reduce the speed of the connections. For example, for UDP Down to 60 Mbps and losses 40% indicating that during the most recent test cycle, the server sent one megabit of data in 10 milliseconds, and the client received 0.6 megabits in 10 milliseconds, with 0.4 megabits lost in transit. It is usually the reason for the loss of packets. There are two primary protocols that can be transmitted: either TCP or User Datagram Protocol (UDP) transport layer protocol. The TCP needs a reliable connection to send traffic. It returns to the packets lost in times with a very high delay and resends them until they reach their destination. When using UDP traffic, there is no automated transmission for lost packets. However, UDP is utilized in live streaming applications (e.g., VoIP and video traffic), handling specific amounts of loss of packets.

- Jitter: Information is transferred to data packets transmitted over the network. Jitter is a measure of delay variance (in milliseconds) experienced by the packets of the same flow. For real-time applications (e.g., voice and video), the packets must be released to the destination in the correct order and at the same rate released at the source. The buffer at the client (called de-jitter buffer) compensates for the jitter introduced by the network if the delay variation is not too much. It is usually caused by congestion on networks, and occasionally, routes change.

3.2. Research Methods

The purpose of empirical study (testbed) was to observe live network performance using real hardware/software. The client–server network testbed is shown on Figure 1. It consists of a Server, an 802.11ax Access point/Router (TP-Link) and a wireless client (802.11ax laptop). The server is connected to TP-Link Router with a category 6 (CAT6) cable (1 Gbps).

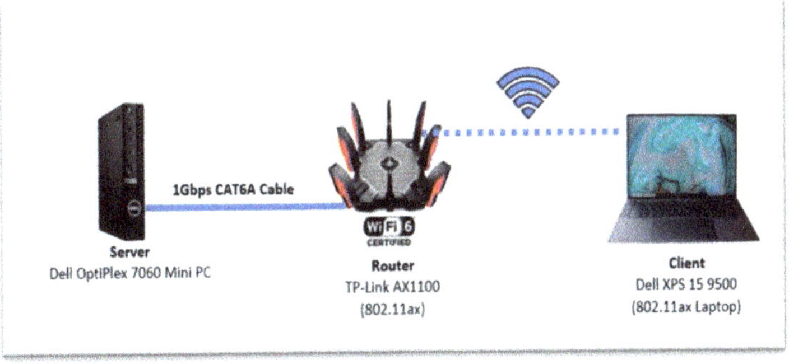

Figure 1. The Gigabit Wi-Fi 6 (802.11ax) client–server network testbed.

The AP provides IEEE 802.11ax MU-MIMO (DL/UL) with explicit beamforming. Experiments used a client–server topology employing two spatial streams; MU-MIMO support remained enabled at the AP throughout, so the measured WPA2/WPA3 overhead reflects a MU-MIMO-capable Wi-Fi 6 deployment, even without scaling to concurrent multi-client traffic. The AP and client were positioned 3 m in a controlled laboratory environment to minimize interference. The testbed operated in the 5 GHz band with a 160 MHz channel width, using channel 48 (5.2 GHz) to ensure interference-free communication. The AX11000 was configured with downlink and uplink MU-MIMO enabled and explicit beamforming active. While our trials exercised a single AP–client flow with two spatial streams, the AP operated under 802.11ax MU-scheduling, so contention/allocation and PHY features active in Wi-Fi 6 were preserved. This ensures measured WPA2/WPA3 effects reflect a MU-MIMO-capable configuration even without concurrent multi-client traffic.

Although the router supported up to eight spatial streams, only two were utilized in our experiments. To enhance reliability, each experiment was repeated ten times and average values were reported. Background interference was further minimized by isolating the AP and conducting tests outside peak usage hours. Link adaptation was active on both AP and client with support up to MCS11 (1024-QAM); in our low-interference 3 m LoS setup, the link typically held high MCS indices, consistent with the high throughputs reported. The AP was run in 802.11ax mode with OFDMA and 1024-QAM enabled, consistent with device defaults. This ensures measurements capture Wi-Fi 6 PHY/MAC efficiencies when assessing WPA2/WPA3 overheads. To isolate the effects of the security protocols, several variables were controlled:

- AP and client were placed at a fixed distance of 3 m in line-of-sight.
- No physical barriers were present.
- Tests used an isolated 5 GHz channel (channel 48 at 5.2 GHz) during low-usage hours to minimize interference.
- All experiments were repeated under identical laboratory conditions.

The evaluation considered the transport layer (TCP/UDP), network layer (IPv4/IPv6), and WPA2/WPA3 security protocols. As a baseline, system performance was first measured in an open configuration (no security), after which WPA2 and WPA3 were enabled for further analysis. In all scenarios, the router was configured solely as an 802.11ax access point, while Windows Firewall and Antivirus were disabled to prevent interference with measurements. This methodology enabled a systematic investigation of Wi-Fi 6 security and its impact on throughput, jitter, and packet loss in a Gigabit client–server environment.

3.3. Protocol Configurations and Measurement Tools

IPerf [21] is as an open-source network analysis tool to measure network bandwidth. For protocol configuration, WPA2 and WPA3 were implemented in Personal mode using WPA2-PSK (AES) and WPA3-SAE (AES-256-GCMP) The main analysis uses Personal mode (WPA2-PSK/AES and WPA3-SAE/AES-256-GCMP). WPA3-Enterprise with RADIUS (192-bit minimum security) was configured and validated for consistency, but quantitative results presented correspond to Personal-mode trials, which dominate client–server deployments. The AP was also tested in Open System mode (no encryption) for baseline comparison. In enterprise scenarios, WPA3-Enterprise was configured with a RADIUS server supporting 192-bit minimum cryptographic strength. Default recommended security configurations were used to ensure alignment with industry practice. This tool offers client/server network functionality to measure throughput between nodes. iPerf generates TCP and UDP traffic loads between two hosts. It determines the maximum network bandwidth (throughput) between a server and a client to perform stress testing on the network's communication channel. It is compatible with Linux and Windows operating systems for various parameters as shown in Table 2, including TCP and UDP with IPv4 and IPv6 protocols. Although industry-standard tools such as Netperf and Nuttcp are widely used, iPerf3 was chosen for its cross-platform compatibility (Linux/Windows), detailed throughput/jitter/loss statistics, and scripting integration for repeatability. For TCP experiments, we used the default congestion control algorithms: CUBIC on Linux and NewReno on Windows. Default flow control and congestion window parameters were retained to reflect typical system configurations. Jitter values are taken from iPerf3 per-UDP-stream reports and represent the variance of inter-packet arrival times at the receiver. For TCP, iPerf3 reports near-zero jitter because reliability mechanisms (ACKs/retransmission/flow control) mask inter-arrival variation at the application layer.

Table 2. Parameters used in the investigation.

Parameter	Value
Network Configuration	Client/Server
Security Protocol	Disable
Transport layer protocol	TCP/UDP
IP Version	IPv4 and IP6
Packet Size	128 Kb
Bandwidth/data rate	1024 Mbps
Time	30 s

3.4. Windows Testbed Setup (Microsoft Windows, 64-Bit)

The objective of the Windows testing method is to assess the performance of the network using iPerf3 as a network testing tool on both the server and client sides. By running iPerf3 on a Windows Server and connecting it with a Windows Client, the experiment measures the network's bandwidth and performance under specific parameters such as packet size, bandwidth, and duration. The test evaluates the effectiveness of IPv4 communication, with a focus on throughput and data transfer efficiency over a 30 s window. The results provide insights into the network's capacity to handle varying packet sizes and bandwidth settings under controlled conditions. The following commands parameters of windows have been set for the testing purposes as shown in Table 3.

Table 3. Technical specifications for setting up a testbed.

Hardware/Software	Function	Technical Specifications
TP-Link AX11000 Tri-Band Router (Ubuntu 22.04 LTS, kernel 5.15)	Wireless router	AX11000 delivers Wi-Fi speed over 10 Gbps
Dell XPS 15 9500	Client	Intel Core i7-10750H@ 2.60 GHz 16 GB DDR4 Ram Intel Wi-Fi 6 AX1650s Wireless Network Adapter 160 MHz
Dell OptiPlex 7060	Server	Intel i5-8500T 2.1-GHz 8 GB DDR4 RAM Intel 7 I219-LM Gigabit Ethernet Adapter
IPerf 3	Traffic generator/collector	
CommView for Wi-Fi	Wireless monitoring tool	802.11 a/b/g/n/ac/ax networks
MS Windows OS (Windows 10 (64-bit))	Server and Client	Windows 10 (64-bit)

4. Results

The client–server network (Windows-based) testbed was set up and configured to study the system performance. The investigation centered on four primary performance metrics including MS Windows TCP and UDP throughput, jitters, and packet losses (IPv4 vs. IPv6). These results and comparative analysis provide a deeper understanding of the impact of security protocols on system performance in varying packet lengths. After the initial observation, we obtain TCP/UDP throughput for open security, WPA2, and WPA3 utilizing both IPv4 and IPv6 traffic. It is important to note that jitter and packet losses are also measured and analyses. The UDP traffic analysis is particularly relevant to connectionless communication protocols where packet timing and loss significantly impact the system performance. This structured approach enabled a thorough evaluation of the interplay between security protocols, transport layers, and IP versions in the Windows environment. The system performance measurement and analysis are structured through six studies presented next.

(i) Study 1: Throughput performance

In Figure 2a, we plot packet length versus TCP throughput for WPA2 and WPA3 security protocols for both IPv4 and IPv6 client–server (MS Windows 10) network. The results for open security (device security turn off) are also presented for comparison purposes. Likewise, the impact of Wi-Fi 6 security on UDP throughput is shown in Figure 2b.

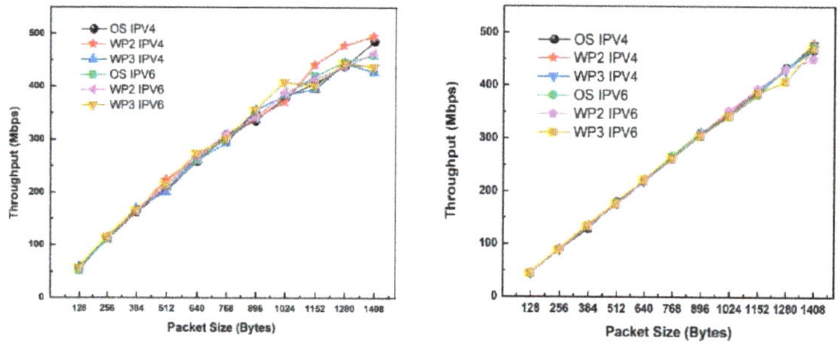

(**a**) TCP Throughput (**b**) UDP Throughput

Figure 2. Effect of Wi-Fi 6 Security (Open system, WPA2 and WPA3) on throughput performance in IPV4 and IPV6 network (**a**) TCP Throughput; and (**b**) UDP Throughput.

Generally, TCP throughput increases as packet length increases. In an open network, IPv4 considerably outperforms IPv6 for all packet sizes. The noticeable difference was observed at packet length of 1024-byte IPv6 outperforms IPv4 by 23% at this packet size (520 Mbps for IPv6 compared to 400 Mbps for IPv4), which offers a 120 Mbps increase in throughput.

For WPA2, IPv6 outperforms IPv4 for all packet sizes. IPv6 outperforms IPv4 by 21% (480 Mbps for IPv6 and 380 Mbps for IPv4) and offers a maximum throughput increase of 100 Mbps. For WPA3, the maximum difference in throughput is spotted at packet length of 1024 bytes. IPv6 offers higher throughput than IPv4 by 20% (490 Mbps for IPv6 and 390 Mbps for IPv4). Therefore, when running IEEE 802.11ax in an open system network, TCP maintains consistent throughput regardless of packet sizes. The most significant difference in throughput between an open system and one with WPA2 security is observed at packet length of 1408 bytes.

By looking at Figure 2b, it is evident that UDP throughput increases with packet size increases. For an open security (no security), IPv6 offers higher throughput than IPv4 across all packet sizes. For instance, IPv6 achieves 16.5% (575 Mbps for IPv6 and 480 Mbps for IPv4) higher UDP throughput than IPv4 at the packet size of 1408 bytes. For WPA2 security, the greatest disparity between IPv6 and IPv4 occurs at packet size of 1280 bytes, with IPv6 surpassing IPv4 by 18.2% (520 Mbps for IPv6 compared to 425 Mbps for IPv4). Similarly, for WPA3 security, the maximum throughput difference is observed at packet size of 1408 bytes, where IPv6 outperforms IPv4 by 17.4% (570 Mbps for IPv6 versus 470 Mbps for IPv4).

When comparing IPv4 performance across the studied security modes (open security, WPA2, and WPA3), the TCP throughput remains approximately consistent, indicating minimal variation. In contrast, IPv6 exhibits slight differences in throughput depending on the security mode. The most notable difference occurs at packet size of 1408 bytes, where WPA2 drops throughput by 7.7% (520 Mbps for open system and 480 Mbps for WPA2). This suggests that while IPv6 generally delivers superior performance, the choice of security mode can influence throughput, particularly at larger packet sizes. These findings highlight the importance of considering IP versions and security configuration when optimizing throughput performance. We observe that WPA3 drops TCP and UDP throughput by 3.8% and 0.9% for IPv6. Overall, IPv6 outperforms IPv4 in both open and protected systems such as WPA2 and WPA3.

(ii) Study 2: Jitter performance

Figure 3 shows the Jitter (ms) for IPv4 and IPv6 on WLAN 802.11ax Client–Server (Windows 10) with WPA2 and WPA3 security and open system. One can observe that this test exhibits no jitter for both IPv4 and IPv6, which correspond to all OS, WPA2, and WPA3 security protocols.

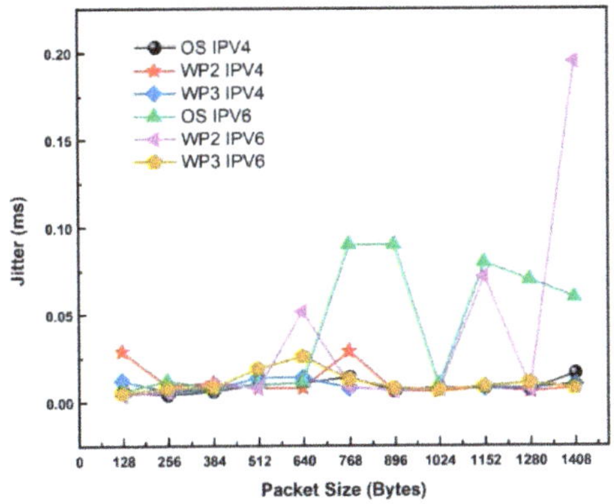

Figure 3. Jitter performance. Comparison of 802.11ax performance for Open System vs. WPA2 and WPA3 security in IPV4 and IPV6 network.

(iii) Study 3: Packet losses

Figure 4 shows the lost datagram for IPv4 and IPv6 in an 802.11ax client–server network for security protocols (WPA2 and WPA3). Operating systems supporting IPv4 and IPv6 were identified by measuring their packet sizes between 128 and 1408 bytes. The results for lost datagrams show that both MS Windows and Linux IPv4 portray the same throughput. For IPv6, the lost datagram (in %) steeply increases as the packet size increases. However, Windows outperforms (about 5%) Linux for most larger packet sizes. The maximum performance difference between Linux and Windows IPv6 is at packet size of 512 bytes. However, Linux outperforms Windows IPv6 by 100%.

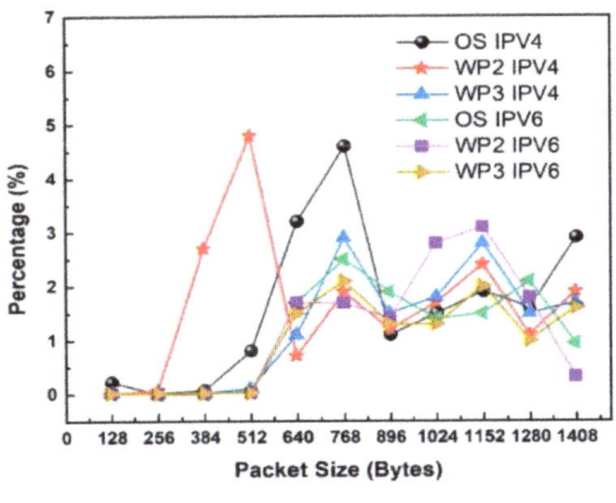

Figure 4. Packet losses. Comparison of WPA2, WPA3 and open security for IPV4 and IPV6 network.

4.1. Comparative Analysis

In this section we study the impact of Windows and Linux on system throughput for various security protocols, including WPA2 and WPA3. We focus on analyzing system performance using both Linux and Windows testbeds for various scenarios, including the effect of WPA3, WPA2, and open security on TCP/UDP throughput (Windows vs. Linux).

(iv) Study 4: Effect of WPA3 on Throughput (Windows vs. Linux)

Figure 5a shows WPA3 TCP throughput for IPv4 and IPv6 on 802.11ax Client–Server Windows 10 operating system (OS). The result for Linux is also shown for comparison purposes. In most scenarios, as packet sizes increase, so does TCP throughput for MS Windows. For Linux, throughput rises with an increase in packet sizes to 900 Mbps, after which the curve flattens. On a WPA3 network, Linux IPv6 and IPv4 significantly outperform Windows 10 by about 40% for all packet sizes, with a maximum difference of 87.6% at packet size of 256 bytes. Linux OS exceeds Windows system by 87.6% (900 Mbps for Linux system and 111 Mbps for windows). For WPA3, in the windows operating system, the TCP throughput increases equally for IPv4 and IPv6 with packet sizes.

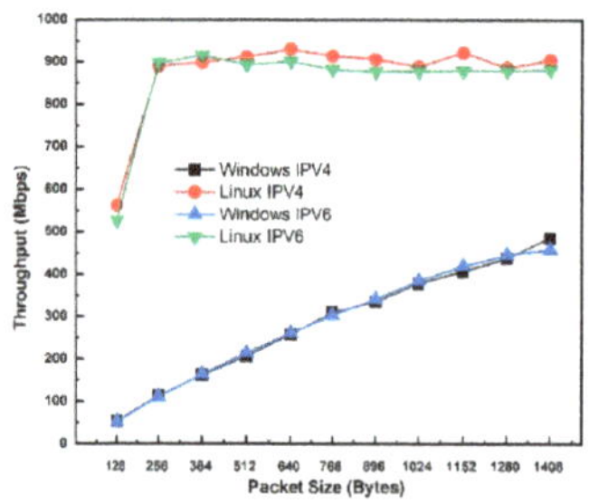

(a) TCP Throughput

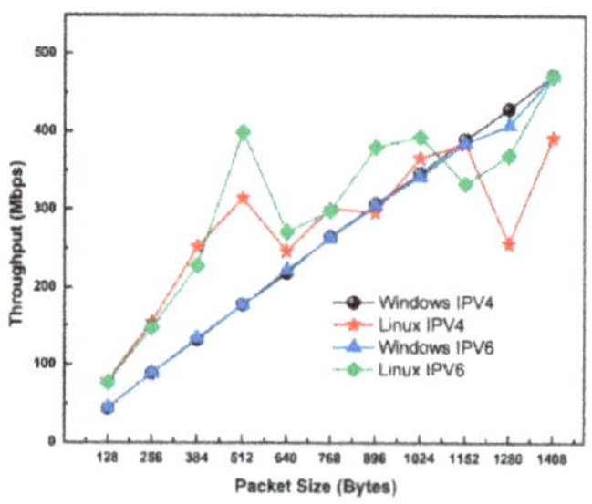

(b) UDP Throughput

Figure 5. Effect of WPA3 Security on Throughput (Windows vs. Linux) in IPV4 and IPV6 network. (**a**) TCP Throughput; and (**b**) UDP Throughput.

Figure 5b shows the UDP throughput for IPv4 and IPv6 on 802.11ax Client–Server (Windows vs. Linux) with WPA3 security. As the packet size changes, UDP's throughput also increases consistently along with them. UDP throughput for Linux with IPv6 outperforms Windows IPv6 for all packet sizes up to 1152 bytes, after which the throughput drops consistently with increasing packet size to 1280 bytes and rises again to 1480 bytes, though at a lower rate than MS Windows. Linux throughput on IPv4 outperforms IPv4 Windows for all packet sizes with an average improvement of 30.6%. For WPA3 in Linux vs. Windows with IPv4, the maximum difference between Linux IPv4 and Windows IPv4 is at packet size of 512 bytes, where IPv6 outperforms IPv4 by 51.7% (369 Mbps for Linux IPv4 vs. 178 Mbps for Windows IPv4), representing a 191 Mbps increase. IPV6's WPA3 security shows that between two OS systems, they are spotted at 512 bytes, where IPV6 Linux shows 372 Mbps over IPV6 Windows at 178 Mbps, which is 52.15% difference. On MS Windows, IPv4 and IPv6 had approximately equal throughput for all packet sizes. Across the board, Linux outperforms MS Windows in WPA3-secured networks.

(v) Study 5: Impact of WPA2 Security on Throughput (Windows vs. Linux)

Figure 6a shows the TCP throughput for IPv4 and IPv6 on 802.11ax Client–Server (Windows 10 vs. Linux) with WPA2 security. In most scenarios, as the packet size increases, the throughput of TCP also increases consistently for Windows. For Linux, the throughput increases with an increase in packet size to 900 Mbps, after which the curve flattens. On the WPA2 network, Linux IPv6 and IPv4 significantly outperform Windows 10 on all packet sizes by about 40%, with the most significant difference at a packet size of 256 bytes. On WPA2 network, Linux IPv6 and IPv4 significantly outperform Windows for all packet sizes by about 40%. The TCP throughput increases equally for IPv4 and IPv6 throughout the packet lengths for Windows. The Linux system with WPA2 outperforms Windows on IPv6 and IPv4, where the maximum difference is spotted at 256 bytes. Overall, Linux outperforms Windows in WPA2 secured system.

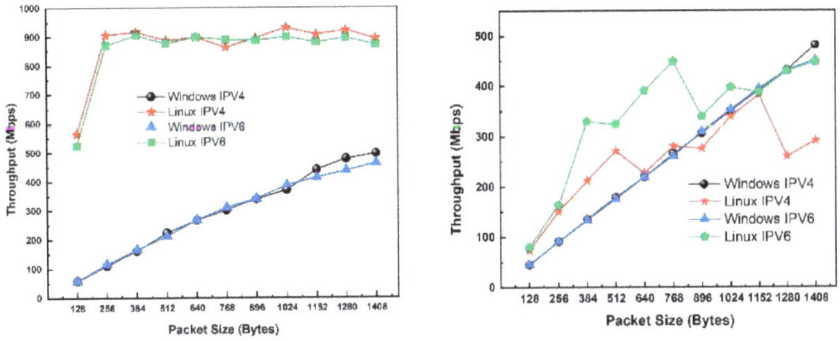

(a) TCP Throughput (b) UDP Throughput

Figure 6. Effect of WPA2 Security on Throughput (Windows vs. Linux) over IPV4 and IPV6 network. (**a**) TCP Throughput; and (**b**) UDP Throughput.

Figure 6b shows the UDP throughput for IPv4 and IPv6 on Linux and Windows operating systems running on WPA2 secured network. In all scenarios, as the size of the packet increases, the performance of UDP also increases proportionally. The Linux Operating system with IPv6 and IPv4 outperforms Windows IPv4 and IPv6 with an average increase of 50.4% on all packet sizes.

(vi) Study 6: Impact of Open Security on Throughput (Windows vs. Linux)

Figure 7a shows IPv4 and IPv6 TCP throughput on Windows and Linux server for Open security. For Windows, increasing the packet size from 128 to 256 bytes improves throughput by 58.7 Mbps. As we increase the packet size, IPv4 performs equally as IPv6 throughout the packet's length, with a slight difference at packet size of 1408 bytes. For Linux, UDP throughput increases with increased packet size consistently, to 898 Mbps, after which the curve flattens. IPv4 performs better than IPv6, with the highest throughput difference of 16 Mbps at 1152 bytes for all packet sizes. As packet size increases, performance remains nearly constant up to 1408 bytes. Linux operating systems with IPv4 and IPv6 have the same throughput for small packet sizes (256 bytes). Still, the throughput increases steeply as the packet size increases. However, for most of the large packet sizes, throughput is slightly constant. Also, IPv4 gives a higher throughput than IPv6 for packet sizes larger than 384 bytes. We observe that Linux outperforms Windows throughout the packet sizes by 60%. The maximum difference is at packet size of 256 bytes, where the Linux server outperforms Windows by 86.6% (898 Mbps for Linux and 111 Mbps for Windows).

Figure 7b compares UDP throughput of IPv4 and IPv6 using Windows and Linux security. We observe that the highest throughput is achieved using Linux client–server network than MS Windows 10 Server. For example, for IPv4 using Linux Server, the throughput is 549 Mbps (13.3% increase from Windows 10, which has a throughput of 476) at a packet size of 1408 bytes. On the other hand, the highest throughput for IPv6 using Linux Server is 514 Mbps (7.4% increase from Windows 10 Server, which is at 476 Mbps) at packet size of 1408 bytes. For open system (no security), the maximum difference in IPv4 and IPv6 between Windows and Linux was observed at packet size of 512 bytes where IPv6 and IPv4 on Linux outperform MS Windows by 52.15%.

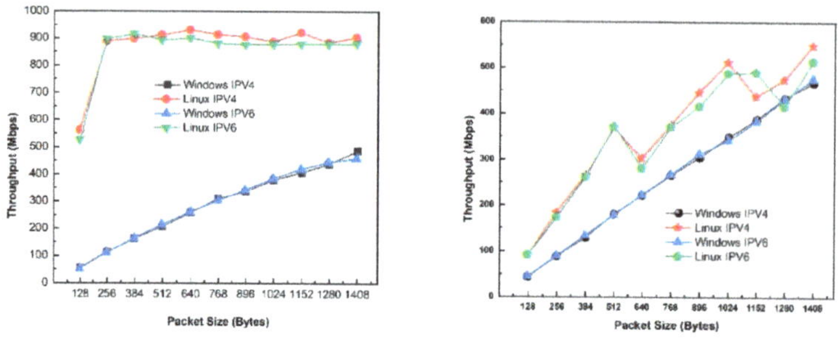

(**a**) TCP IPv4/IPv6 Throughput (**b**) UDP Throughput

Figure 7. Effect of Open security on throughput (Windows vs. Linux) over IPv4/IPv6 network (**a**) TCP IPv4/IPv6 Throughput; and (**b**) UDP Throughput.

Each experiment was repeated ten times under identical conditions, and the reported throughput values represent the averaged results. During repetitions, the variation across runs was minimal (within ±2–3% of the mean), indicating stable system performance. Given this consistency, error bars or confidence intervals were not included in the graphs, as they would overlap with the plotted values and provide limited additional insight. Instead, the averages reported in both the figures and accompanying summary tables reliably capture the system performance trends across WPA2 and WPA3 configurations.

The observed differences between Windows and Linux performance can be attributed to differences in network stack design and NIC driver implementations. Linux employs a more streamlined kernel-level network stack with efficient buffer management, faster context switching, and optimized NIC drivers, which reduces processing overhead. Windows, by contrast, relies on additional abstraction layers (e.g., WinSock API) and background services, which increase latency and reduce throughput. Furthermore, Linux supports more advanced offloading features (e.g., TCP Segmentation Offload, Large Receive Offload), which improve packet handling efficiency. These architectural distinctions explain the higher throughput and smoother convergence trends observed in Linux compared to Windows across WPA2/WPA3 scenarios.

4.2. Summarization of Results

The summary of key research findings is presented in Table 4. The TCP and UDP throughput (Mbps) for open system (no security), WPA2, and WPA3 for both IPV6 and IPv4 are shown in Row 2 and Row 3, respectively. Column 5 shows average throughput drops because of Wi-Fi 6 WPA3 security protocol. For instance, WPA3 TCP throughput drops by 3.8% $\left[\frac{520-500}{520} \times 100\%\right]$ for IPv6. This throughput degradation is due to encryption overheads.

Table 4. Effect of WPA3 security on TCP/UDP throughput dropping.

	Open System	WPA2	WPA2 Throughput Drops (%)	WPA3	WPA3 Throughput Drops (%)
TCP Throughput (Mbps)	520 IPv6	480 IPv6	7.7	500 IPv6	3.8
	400 IPv4	380 IPv4	5.0	390 IPv4	2.5
UDP Throughput (Mbps)	575 IPv6	520 IPv6	9.6	570 IPv6	0.9
	480 IPv4	425 IPv4	11.5	470 IPv4	2.1

Note: (1) WPA3 UDP offers 12.3% higher throughput than TCP for IPv6. (2) For WPA3, IPv6 outperforms IPv4 by 23% and 16.5% for TCP and UDP throughput, respectively.

The performance fluctuation and convergence trends observed in Figures 5–7 can be attributed to the distinct design strategies of Windows and Linux operating systems. Linux employs a lightweight, modular kernel-level network stack that emphasizes efficiency in packet scheduling, buffer management, and interrupting handling. This design allows Linux to achieve smoother convergence and reduced variance in throughput as packet sizes increase. By contrast, Windows incorporates additional abstraction layers (e.g., WinSock API) and background processes for security and compatibility, which can introduce latency and variability in data handling. Furthermore, Linux NIC drivers typically expose more advanced offloading features (e.g., TCP Segmentation Offload, Large Receive Offload), whereas Windows applies stricter consistency and verification mechanisms that increase overhead. These architectural differences explain why Linux demonstrates more stable performance trends with minimal fluctuation, while Windows shows greater variance and slower convergence under the same WPA2/WPA3 security configurations.

To complement the graphical results, two summary tables are provided for quick reference. Table 5 presents the average throughput values for WPA2 and WPA3 across TCP/UDP and IPv4/IPv6 environments. The results confirm that WPA3 introduces only minimal performance degradation (<4%) compared to WPA2, with IPv6 consistently achieving higher throughput than IPv4.

Table 5. Average Throughput (Mbps) for WPA2 and WPA3 across TCP/UDP and IPv4/IPv6.

Security	Protocol	TCP (IPv4)	TCP (IPv6)	UDP (IPv4)	UDP (IPv6)
Open	Baseline	400	520	480	575
WPA2	Enabled	380	480	425	520
WPA3	Enabled	390	500	470	570

Note: Values represent averages across 10 test runs. WPA3 shows minimal degradation compared to WPA2, with IPv6 consistently outperforming IPv4.

Table 6 compares the performance of Windows and Linux under WPA2 and WPA3 in terms of throughput, jitter, and packet loss. The findings demonstrate that Linux achieves higher and more stable throughput with negligible jitter and lower packet loss, whereas Windows shows greater fluctuation due to additional abstraction layers in its network stack. These results align with the figures presented earlier and provide a concise numerical reference to support the observed trends.

Table 6. Comparative Performance of Windows vs. Linux under WPA2 and WPA3 (Throughput, Jitter, Packet Loss).

Security	OS	TCP (Avg. Mbps)	UDP (Avg. Mbps)	Jitter (ms)	Packet Loss Trend
WPA2	Windows	~380–420	~425–450	~0	Low (IPv4), Moderate ↑ with IPv6 size
WPA2	Linux	~600–900	~650–950	~0	Very Low overall
WPA3	Windows	~390–430	~440–470	~0	Low (IPv4), Moderate ↑ with IPv6 size
WPA3	Linux	~650–900	~700–950	~0	Very Low overall

5. Practical Implications

The results from both Windows and Linux testbeds reveal important insights into the impact of Wi-Fi 6 security protocols (Open security, WPA2, and WPA3) on system performance, especially TCP/UDP throughput for IPv4 and IPv6. While both operating systems showed consistent patterns, MS Windows demonstrated slightly lower throughput than Linux, especially for IPv6 traffic. The higher efficiency of Linux, particularly in handling

IPv6 traffic, can be attributed to its more optimized network stack and reduced overheads. For TCP throughput, the Linux-based testbed consistently outperformed MS Windows, with a significant performance gap observed at larger packet sizes demonstrating a 49% increase in throughput for IPv4 at packet size of 1408 bytes. Similarly, UDP throughput on Linux was notably higher, especially for IPv6, where Linux achieved an 87.7% increase compared with Windows at a packet size of 256 bytes.

WPA3 achieves optimized performance in high-density environments primarily through its Simultaneous Authentication of Equals (SAE) handshake and Opportunistic Wireless Encryption (OWE), which reduce the time and overhead of key exchange in crowded networks. When combined with 802.11ax MU-MIMO and OFDMA, these mechanisms allow multiple devices to authenticate and transmit securely with minimal encryption-induced delays. Our results confirm this: WPA3 introduced only a 3.8% throughput drop for TCP and 0.9% for UDP in IPv6 environments, which demonstrates that WPA3's overhead remains negligible even in multi-user scenarios.

We observe that WPA3 introduced small overheads, as expected, due to its more advanced encryption techniques. However, both Linux and Windows testbeds showed that the performance degradation caused by WPA3 was minimal, particularly for IPv6 traffic, where the simplified and more efficient header structure mitigated the impact. This result highlights the robustness of WPA3 in maintaining high throughput and low latency, even in more secure environments. Jitter and packet losses remained minimal in both operating systems, with slight differences in UDP packet delays. Linux's efficient socket layer and faster kernel switches provide better performance for all security protocols with respect to packet transmission and reception.

Our findings suggest that while both Windows and Linux can handle the demands of 802.11ax networks (Wi-Fi 6), Linux outperforms Windows in most scenarios, particularly when dealing with IPv6 traffic and larger packet sizes. This performance gap is likely due to the inherent differences in the network stack and system architecture between the two operating systems investigated. However, the relatively small differences in throughput, jitter, and packet losses contributing to dropping system performance for all security protocols indicate that 802.11ax wireless network is designed to maintain consistent performance, regardless of the security features enabled. These results highlight the scalability and reliability of 802.11ax, making it suitable for complex, high-demand wireless network environments. The security-related impact of WPA2 and WPA3 is reflected in system-level metrics such as throughput, jitter, and packet loss. Encryption introduces additional computation at both transmitter and receiver, which can lead to reduced throughput and increased packet processing delays. However, our results show that WPA3 overhead was minimal ($\leq$3.8%), indicating that the security mechanisms are efficient and do not compromise quality of service. Thus, throughput, jitter, and packet loss serve as indirect indicators of security-performance trade-offs, confirming that WPA3 maintains robust protection without significantly burdening system performance.

Our empirical testbed results are consistent with prior simulation-based studies [4,5], which also reported throughput degradation when encryption mechanisms were applied. However, unlike earlier simulation work conducted in IEEE 802.11ac environments, where WPA3 introduced noticeable reductions in throughput, our IEEE 802.11ax testbed results show only minimal degradation (<4%). This indicates that the enhanced MAC/PHY layer efficiency of Wi-Fi 6, including OFDMA and MU-MIMO that effectively compensates for the additional processing overhead introduced by WPA3's advanced encryption. Thus, our findings not only confirm but also extend simulation-based evidence, providing practical validation in real-world deployments and demonstrating that WPA3 can achieve strong security while maintaining near-baseline throughput in Wi-Fi 6 networks.

6. Conclusions

This study comprehensively analyzed the security features of 802.11ax (Wi-Fi 6) network across both MS Windows and Linux operating systems. We have measured throughput, packet loss, and packet jitter using iPerf3 tool and provided a detailed assessment of network behavior. The research findings revealed that IPv6 consistently outperformed IPv4, attributed to its streamlined header structure, absence of packet fragmentation, and efficient checksum processing. The testbed was set up to study the system performance and to simulate real-world scenarios, facilitated precise data collection across a range of packet sizes, enabling a robust evaluation of system performance in both Linux and MS Windows server environments. The obtained results have shown that the impact of WPA3 security on TCP/UDP throughput is not very significant. For instance, WPA3 drops TCP throughput and UDP throughput by 3.8% and 0.9%, respectively, for IPv6. This decrease in throughput is due to overheads introduced by advanced encryption technology. IPv6 consistently outperforms IPv4 in both TCP and UDP throughput. UDP offers higher throughput than TCP in IPv6 environments. Linux outperforms MS Windows in all scenarios, especially with larger packet sizes and IPv6 traffic.

However, as networks continue to grow in complexity, further research is recommended to explore potential challenges and optimizations. Future studies could investigate energy efficiency and scalability aspects of 802.11ax networks across both MS Windows and Linux operating systems, particularly in more diverse and demanding network conditions. Such investigations would provide valuable insights into enhancing the deployment and performance of next-generation wireless networks. While full-duplex transmission is being explored in next-generation standards such as IEEE 802.11be (Wi-Fi 7), our study focused on 802.11ax, which primarily enhances performance using OFDMA and MU-MIMO. At present, 802.11ax devices do not implement true MAC/PHY full-duplex capability, and therefore this feature was not included in our experiments. Future studies will investigate the impact of WPA3 when combined with full-duplex technology as it becomes available in Wi-Fi 7 deployments. This study focused on baseline performance under benign conditions to isolate the impact of security protocols. Future work will extend this evaluation to real-world security threats such as de-authentication attacks, man-in-the-middle (Evil Twin) attacks, and offline dictionary attacks. Such experiments will help to assess WPA3's resilience and performance trade-offs under adversarial conditions.

Author Contributions: Conceptualization, N.F.; methodology, N.F. and N.I.S.; software, N.F. and N.I.S.; validation, N.F., N.I.S. and M.J.A.; formal analysis, N.F., N.I.S. and M.J.A.; investigation, N.F., N.I.S. and M.J.A.; resources, N.I.S.; data curation, N.F., N.I.S. and M.J.A.; writing—original draft preparation, N.F.; writing—review and editing, N.I.S. and M.J.A.; visualization, N.F., N.I.S. and M.J.A.; supervision, N.I.S.; project administration, N.I.S. All authors have read and agreed to the published version of the manuscript.

Funding: This research received no external funding.

Data Availability Statement: The original contributions presented in the study are included in the article. Further inquiries can be directed to the corresponding author.

Conflicts of Interest: The authors declare no conflicts of interest.

References

1. Bellalta, B. IEEE 802.11ax: High-efficiency WLANs. *IEEE Wirel. Commun.* **2016**, *23*, 38–46. [CrossRef]
2. Mozaffariahrar, E.; Theoleyre, F.; Menth, M. A Survey of Wi-Fi 6: Technologies, Advances, and Challenges. *Future Internet* **2022**, *14*, 293. [CrossRef]

3. Tsetse, A.; Bonniord, E.; Appiah-Kubi, P. Performance Study of the Impact of Security on 802.11ac Networks. In *Information Technology—New Generations*; Advances in Intelligent Systems and Computing; Springer: Cham, Switzerland, 2018; Volume 738, pp. 11–17.
4. Kolahi, S.S.; Almatrook, A.A. Impact of Security on Bandwidth and Latency in IEEE 802.11ac Client-to-Server WLAN. In Proceedings of the 2017 Ninth International Conference on Ubiquitous and Future Networks (ICUFN), Milan, Italy, 4–7 July 2017; pp. 893–897.
5. Alghamdi, S.A. Throughput Analysis of IEEE WLAN 802.11ac under Security Protocols. *Int. J. Comput. Netw. Commun. IJCNC* **2018**, *9*, 1–13.
6. Wen, J.; Pettersson, C.; Max, S.; Sung, K.W.; Slimane, S.B. Wi-Fi Performance Evaluation in Industrial Scenarios. In Proceedings of the 2025 IEEE 21st International Conference on Factory Communication Systems (WFCS), Munich, Germany, 4–6 June 2025; pp. 1–8.
7. Qu, Q.; Li, B.; Yang, M.; Yan, Z.; Yang, A.; Deng, D.J.; Chen, K.C. Survey and Performance Evaluation of the Upcoming Next Generation WLANs Standard—IEEE 802.11ax. *Mob. Netw. Appl.* **2019**, *24*, 1461–1474.
8. Afaqui, M.S.; Garcia-Villegas, E.; Lopez-Aguilera, E. IEEE 802.11ax: Challenges and Requirements for Future High Efficiency Wi-Fi. *IEEE Wirel. Commun.* **2016**, *24*, 130–137.
9. Deng, C.; Fang, X.; Han, X.; Wang, X.; Yan, L.; He, R.; Guo, Y. IEEE 802.11be Wi-Fi 7: New Challenges and Opportunities. *IEEE Commun. Surv. Tutor.* **2020**, *22*, 2136–2166.
10. Hadiwinata, S.D.; Muhammad, A.H.; Budi, I.S. Analysis of the Impact of Implementing Wireless Security Protocol (WPA2-PSK and WPA3-SAE) on Handover Performance on 5 GHz Networks. *Bul. Poltanesa* **2025**, *26*, 59–72.
11. Hoefel, R.P.F. IEEE 802.11ax (Wi-Fi 6): DL and UL MU-MIMO Channel Sounding Compression Schemes. In Proceedings of the IEEE Vehicular Technology Conference, Antwerp, Belgium, 25–28 May 2020; pp. 1–6.
12. Banerji, S.; Chowdhury, R.S. On IEEE 802.11: Wireless LAN Technology. *Int. J. Mob. Netw. Commun. Technol.* **2013**, *3*, 45–64. [CrossRef]
13. Khorov, E.; Kiryanov, A.; Lyakhov, A.; Bianchi, G. A Tutorial on IEEE 802.11ax High Efficiency WLANs. *IEEE Commun. Surv. Tutor.* **2019**, *21*, 197–216. [CrossRef]
14. Sarkar, N.I.; Ali, M.J. A Study of MANET Routing Protocols in Heterogeneous Networks: A Review and Performance Comparison. *Electronics* **2025**, *14*, 872. [CrossRef]
15. Weller, D.; Vegt, A.V.D. Wi-Fi 6 Performance Measurements of 1024-QAM and DL OFDMA. In Proceedings of the IEEE International Conference on Communications, Dublin, Ireland, 7–11 June 2020; pp. 1–7.
16. Morais, D.H. Wi-Fi 6/6E and Wi-Fi 7 Overview. In *5G/5G-Advanced, Wi-Fi 6/7, and Bluetooth 5/6: A Primer on Smartphone Wireless Technologies*; Springer: Cham, Switzerland, 2025; pp. 149–179.
17. Alghamdi, T.M. Throughput Analysis of IEEE WLAN "802.11ac" Under WEP, WPA, and WPA2 Security Protocols. *Int. J. Comput. Netw.* **2019**, *11*, 35–50.
18. Bazzi, A.; Slock, D.T.M.; Meilhac, L. JADED-RIP: Joint Angle and Delay Estimator and Detector via Rotational Invariance Properties. In Proceedings of the 2016 IEEE International Symposium on Signal Processing and Information Technology (ISSPIT), Limassol, Cyprus, 12–14 December 2016.
19. Deng, D.-J.; Lin, Y.P.; Yang, X.; Zhu, J.; Li, Y.B.; Luo, J.; Chen, K.C. IEEE 802.11ax: Highly Efficient WLANs for Intelligent Information Infrastructure. *IEEE Commun. Mag.* **2017**, *55*, 52–59. [CrossRef]
20. Deng, D.J.; Lien, S.Y.; Lee, J.; Chen, K.C. On Quality-of-Service Provisioning in IEEE 802.11ax WLANs. *IEEE Access* **2016**, *4*, 6086–6104. [CrossRef]
21. Afaqui, M.S.; Garcia-Villegas, E.; Lopez-Aguilera, E.; Smith, G.; Camps, D. Evaluation of Dynamic Sensitivity Control Algorithm for IEEE 802.11ax. In Proceedings of the 2015 IEEE Wireless Communications and Networking Conference, WCNC 2015, New Orleans, LA, USA, 9–12 March 2015; pp. 1060–1065. [CrossRef]

electronics

Article

A Digital Twin-Assisted VEC Intelligent Task Offloading Approach

Yali Wang [1,2,*], Hongtao Xue [3] and Meng Zhou [3]

1 Computing Science and Artificial Intelligence College, Suzhou City University, Suzhou 215104, China
2 Suzhou Key Lab of Multi-Modal Data Fusion and Intelligent Healthcare, Suzhou City University, Suzhou 215104, China
3 School of Computer and Information Engineering, Henan Normal University, Xinxiang 453007, China
* Correspondence: ylwang@szcu.edu.cn

Abstract

Vehicular edge computing (VEC) represents a concrete application of mobile edge computing (MEC) in the field of intelligent transportation, with task offloading serving as one of its core components. The design of efficient task offloading strategies poses significant challenges due to the dynamic network topology, stringent low-latency requirements, and massive data processing demands. This paper proposes a digital twin (DT)-assisted intelligent task offloading approach, which establishes a dynamic interaction and mapping between the virtual and physical worlds to enable real-time monitoring of VEC network states, thereby optimizing offloading decisions. First, to meet diverse user service requirements, an optimization model is formulated with the objective of minimizing task processing latency and energy consumption. Next, a gravity model-based vehicle clustering algorithm is integrated with digital twin technology to find the optimal offloading space and ensure link stability among vehicles within aggregated clusters. Furthermore, to minimize overall system costs, the Twin Delayed Deep Deterministic Policy Gradient (TD3) algorithm is utilized to train the offloading policy, enabling automatic optimization of both latency and energy consumption. consumption. Finally, a feedback mechanism is introduced to dynamically adjust parameters and enhance the robustness of the clustering process. Simulation results demonstrate that the proposed approach significantly outperforms baseline methods in terms of task completion cost, energy consumption, delay, and success rate, thereby validating its potential and superior performance in dynamic vehicular network environments.

Keywords: vehicular edge computing; task offloading; deep reinforcement learning; clustering; digital twin

1. Introduction

The widespread adoption of 5G and the continuous advancement of 6G technologies are driving the swift advancement of the Internet of Vehicles (IoV) [1]. As a representative scenario of the Internet of Things (IoT) [1] in transportation systems, IoV is showing unprecedented growth potential. Diverse vehicular applications have become deeply integrated into everyday life, ranging from driving safety and in-vehicle entertainment to mobility services [2]. However, vehicles with constrained computational resources may face significant challenges in processing these tasks efficiently. Cloud servers are typically located far from end users [3]. Transmitting the exponentially growing vehicular application data to centralized cloud servers imposes a substantial burden [4] on the network and leads to unpredictable latency, making it unsuitable for IoV scenarios with strict real-time requirements. Mobile edge computing (MEC) [5] addresses this issue by relocating data processing from remote cloud centers to edge nodes closer to the data source, significantly lowering communication delay and enhancing response times [6]. Vehicle edge computing (VEC), an emerging paradigm integrating MEC with IoV, enables the offloading of computationally intensive and latency-sensitive tasks to VEC servers or roadside units, thereby reducing latency and improving service quality for users [7]. However, the increasing number of service-requesting vehicles intensifies competition for limited edge resources, resulting in excessive load pressure on edge servers (ES). With advancements in vehicle intelligence, smart vehicles now possess certain levels of computational and caching capabilities. Aggregating and utilizing the idle resources [4] of these vehicles can both expand the computational capacity of the VEC system and alleviate the burden on edge servers. Nonetheless, the high mobility of vehicles and the dynamic environment often cause existing task offloading approaches to perform poorly in such unpredictable and rapidly changing systems.

Edge intelligence, which integrates edge computing with artificial intelligence, is a promising emerging technology. Deep reinforcement learning (DRL), a subfield of artificial intelligence, fuses the powerful perceptual abilities of deep learning with the decision-making capabilities of reinforcement learning. It is increasingly used to tackle decision-making problems in dynamic and complex environments, offering an effective solution for tasks such as offloading and resource allocation. Compared with heuristic algorithms, DRL offers greater robustness and more stable convergence, enabling instant and dynamic decision-making. Digital twin (DT) is an emerging technology that creates digital replicas of physical entities based on real-time status and historical data. Until 2025, DT technology has been widely adopted in a large variety of domains [8], such as smart community, healthcare and intelligent transportation systems. By ensuring reliable communication between the physical and digital domains, DT bridges the gap [2] between physical space and its digital representation, enhancing real-time interaction and enabling close monitoring [9]. The mapping between virtual models and physical entities provides comprehensive insights into the VEC network, enabling feature extraction and predictive analysis of physical vehicles and dynamic environments [10,11].

In recent years, some studies have started to explore the integration of DT technology with DRL to solve complex problems in practical applications. The role of DT varies across different use cases. For instance, one study [12] utilizes DT to predict the arrival capabilities of future tasks and then applies DRL algorithms to optimize offloading strategies, determining whether tasks should be offloaded to cloud centers, edge servers, or local computing resources. Another study [13] leverages DT's ability to sense global and historical information, assisting in vehicle clustering, and then employ DRL algorithms to identify the optimal offloading location for tasks. Additionally, a further study [14] uses DRL to make resource allocation [15] and task offloading decisions, while DT simulates the real-world environment of autonomous vehicles to gather global information and optimize resource distribution. The combination of these technologies provides theoretical support for efficient vehicle management and demonstrates high quality and feasibility in practical applications.

Research on DT-based solutions for VEC networks is still in its early stages. First, most existing DT-assisted vehicular task offloading approaches rely on full offloading, whereas partial offloading strategies have shown greater potential in reducing latency. Second, the majority of current studies focus on single-objective optimization, typically minimizing latency. However, user requirements can vary, and single-objective approaches may not adequately address the diverse needs of all users. Furthermore, few studies have investigated the integration of DT technology with DRL approaches in the context of VEC networks. To deeply explore the performance of the combination of these two technologies in VEC, this paper proposes a novel digital twin-assisted intelligent task offloading (DTAITO) approach for VEC networks to support efficient offloading decision-making. The primary contributions of this paper can be outlined as follows:

(1) The partial task offloading optimization model is proposed to jointly minimize latency and energy consumption. This model balances computational performance with energy efficiency while accommodating the diverse requirements of IoV users.

(2) The digital twin network is used to capture real-time, system-wide information on vehicles and network conditions. A Gravity-Inspired Vehicle Clustering (GIVC) algorithm is applied to dynamically form highly resource-compatible clusters, ensuring reliable and stable communication links among vehicles within each cluster. This approach significantly lowers the complexity of task offloading, increases task scheduling success rates, and improves overall system performance under highly dynamic IoV environments.

(3) The TD3 algorithm is introduced to make real-time task offloading decisions in complex and dynamic vehicular networks, improving both the efficiency and stability of decision-making.

(4) A feedback mechanism is incorporated to dynamically tune the parameters of the GIVC algorithm according to task offloading outcomes. This enhances the adaptability and robustness of the clustering process across varying scenarios, further increasing offloading success rates and improving network performance.

The organization of this paper is outlined as follows: Section 2 reviews related work, Section 3 describes the system model and optimization problems, Section 4 describes the DTAITO approach in detail, Section 5 analyzes the experimental evaluation, and Section 6 concludes the study.

2. Related Work

In this section, a comprehensive review of the task offloading literature in V2V scenarios is reviewed. Additionally, methods that leverage DRL and DT technologies to assist task offloading are also discussed. Moreover, the limitations of existing studies are summarized, and the innovative contributions of this work are emphasized.

2.1. Task Offloading in V2V

VEC has emerged as a highly promising computing paradigm, offering a feasible solution to the limitations of on-board computational capabilities that hinder the efficient execution of computation-intensive applications. Consequently, it has attracted significant attention from both academia and industry in recent years. Considering offloading scenarios, the majority of existing studies have primarily focused on V2I environments [16,17]. However, when the number of ES near the vehicle is limited or the load on the edge servers is high, the offloading and execution of vehicle tasks can be significantly affected. To address this issue, several studies have explored task offloading in V2V scenarios, leveraging the idle resources of nearby vehicles to execute tasks. Wu et al. [18] propose a V2V-based secure computation offloading algorithm, R-MDDQN, for video analysis. It ensures data security through Wyner's wiretap coding approach, dynamically adjusts multi-objective weights using a Radial Basis Function (RBF) network, and optimizes the offloading strategy with a Double Deep Q-Network (DDQN). Chen et al. [19] regard nearby vehicles with idle resources as a resource pool and propose a distributed computation offloading strategy based on the DQN algorithm to minimize the execution time of composite tasks in V2V scenarios. In another work, Chen et al. [5] formulate the problem of offloading as a generalized allocation model with constraints which is solved by the discrete bat algorithm and greedy algorithm, respectively. However, although the above studies utilize the idle computing resources of vehicles, they focus solely on minimizing latency without jointly considering energy consumption.

2.2. Task Offloading with DRL

Numerous studies have proposed a variety of solutions to solve the task offloading problem in VEC. To effectively address the complexity and vast search space associated with task offloading in IoV scenarios, some studies have adopted swarm intelligence-based heuristic approaches. Cong et al. [20] propose a two-stage heuristic task offloading strategy to address the issue of inefficient resource allocation resulting from offloading decisions in multi-vehicle, multi-server IoV scenarios. The strategy integrates an improved artificial fish swarm algorithm with an improved hybrid genetic algorithm, using iterative optimization to allocate resources efficiently in task offloading, thereby achieving joint optimization of average cost, energy consumption and latency. Chen et al. [21] propose an enhanced heuristic task offloading strategy to improve offloading and resource allocation in IoV environments. They employ an improved dual-population immune genetic algorithm, which retains elite populations while introducing an adaptive migration operator. The approach considers constraints such as the maximum tolerable delay of vehicles and the allocatable resources of the roadside units to optimize system energy consumption and latency. However, the scenarios addressed by the aforementioned approaches are overly idealized. In contrast, real-time vehicular network scenarios are dynamic and complex, making it difficult for these solutions to effectively adapt to practical environments.

Recently, DRL has been regarded as an effective technique for addressing task offloading problems in dynamic vehicular network scenarios. Among the studies employing DRL for task offloading, some have adopted binary offloading strategies. Shi et al. [22] propose a blockchain-enabled VEC framework and develop a computation offloading approach based on the soft actor–critic (SAC) algorithm. Several studies have focused on partial task offloading, under the premise that it offers greater potential and flexibility than full offloading. Yao et al. [23] formulate the dynamic computation offloading problem as a Markov Decision Process and applied the TD3 algorithm in an IoV context to support real-time decision-making and prediction for optimal offloading strategies. Some studies have focused on partial task offloading. Huang et al. [24] consider a cloud-edge-end architecture in a dynamic network environment and introduced the CORA algorithm to minimize system costs under task latency and transmission power constraints, jointly optimizing resource allocation and task offloading. Gao et al. [25] propose a federated learning-assisted DRL approach that allows tasks to be partially offloaded to the ES, enabling concurrent execution on both the local device and ES to reduce task completion time. However, the aforementioned studies have not taken into account that, as the number of edge servers and vehicles increases, the size of the decision space also expands, thereby affecting the real-time capability of obtaining the optimal offloading strategy.

2.3. Task Offloading with DT

Digital twin is a technology that enables real-time mapping and interaction between virtual models and their corresponding physical entities, processes, systems, and environments. It has been widely applied in various fields such as manufacturing, transportation, and smart cities [26,27]. Dai et al. [28] propose a DRL-based resource allocation approach for digital twin-enabled VEC networks. They jointly optimize computational resource allocation and task offloading to minimize overall system offloading latency and enhance network performance and computational efficiency. Cao et al. [29] apply digital twin technology to vehicular task offloading scenarios, addressing vehicle mobility challenges through the formulation of a multi-objective joint optimization problem. Sun et al. [30]

introduce a mobility-aware offloading approach for digital twin-enhanced networks. By constraining service migration costs, the approach aims to minimize offloading waiting time. They employ Lyapunov optimization to convert long-term migration cost constraints into a multi-objective dynamic optimization problem, which is then solved using a DRL algorithm. In addition, several other notable studies have explored the role of DT in various scenarios. For instance, some studies use DT to predict the arrival rate of tasks [12] at future edge servers, simulate resource allocation [13], or monitor global information and acquire historical data [14] through DT. Subsequently, these studies integrate DRL algorithms to make decisions regarding task offloading locations or resource allocation. The aforementioned studies employ DT technology as an auxiliary approach to address task offloading in vehicular networks. Although this represents an innovative attempt, other aspects of the proposed approaches still suffer from limitations such as relying on a single optimization objective or neglecting the reduction of the decision space.

2.4. Summary

By analyzing prior studies, the related work is summarized as follows. First, leveraging the idle computing resources [31] of vehicles can alleviate the load pressure on edge servers in V2I scenarios. Second, DRL algorithms have proven effective in addressing task offloading problems in dynamic and heterogeneous environments. Third, DT technology provides valuable support for tackling high-risk or challenging tasks in real-world scenarios. Nevertheless, the core challenge of vehicular task offloading remains how to deliver efficient real-time services in highly dynamic vehicular environments. To this end, this paper integrates DRL and DT technologies and proposes the DTAITO approach, which optimizes task offloading decisions in VEC scenarios and enables efficient real-time services in dynamic vehicular networks while simultaneously improving overall system performance.

3. System Model

3.1. Network Model

The digital twin-assisted VEC architecture is illustrated in Figure 1. The digital twin network (DTN) is structured into two parts: a digital twin layer and a physical entity layer. Meanwhile, the vehicular edge computing system is organized into three tiers, namely the cloud, edge, and user layers. Vehicles in the user layer are responsible for collecting and analyzing data, and they offload tasks to other vehicles when computational resources are insufficient, thereby reducing the burden on roadside units (RSUs). RSUs in the edge layer communicate wirelessly with surrounding vehicles, acquiring real-time vehicle information and generating digital twin models to reflect and predict the physical state of vehicles in real time. The cloud layer consists of high-performance servers responsible for efficiently managing the edge servers. The architecture of the DTN comprises three fundamental modules: model mapping, data storage and digital twin management. These modules are intended to facilitate real-time updates and sustain synchronization across the physical and digital layers.

By utilizing a clustering algorithm assisted by the DTN deployed on RSUs, the comprehensive information of all vehicles on the road can be acquired, enabling the dynamic grouping of vehicles into distinct aggregation clusters. Each aggregation group consists of an RSU connected to an edge server and K vehicles, denoted by the set $V = \{1, 2, \ldots, V\}$. All vehicles in the cluster have access to the RSU. When a vehicle lacks sufficient resources to execute a task locally, it initiates constrained offloading within the group, thereby narrowing the candidate offloading targets in advance. Vehicles within the group that lack the computational capacity to handle intensive tasks [32] send task requests to the RSU. The RSU then makes optimal offloading decisions based on factors such as the available resources and load of the connected ES, as well as the idle resources of other vehicles, thereby reducing both task execution energy consumption and delay.

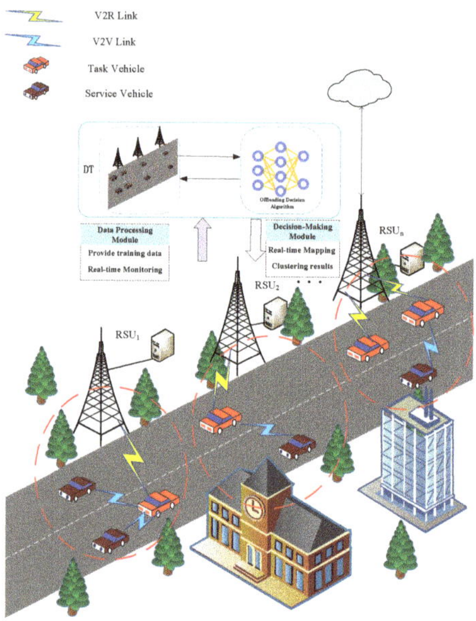

Figure 1. The VEC network assisted by digital twins.

Based on their roles in requesting or providing computational resources, vehicles within an aggregation group are categorized as service vehicles (SVs) and task vehicles (TVs). Assume there are K vehicles on the road. Among them, i vehicles request task offloading during a given period and are represented by $TV = \{TV_1, TV_2, \ldots, TV_I\}$, while j vehicles provide computational resources and are represented by $SV = \{SV_1, SV_2, \ldots, SV_J\}$. We let $H_i = \{D_i, C_i, T_i^{tolerate}\}$ express the task of vehicle, where C_i represents the number of CPU cycles required to complete task H_i, D_i represents the size of the input data and $T_i^{tolerate}$ represents the maximum tolerable latency of task H_i. This work adopts a partial offloading approach, whereby the task of TV_i can be offloaded to either the RSU or an SV according to an optimal offloading ratio. We let θ_i represent the proportion of the task offloaded, and $1 - \theta_i$ represent the proportion executed locally, with $\theta_i \in [0, 1]$. $\theta_i = 1$ means that it will be fully offloaded, $\theta_i = 0$ denotes that the task will be executed entirely locally. $0 < L < 1$ represents partial task offloading, in which the task is partially executed locally and partially at the ES, enabling collaborative processing between the local device and the ES.

3.2. Social Relationship Model

Considering the highly dynamic properties of VEC networks, unstable communication links can significantly increase both energy consumption and latency. Therefore, ensuring the stability of inter-vehicle communication links is critical. To address this, the DTAITO approach introduces a social relationship model that integrates multi-scale factors within the VEC network. It constructs social trust values from raw data and represents them as a social trust matrix, which serves as a quantitative indicator of inter-vehicle social relationships. This matrix is used to describe the stability of communication links between vehicles, thereby mitigating the challenges posed by vehicular mobility. The core idea of the social trust value is to assess the level of trust between two vehicles based on their proximity, evaluated using two key parameters: directional similarity and velocity similarity.

(1) *Directional Similarity*: $o_{i,j}^{d}$ is used to indicate whether the directions of vehicles TV_i and SV_j are aligned. It is defined by the following expression:

$$o_{i,j}^{d} = \begin{cases} 0, & \text{if } i \text{ has the same direction as } j \\ 1, & \text{if } i \text{ has no same direction as } j \end{cases} \tag{1}$$

(2) *Velocity Similarity*: Let v_i and v_j represent the speeds of vehicle i and j, respectively. The velocity similarity between the two vehicles is denoted by $o_{i,j}^{v}$, and it is defined by the following expression:

$$o_{i,j}^{v} = \begin{cases} 0, & \text{if } v_i = 0 \text{ or } v_j = 0 \\ \frac{v_j}{v_i}, & \text{if } v_j < v_i \\ \frac{v_i}{v_j}, & \text{if } v_i < v_j \\ 1, & \text{if } v_i = v_j \end{cases} \tag{2}$$

Based on directional similarity and velocity similarity, the social trust value between vehicle i and j is expressed as:

$$o_{i,j} = \eta_1 o_{i,j}^{d} + \eta_2 o_{i,j}^{v} \tag{3}$$

where η_1 and η_2 are the weighting coefficients for directional and velocity similarity, respectively. A higher value of $o_{i,j}$ indicates a stronger trust level between vehicle i and j . For ease of representation, $U = [o_{i,j}]_{M \times M}$ is introduced to describe the trust relationships among vehicles within a given region.

By clustering vehicles according to the social relationship model, communication links within each aggregation group are stabilized, thereby mitigating the latency and energy overhead caused by link instability or disconnection. When applying the DRL algorithm for offloading decisions, this approach significantly reduces the decision space and improves the efficiency of V2V task offloading.

3.3. Communication Model

When the task of TV_i is offloaded to the ES, data transmission is required. The communication model we adopt is similar to that presented in [33]. Let R_i represent the data transmission rate from TV_i to RSU or SV_j, and it is calculated as follows:

$$R_i = W_i \log_2\left(1 + \frac{P_i d_i^{-\beta} |h_i|^2}{N_0 + I_n}\right) \tag{4}$$

where W_i represents the bandwidth of the wireless channel, d_i indicates the distance between TV_i, P_i represents the transmission power used by the vehicle to upload data. β is the exponent of path loss, d_i indicates the distance between TV_i and ES or another vehicle SV_j, h_i denotes the wireless channel gain, I_i indicates the inter-cell interference of the uplink [34], and N_0 refers to the Gaussian noise power in the channel. Given that the delay in returning the results is minimal and can be disregarded, the transmission rate for result delivery is not considered in this study.

Offloading an excessive number of tasks to the SVs can cause significant interference, impacting communication efficiency. Additionally, interference in the communication link may result in fluctuations in the V2V communication range. The instant V2V communication, denoted as $\mathcal{D}$, is given by the following expression:

$$\mathcal{D} = \mathcal{D}_0 \times \ell\left(1 + \frac{P_i d_i^{-\beta} |h_i|^2}{N_0 + I_n}\right) \tag{5}$$

where ℓ is the adjustment coefficient and $\mathcal{D}_0$ is the initial communication distance.

3.4. *Task Offloading Model*

3.4.1. Local Computing Model

When a vehicle has sufficient computational resources to process its own tasks, it does not need to rely on the ES or other vehicles. Under this circumstance, the local computation of the task involves both latency and energy consumption, denoted as T_i^{local} and E_i^{local}, respectively. The corresponding formulas are given as follows:

$$T_i^{local} = \frac{(1-\theta_i)C_i}{f_i} \tag{6}$$

$$E_i^{local} = \kappa(f_i)^2(1-\theta_i)C_i \tag{7}$$

where f_i represents the computational capability of TV_i, and κ denotes the power consumption coefficient of the vehicle.

3.4.2. Edge Computing Model

When the task of TV_i is offloaded, and the RSU has sufficient computational resources with low load, the DTAITO approach allows the requesting vehicle to offload its task to the edge server associated to the RSU for processing. In this case, the total delay is primarily composed of the transmission delay from the vehicle to the RSU and the computation delay at the ES. The energy consumption includes both the transmission energy to the RSU and the execution energy at the ES. The transmission and computation delays for tasks offloaded to the ES are expressed as follows:

$$T_i^{trans,es} = \frac{\theta_i D_i}{R_i^{v2r}} \tag{8}$$

$$T_i^{exe,es} = \frac{\theta_i C_i}{f_i^{es}} \tag{9}$$

The total delay for task processing at the ES can be expressed as:

$$T_i^{total,es} = T_i^{trans,es} + T_i^{exe,es} \tag{10}$$

where f_i^{es} represents the computational resources allocated by the ES to task H_i, which must be less than f^{es}. f^{es} denotes the computational capacity of the ES, measured in CPU cycles per second. As the output data size after task execution is much smaller than the input data size, the result return delay in the DTAITO approach will be reasonably ignored. The transmission energy to the RSU and the execution energy at the ES are expressed as follows:

$$E_i^{trans,es} = P_i^{trans} T_i^{trans,es} \tag{11}$$

$$E_i^{exe,es} = P_i^{exe} T_i^{exe,es} \tag{12}$$

The total energy consumption for task execution at the ES is displayed by:

$$E_i^{total,es} = E_i^{trans,es} + E_i^{exe,es} \tag{13}$$

When the RSU lacks sufficient computational resources or is heavily loaded, the task is offloaded to a service vehicle with available computing capacity for execution. Under this circumstance, the total delay $T_{i,j}^{total,sv}$ for completing the task comprises the transmission delay $T_{i,j}^{trans,sv}$ for sending H_i to SV_j, and the computation delay $T_{i,j}^{exe,sv}$ for executing it on SV_j. The corresponding expressions are given as follows:

$$T_{i,j}^{trans,sv} = \frac{\theta_i D_i}{R_i^{v2v}} \tag{14}$$

$$T_{i,j}^{exe,es} = \frac{\theta_i C_i}{f_{i,j}^{sv}} \tag{15}$$

where $f_{i,j}^{sv}$ represents the computational resources allocated by SV_j to TV_i, and $f_{i,j}^{sv}$ must be less than f_j^{sv}. f_j^{sv} denotes the computational capability of SV_j, measured in CPU cycles per second. Therefore, the total delay for executing task H_i offloaded to SV_j is given by:

$$T_{i,j}^{total,sv} = T_{i,j}^{trans,sv} + T_{i,j}^{exe,sv} \tag{16}$$

Under the assistance of SV_j, the total energy consumption $E_{i,j}^{total,sv}$ for completing the task includes the transmission energy from TV_i to SV_j and the computation energy consumed by H_i when processing the task on SV_j. The respective expressions are given as follows:

$$E_{i,j}^{trans,sv} = P_i^{trans} T_{i,j}^{trans,sv} \tag{17}$$

$$E_{i,j}^{exe,sv} = P_j^{exe} T_{i,j}^{exe,sv} \tag{18}$$

Therefore, the total energy consumption $E_{i,j}^{total,sv}$ for task H_i offloaded to SV_j for processing is expressed as:

$$E_{i,j}^{total,sv} = E_{i,j}^{trans,sv} + E_{i,j}^{exe,sv} \tag{19}$$

Therefore, when task H_i of TV_i is offloaded, the delay T_i^{off} and energy consumption E_i^{off} for the offloaded portion are given by the following expressions:

$$T_i^{off} = \begin{cases} T_i^{total,es}, & \text{if the task is offloaded to } ES \\ T_{i,j}^{total,sv}, & \text{if the task is offloaded to } SV_j \end{cases} \tag{20}$$

$$E_i^{off} = \begin{cases} E_i^{total,es}, & \text{if the task is offloaded to } ES \\ E_{i,j}^{total,sv}, & \text{if the task is offloaded to } SV_j \end{cases} \tag{21}$$

Since partial offloading allows local and offloaded computations to be executed in parallel, the execution delay and energy consumption for task H_i can be formulated based on the above equations as follows:

$$T_i = \max\{T_i^{local}, T_i^{off}\} \tag{22}$$

$$E_i = E_i^{local} + E_i^{off} \tag{23}$$

3.5. Problem Formulation

In line with most existing studies, this paper adopts energy consumption and delay as the key performance metrics for evaluating system efficiency. Two weighting parameters are introduced to transform the multi-objective optimization problem of energy consumption and delay into a single-objective one. By adjusting these weights, the model can accommodate varying user [35] preferences. The total cost incurred by all vehicles within a cluster can be formulated as Equation (24):

$$\min Z = \sum_{i=1}^{I} (\alpha_1 T_i + \alpha_2 E_i) \tag{24}$$

$$\text{s.t. } I \cup J = K, \tag{25}$$

$$T_i \leq T_i^{tolera}, \forall i \in I, \tag{26}$$

$$\theta_i \in [0,1], \forall i \in I, \tag{27}$$

$$0 \leq (f_{i,j}^{sv} | \theta_i \neq 0) \leq f_j^{sv}, \forall i \in I, \forall j \in J, \tag{28}$$

$$0 \leq (f_i^{es} | \theta_i \neq 0) \leq f^{es}, \forall i \in I, \tag{29}$$

$$\sum_{i=1}^{I} (f_i^{es} | \theta_i \neq 0) \leq f^{es}, \forall i \in I, \tag{30}$$

$$\alpha_1 + \alpha_2 = 1, \alpha_1 \in [0,1], \alpha_2 \in [0,1], \forall i \in I, \tag{31}$$

where constraint (25) requires that TV_i must select SV_j within the aggregation group to provide computational services. Constraint (26) ensures that the execution time of task H_i does not surpass its maximum tolerable latency. Constraint (27) stipulates that the offloading ratio of task H_i must not exceed 1, allowing any proportion of the task to be processed locally or offloaded. Constraints (28) and (29) ensure that the computing resources allocated to TV_i by SV_j and ES do not exceed their respective maximum computational capacities. Constraint (30) requires that the total computing resources allocated by the RSU to task H_i do not exceed its available computational capacity. Constraint (31) defines α_1 and α_2 as the relative weights of delay and energy consumption, which can be adjusted according to different users' service requirements.

When $\theta_i = 0/1$, the time complexity of obtaining the optimal solution increases exponentially with the number of TV. This problem has been proven to be NP-hard [36]. With the introduction of the partial offloading problem, where $\theta_i \in (0,1)$, the problem becomes more complex. Therefore, this study employs a DRL algorithm to solve it.

4. Proposed Approach

The DTAITO approach proposed in this study addresses the aforementioned problems through the GIVC algorithm and TD3 algorithm. First, the approach uses the GIVC algorithm assisted by DT for vehicle clustering, ensuring the stability of the links between vehicles within the aggregation group. Then, the TD3 algorithm is employed to obtain the optimal offloading decision, with the design of the action space, state space, and reward function for the partial offloading problem. By training a neural network, the optimal solution for the task offloading problem is obtained. In the end, a feedback mechanism is introduced to adjust the parameters of clustering according to the offloading results, enhancing the robustness of the GIVC algorithm in various environments.

4.1. Gravity-Inspired Vehicle Clustering (GIVC) Algorithm

Given the high vehicle density, direct large-scale scheduling is impractical. Aggregation groups are formed based on the availability and demand for computational resources, using the DT and GIVC algorithms to determine the optimal offloading space, thereby effectively reducing the complexity of task scheduling. A DT node for the VEC is established in each RSU, where each RSU collects the topology of vehicles and computational capabilities in the surrounding environment. Data is transmitted through wired communication, constructing the overall DT network of the VEC. For clarity, the DTAITO approach in this paper defines the elements of the DT network as $\{\Lambda, \Theta, \Psi\}$, where Λ represents the digital model of the vehicle, consisting of the task set $\{H_i\}$, the social trust value set $\{o_i^j\}$, the computational resource set $\{f_i\}$ and the transmission rate set $\{R_i\}$. $\Theta = \{\Theta_1, \Theta_2, \Theta_3\}$ denotes the correlation coefficient between computational resources, social trust values, and transmission rates in the DT network. Ψ is the cyclic sequence number, which assists in parameter updates.

The GIVC algorithm used for clustering in the DTAITO approach is an improvement based on the K-Means algorithm, inspired by Newton's law of gravitation. This paper uses the algorithm to generate optimal aggregation groups, each consisting of one RSU and V vehicles. In this study, the "mass" of a vehicle i is defined as:

$$M_i = \frac{C_i}{f_i} \tag{32}$$

where C_i denotes the number of CPU cycles required by vehicle i to complete task H_i and f_i represents the computational capability of each vehicle. This variable is used to estimate the computational demand of vehicle i, which is supplemented by offloading tasks to address resource deficiencies. When vehicle i acts as the service vehicle, its "mass" becomes M_i^{-1}. Next, according to Equation (32), the gravitational force between vehicle i and vehicle j can be expressed as:

$$F_{i,j} = \frac{\Theta_1 \max(M_i/M_j, M_j/M_i)}{(\Theta_2/\omega_{i,j} + \Theta_3/R_{i,j})^2} \tag{33}$$

where the numerator of Equation (33) primarily represents the supply–demand relationship strength between vehicle i and vehicle j, reflecting their relative strength in terms of computational resource requirements. The proposed method modifies the K-Means algorithm by replacing its distance metric in the denominator with social trust values and communication rates. Through the incorporation of the gravitational formula (33) in place of the distance element, enhanced clustering performance for vehicles is achieved.

Let the ensemble of vehicles in the region excluding the cluster centers be denoted as $\bar{X} = \{v_1, v_2, \ldots, v_n\}$, and the set of vehicles serving as the cluster centers be denoted as $\bar{Y} = \{v'_1, v'_2, \ldots, v'_m\}$. Ultimately, the aggregation groups produced by the algorithm are collectively denoted as $\overline{\Gamma} = \{\overline{\Gamma}_1, \overline{\Gamma}_2, \ldots, \overline{\Gamma}_m\}$. The specific procedure of Algorithm 1 is as follows.

Algorithm 1 GIVC Algorithm

Input: Desired number of aggregation groups; number of vehicles
Output: A set of m aggregation groups $\overline{\Gamma} = \{\overline{\Gamma}_1, \overline{\Gamma}_2, \ldots, \overline{\Gamma}_m\}$

```
Initialize model parameters Θ1, Θ2, Θ3, and the value of the number of aggregation groups m ;
Initialize the aggregation group set Γ̄ = ∅;
Randomly select m vehicles as cluster centers Ȳ = {v'1, v'2, ..., v'm};
for k = [1, 2, ..., m] do
    Update Γ̄k to Γ̄k = {v'k};
end for
for p = [1, 2, ..., n] do
    Calculate the gravitational set {F_{vi,vj}}, ∀vj ∈ Ȳ using Equation (33);
    Select the vehicles vj that make {F_{vi,vj}} = max{F_{vi,vj}};
    Update Γ̄j to Γ̄j = Γ̄j ∪ {vi};
end for
return Γ̄ = {Γ̄1, Γ̄2, ..., Γ̄m}.
```

4.2. Task Offloading Decision Approach

The Markov Decision Process (MDP) is formulated as a mathematical model to capture sequential decision-making in stochastic environments. First, the DTAITO approach models the above optimization problem as an MDP, and then uses the TD3 to make task offloading decisions.

4.2.1. Markov Decision Process

The MDP model is typically represented by a four-tuple (S, A, T, R), where S denotes the state space, A represents the action space, T is the state transition probability function (which is unknown in this paper), and R is the immediate reward obtained by performing action A in state S. Based on the above definitions, the problem under study is modeled as the following MDP model.

(1) **State Space**: The state space of the entire system is obtained through the DT-assisted clustering process, which includes the vehicles number in the aggregation group, the task information of TV, the related information between SV and TV, and the information of ES. Therefore, the system state is expressed as:

$$S = \{S_{H_i}, S_i, S_j, S_{es}\} \tag{34}$$

where S_{H_i} can further be expressed as (D_i, C_i, T_i^{tolera}), which includes the task size, the required computational resources, and the maximum tolerable delay. S_i denotes the information of task vehicle TV_i, including its transmission power P_i^{trans}, computation power P_i^{exe}, and remaining computational resources f_i^{remain}. S_j represents the information of service vehicle SV_j, including its computation power P_j^{exe} and remaining computational resources f_j^{remain}. S_{es} denotes the information of the ES connected to the RSU, including its computation capacity f^{es} and remaining computational resources f_{es}^{remain}.

(2) **Action Space**: To determine the offloading ratio and offloading target for each vehicle, $\theta_i \in [0,1]$ can represent three scenarios: full local execution, partial task offloading, and complete offloading. x_i^j denotes the task offloading location for TV_i, where $j \in \{0, 1, \ldots, J\}$ indicates offloading to the ES connected to the RSU or to an eligible SV_S. Therefore, the action space is expressed as:

$$A = \{\theta_i, x_i^j\} \tag{35}$$

(3) **Reward**: After executing action A in state S, the agent receives the corresponding reward $R(S, A)$. The goal of the DRL algorithm is to maximize cumulative rewards. To align the objective function with the goal of the algorithm, this study designs the following reward function:

$$R(S, A) = \begin{cases} -\sum\limits_{i=1}^{I} (\alpha_1 T_i + \alpha_2 E_i) \\ \vartheta \end{cases} \tag{36}$$

In this case, when the agent successfully completes the task as required, it receives reward $-\sum\limits_{i=1}^{I} (\alpha_1 T_i + \alpha_2 E_i)$. If the agent fails to complete the task as required, it incurs a corresponding penalty ϑ. Under this setup, the larger the reward value, the smaller the offloading cost Z that is focused on, thus achieving effective optimization of the system's performance.

4.2.2. Vehicle Partial Task Offloading with TD3

Given that the DQN [37] method is not well-suited for continuous action control problems and that the Deep Deterministic Policy Gradient (DDPG [38]) algorithm exhibits poor robustness in hyperparameter selection and tuning, the DTAITO approach chooses the TD3 algorithm to make partial offloading task decisions for vehicles. TD3 addresses issues such as value function overestimation bias, training instability, and slow convergence speed that exist in DDPG during policy optimization. Several improvements have been proposed to enhance the performance and stability of algorithm: First, a dual Q-network architecture is used, with two independent critic networks learning two Q-functions in parallel. When calculating target values, the smaller of the two Q-function estimates is chosen to effectively suppress the overestimation problem caused by value function approximation errors. Secondly, a target policy smoothing mechanism is introduced during the target policy calculation process. By adding truncated Gaussian noise to the target action, the tendency of the policy function to overfit in the steep regions of the Q-value function is reduced, thus improving the stability and robustness of the learning process. Finally, a delayed policy update mechanism is introduced, where the actor network is updated once for every several updates to the critic network. Consequently, the policy network benefits from more reliable value estimates, leading to reduced variance and improved training efficiency.

The flowchart of the TD3 algorithm is shown in Figure 2. First, the TD3 algorithm employs a DRL model composed of a main and a target network. Each network is composed of two critic networks and an actor network, which are used to approximate the policy function and the value function, respectively. At the same time, the parameters of the critic and actor networks in the target network are denoted as θ_1', θ_2' and ϕ'. The role of the actor network $\pi_\phi$is to generate action $a(t)$, that is:

$$a(t) = \pi_\phi(s) + \varepsilon, \varepsilon \sim N(0, \mu) \tag{37}$$

where ε represents the noise, which plays a crucial role in promoting exploration within the DRL model. It follows a normal distribution, characterized by a mean of 0 and a variance of μ .

The actor network receives its input from the state space, which is derived from the data provided by the DT. The actor network selects action $a(t)$ based on the present state $s(t)$, then engages with the environment, leading to the next state $s(t+1)$ and producing the reward $r(t)$ associated with performing that action in the given state. The resulting four-tuple $< s(t), a(t), r(t), s(t+1) >$ is then stored in the experience replay buffer for updating the TD3 network parameters. To update the parameters of the main actor network, the TD3 algorithm utilizes the deterministic policy gradient. The expression for the deterministic policy gradient is as follows:

$$\nabla_\phi J(\phi) = N^{-1} \sum \nabla_a Q_{\theta_1}(s, a)|_{a=\pi_\phi(s)} \nabla_\phi \pi_\phi(s) \tag{38}$$

where Q_{θ_1} represents the first critic network of the main network, and π_ϕ represents the actor network of the main network, which is used to approximate the optimal policy.

The parameter update formula for the main network is as follows:

$$\theta_i = \arg\min_{\theta_i} N^{-1} \sum (y - Q_{\theta_1}(s, a))^2 \tag{39}$$

where $Q_{\theta_1}(s, a)$ represents the actual value of the Q-function, and y represents the target Q-value of the target critic network. The calculation formula for y is as follows:

$$y = r + \gamma \min_{i=1,2} Q_{\theta_i'}(s', \tilde{a}) \tag{40}$$

where γ represents the discount factor, which lies within the range $[0, 1]$. r represents the immediate reward. $\tilde{a}$ is the action generated by $\pi_{\phi 1}$ based on state s'.

The parameters of the target network will be updated using soft updates, ensuring smoother and more stable parameter updates. The update formula is as follows:

$$\theta_i' \leftarrow \tau\theta_i + (1-\tau)\theta_i' \tag{41}$$

$$\phi' \leftarrow \tau\phi + (1-\tau)\phi' \tag{42}$$

where τ represents the soft update rate of the target network, which is typically set to a small value, such as 0.01 in this study. The specific details are shown in Algorithm 2.

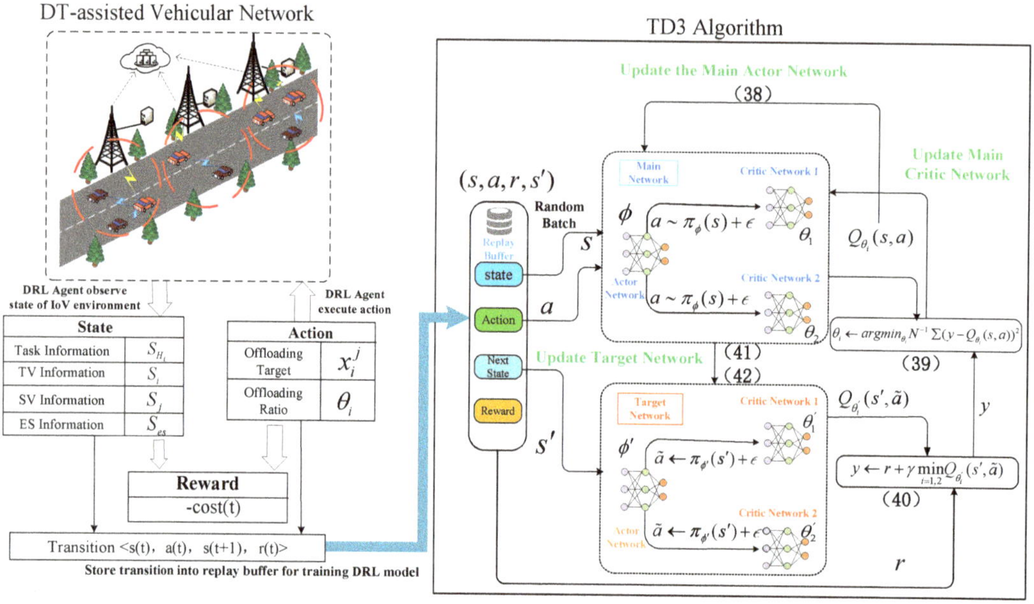

Figure 2. TD3 algorithm training process.

The computational complexity of the TD3 algorithm for partial offloading based on VEC can be analyzed by considering the operations performed at each step. The initialization of networks and the replay buffer has a complexity of $O(1)$. For each episode, initializing the exploration process and the environment is a constant time operation, giving a complexity of $O(1)$. Within each episode, there are T timesteps. Each timestep involves action selection, execution, observation, storing transitions, sampling mini-batches, target action calculation, target Q-value computation, and critic network update, each contributing $O(1)$ or $O(N)$, where N is the mini-batch size. Every d timesteps, the policy is updated, involving the actor network update and target network soft update, contributing complexities of $O(N)$ and $O(1)$. Summing up the complexities, the overall complexity is $O(1) + M \times (O(1) + T \times O(N)) + M \times (T/d) \times O(N)$. Upon simplification, the dominant term is $M \times T \times O(N)$, indicating that the computational complexity of TD3 algorithm is $O(M \times T \times N)$, showing that the complexity scales linearly with the number of episodes M, the number of timesteps per episode T, and the mini-batch size N.

Algorithm 2 TD3 Algorithm for Partial Offloading Based on VEC

Input: Task information and resource information
Output: Optimal task offloading strategy
Initialize the actor network π_ϕ and critic network Q_{θ_1}, Q_{θ_2} using random parameters ϕ, θ_1, θ_2;
Initialize the target network parameters $\theta'_1 \leftarrow \theta_1$, $\theta'_2 \leftarrow \theta_2$, $\phi' \leftarrow \phi$;
Initialize the mini-batch S and the experience replay buffer B;
Initialize the soft update factor τ and the discount factor γ;
for *episode* $\leftarrow 1$ **to** M **do**
  Reset simulation environment of VEC and obtain clustering results;
  Get initial state s_0;
  for $t \leftarrow 1$ **to** T **do**
    Obtain action $a(t)$ using Equation (37);
    Execute action $a(t)$, obtaining reward $r(t)$ and the next state $s(t+1)$;
    if B is not full **then**
      Store $< s(t), a(t), r(t), s(t+1) >$ into B for training the network;
    else
      Randomly replace $< s(t), a(t), r(t), s(t+1) >$ in B;
    end if
    Randomly sample mini-batch of N transitions from replay memory B;
    Update ϕ with Equation (38);
    Update θ_1 and θ_2 with Equation (39);
    if $t \mod d = 0$ **then**
      Update the target network parameters $\theta'_1, \theta'_2, \phi'$ using soft updates based on Equations (41) and (42);
    end if
  end for
end for

4.2.3. Feedback Mechanism

To further improve the robustness of the GIVC algorithm in dynamic and complex scenarios, a feedback mechanism is introduced, dynamically adjusting the parameters of the next cycle based on the offloading results from the previous cycle. Let $\Theta_T = \{\Theta_{1,T}, \Theta_{2,T}, \Theta_{3,T}\}$ denote the set of gravitational parameters within cycle T, which is updated according to the comparison results of the adjacent cycles.

First, the update formula for $\Theta_{1,T}$ is as follows:

$$\Theta_{1,T} = \Theta_{1,T-1} \cdot \frac{\sum_{i=1}^{m \cdot M} C_i}{\sum_{\Gamma_m \in \Gamma} \cdot \sum_{n=1}^{N} C'_n} \tag{43}$$

where Equation (43) demonstrates the role of resource factors in the gravitational model. In the formula, the coefficient denotes the ratio of computational resources of the current DT network to those of the final DT network within cycle T. If this ratio is above 1, it implies that the average resource requirement of the aggregation group has increased during the new mapping cycle. Therefore, $\Theta_{1,T}$ must be adjusted upward to strengthen the sensitivity of resource alignment in clustering.

$\Theta_{2,T}$ is used to measure the role of social trust values in the gravitational model. The update expression is given by:

$$\Theta_{2,T} = \Theta_{2,T-1} \cdot \frac{\sum_{\Gamma_m \in \Gamma} \sum_{m=1}^{M} \sum_{n=1}^{N} o'_{m,n}}{\sum_{i=1}^{k \cdot K} \cdot \sum_{j=1}^{k \cdot K} o_{i,j}} \tag{44}$$

where $o'_{m,n}$ and $o_{i,j}$ denote the social trust values between the two vehicles during cycles $T-1$ and T, respectively. When the coefficient in the formula is less than 1, it indicates that the social trust level within the aggregation group has increased in the new cycle. Therefore, $\Theta_{2,T}$ can be reduced to enhance the role of social trust values in the clustering process.

$\Theta_{3,T}$ denotes the impact of data transmission capability in the gravitational model. The update formula can be expressed as follows:

$$\Theta_{3,T} = \Theta_{3,T-1}\frac{\sum_{\Gamma_m \in \overline{\Gamma}} \sum_{m=1}^{M} \sum_{n=1}^{N} r'_n T'_{n,m}}{\sum_{i=1}^{k \cdot K} D_i} \tag{45}$$

where the coefficient in the formula represents the ratio of data transmission capability between the current cycle and the previous cycle. $T'_{n,m}$ represents the transmission time between vehicle m and n in cycle $T-1$. If this value is below 1, reducing $\Theta_{3,T}$ can increase the relative importance of data transmission capability during the clustering process.

Dynamically adjusting the parameters of the gravitational model can better reflect computational resource demands, social trust values, and data transmission capabilities, thereby effectively improving the accuracy of clustering and further optimizing the performance of the VEC network.

5. Simulation and Evaluation

5.1. Simulation Environment Setup

All experiments were performed on a machine with a GTX 1050 Ti (4 GB VRAM) graphics card and an Intel Core(TM) i7-8750H processor. The code and training weights of the tested algorithm did not use the official pre-trained version. Instead, a customized version of the code was employed to construct the base network architecture of the corresponding algorithm and implement the optimization functionalities. The experimental environment simulates a 2000 m long two-way road, with a total of 25 vehicles in the area, including task vehicles and service vehicles. Each aggregation group contains 15 vehicles. In the experiment, the RSUs are uniformly distributed, with a distance of 500 m between two RSUs, and each RSU has a coverage radius of 250 m. The noise power density is set to −174 dBm/Hz, the transmission bandwidth is 10 MHz, the channel gain range is (10^{-8}, 10^{-7}), and the vehicle's upload power is 0.1 W. For offloading tasks, the maximum tolerable delay is 1.5 s, the data size ranges from 0.8 MB to 1.2 MB, and the required CPU cycles for task execution range from 0.1 G to 1.0 G. The CPU frequencies of the ES and vehicles are 2.0 GHz to 2.8 GHz and 0.5 GHz, respectively. The algorithm implementation uses Python 3.8, PyTorch 1.11.0, as well as libraries such as NumPy 1.22.4 and pandas 1.4.2. The Adam optimizer is used for training the deep reinforcement learning model. Some experimental simulation parameters are shown in Table 1.

Table 1. Environmental simulation parameters.

Parameters	Value	Parameters	Value
N_0	−174 dBm/Hz	C_i	(0.1, 1.0) G
W_i	10 MHz	D_i	(0.8, 1.2) MB
W_i	0.1 W	f_i	0.5 GHz
$T_i^{tolerate}$	1.5 s	f_{rsu}	(2.0, 2.8) GHz

For the TD3 network structure shown in Figure 2, key parameters have been carefully designed to ensure the algorithm's stability and efficiency. The discount factor γ is set to 0.99 to achieve a reasonable trade-off between long-term and short-term returns, and to control the range of noise through the discount factor, thereby enhancing the robustness of the policy. The soft update coefficient τ is also set to 0.01 in the experiments to ensure the smooth updating of the target network parameters and avoid policy instability caused by too rapid parameter changes. Furthermore, to suppress noise interference during the policy optimization process, the noise clipping parameter is set to 0.5, which limits the range of random noise and ensures the rationality of the exploration behavior. The policy update delay is set to 2, which delays the update frequency of the actor network, allowing the critic network enough time to learn, thereby improving the accuracy of the Q-function. To improve the performance of the TD3 algorithm, some experiments are conducted to select the optimal values for several key parameters.

The experimental results in this study are presented through bar charts and line charts. The data source for these result graphs is explained as follows: Since the different approaches used in this experiment all include DRL algorithms, the rewards obtained in each round after training the DRL algorithm typically form a fluctuating curve. To evaluate the performance of the tested approaches, it is crucial to observe the overall trend of this curve. Therefore, we choose to average the results every 100 episodes to smooth the fluctuations and present them as a line chart. This method clearly demonstrates the trends of different approaches, making it easier to visually compare their performance. Additionally, the experimental results also include bar charts, where each value in the bar chart represents the average reward of each approach over the last 100 episodes.

5.1.1. Selection of Experience Replay Buffer Size

In Figure 3a, the total cost is compared for different experience replay buffer sizes (1600, 3200, 6400, 8400). Experimental results demonstrate that the total cost is minimized when the experience replay buffer size is 6400. Therefore, the buffer capacity is fixed at 6400 to optimize network performance, as it provides sufficient storage for diverse samples and alleviates excessive sample correlation during training.

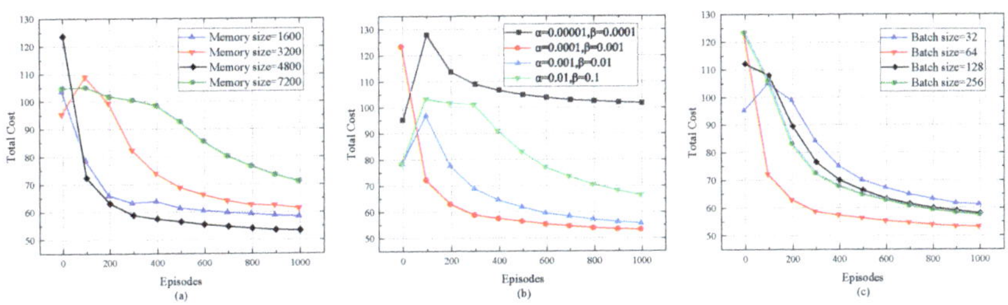

Figure 3. (**a**) The impact of experience replay pool size on total cost. (**b**) The impact of different batch sizes on total cost. (**c**) The impact of different learning rates on total cost.

5.1.2. Selection of Batch Size

In Figure 3b, the total cost is compared for different batch sizes (32, 64, 128, 256). The results show that the total cost is minimal when the batch size is 64. Therefore, the batch size is set to 64, which helps strike a balance between computational efficiency and the stability of gradient estimation.

5.1.3. Selection of Learning Rate Size

In Figure 3c compares the effect of varying learning rates on the total cost. The results indicate that assigning learning rates of 0.001 to the critic network and 0.0001 to the actor network leads to the minimum total cost. This helps balance the training speed of the network with convergence performance, reducing the likelihood of divergence due to an overly high learning rate or inefficiency from a low one.

5.2. Approach Evaluation

5.2.1. Comparison Approaches

The proposed GIVC-TD3 algorithm is compared with the following algorithms: No Clustering + TD3 (NC-TD3), K-Means + TD3 (K-TD3), Gravitational Model-based Clustering + DDPG (GIVC-DDPG), Gravitational Model-based Clustering + PPO (GIVC-PPO), Gravitational Model-based Clustering without feedback mechanism + TD3 (GIVC-NF-TD3), and Gravitational Model-based Clustering + Local Computation (GIVC-LOCAL). Except for the GIVC-NF-TD3 method, all other methods using the GIVC algorithm default to employing a feedback mechanism. The specific details are as follows:

(1) NC-TD3: This algorithm does not consider the use of clustering algorithms by DT to find the optimal decision space before offloading. The comparison demonstrates the benefit of pre-determining the optimal decision space using clustering algorithms.

(2) K-TD3: Leveraging DT assistance, this approach integrates K-Means clustering with TD3-based offloading decisions. Comparative analysis confirms the effectiveness and benefits of the GIVC algorithm.

(3) GIVC-DDPG: The vehicle clustering algorithm uses the GIVC algorithm, and the DRL algorithm for offloading decisions uses DDPG. The comparison with the TD3 algorithm in this study reflects whether the TD3 algorithm yields better results.

(4) GIVC-PPO: The GIVC algorithm is used for clustering, and the PPO algorithm is used for task offloading decisions.

(5) GIVC-NF-TD3: This method employs a clustering algorithm for clustering but does not use the feedback mechanism to dynamically adjust the parameters within the clustering algorithm. Instead, it utilizes the TD3 algorithm for offloading decisions.

(6) GIVC-LOCAL: In this approach, the task is executed only locally on the task vehicle. When computational resources are inadequate or the task surpasses the delay threshold, task execution will fail. This highlights the importance of task offloading technology.

5.2.2. Evaluation Metrics

(a) Total Cost (TC): This is the optimization objective of the system, representing the weighted sum of energy consumption and delay during the task offloading process. The value of TC reflects the quality of the offloading approach.

(b) Total Completion Delay (TCD): This refers to the sum of the computation delays for all vehicle tasks within the aggregation group, reflecting the performance of the task offloading approach in terms of delay.

(c) Total Energy Consumption (TEC): This is the total energy consumption for task execution within the aggregation group, reflecting the effectiveness of this approach in energy saving.

(d) Success Rate (SR): This is the ratio of tasks completed within the delay constraint to the total number of tasks requested, reflecting the stability of the approach.

5.3. Performance Evaluation

This section compares the proposed approach in this study with the aforementioned comparison approaches. The analysis is conducted by providing the average results of 10 independent runs under the same configuration.

5.3.1. Approach Optimization Performance Analysis

(1). Optimization Effect of Different Approaches on Total Cost

As shown in Figure 4a, different algorithms exhibit significant differences in optimizing total cost, with the GIVC-TD3 approach showing a distinct advantage. First, in the initial stage of the algorithm (0–200 episodes), GIVC-TD3 and GIVC-DDPG optimize significantly faster than the other approaches, with their total cost decreasing the most, demonstrating strong initial convergence ability. This is because the gravitational model-based vehicle clustering algorithm comprehensively considers factors such as communication, resources and social aspects, allowing it to obtain a reasonable aggregation group in advance. This reduces the decision space range, effectively lowering the complexity of the state space and reducing high system overhead costs caused by erroneous decisions to some extent. Secondly, in the mid-stage (200–600 episodes), the approaches using TD3 continue to optimize, while the GIVC-DDPG approach stabilizes around episode 400. Finally, in the later stage (600–1000 episodes), GIVC-TD3 shows the best convergence performance, with the total cost stabilizing around 56. Compared to K-TD3, NC-TD3, GIVC-DDPG, GIVC-NF-TD3 and GIVC-PPO, it reduces the total cost by 7.35%, 19.21%, 22.85%, 11.28% and 27.83%, respectively. The GIVC-NF-TD3 approach, due to the absence of a feedback mechanism, exhibits suboptimal performance in comparison to the GIVC-TD3 approach in terms of optimization effectiveness. In conclusion, the GIVC-TD3 approach demonstrates significant advantages both in terms of initial convergence speed and later-stage stability.

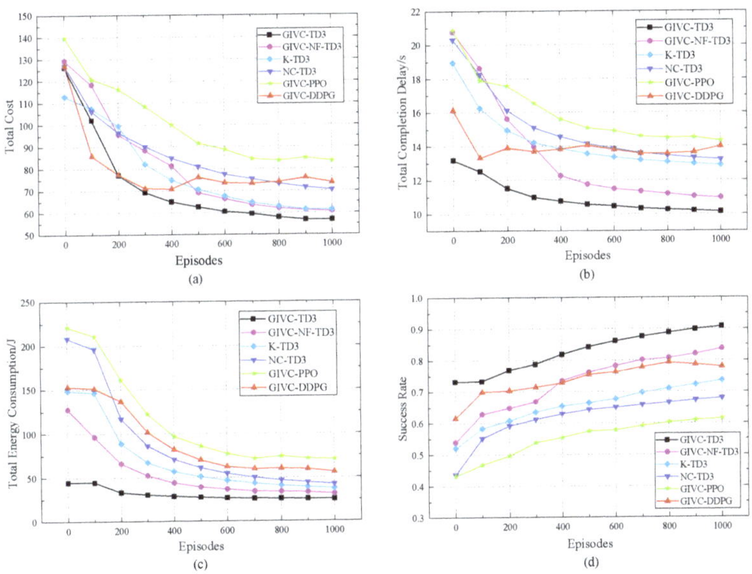

Figure 4. (**a**) Optimization effects of different approaches on total cost. (**b**) Impact of different approaches on latency. (**c**) Impact of different approaches on total energy consumption. (**d**) Impact of different approaches on offloading success rate.

(2). Optimization Effect of Different Approaches on Total Completion Delay

Figure 4b compares the impact of different approaches on the total completion delay. In the figure, the number of episodes is shown on the x-axis, and the total completion delay is shown on the y-axis. As the number of episodes increases, the delay of the NC-TD3, K-TD3, and GIVC-TD3 approaches decreases, while the GIVC-DDPG approach shows limited improvement. The total completion delay of the GIVC-TD3 approach is reduced by 21.10%, 23.02%, 27.05%, 18.74% and 31.34% compared to the GIVC-DDPG, K-TD3, NC-TD3, GIVC-NF-TD3 and GIVC-PPO approach, respectively. In contrast, the GIVC-TD3 approach proposed in this study achieves the lowest total completion delay. The reason for this is that the proposed approach uses the GIVC algorithm to obtain the most reasonable aggregation group, reducing the decision space, and applies the TD3 algorithm to make optimal offloading decisions. This allows tasks to be offloaded at the best ratio to the most suitable service vehicles or edge servers for computation. The results show that the GIVC-TD3 approach maximizes the utilization of computational resources and minimizes the total completion delay.

(3). Optimization Effect of Different Approaches on Total Energy Consumption

Figure 4c compares the energy consumption of the GIVC-TD3, K-TD3, NC-TD3 and GIVC-DDPG approaches. The results show that the proposed approach in our study effectively decreases the energy consumption of task computation. Specifically, the GIVC-TD3 approach reduces energy consumption by 31.81%, 39.64%, 42.76% and 73.07% compared to the K-TD3, NC-TD3, GIVC-NF-TD3 and GIVC-PPO approach, respectively. This can be attributed to the clustering algorithm employed in this study, which determines the optimal aggregation group by taking into account factors such as resources and speed, thus significantly reducing the high energy consumption caused by task failures resulting from unstable vehicle links. At the same time, compared to the GIVC-DDPG approach, the proposed approach in this study reduces energy consumption by 54.62%. This effect arises from the introduction of a dual Q-network in the TD3 algorithm, which effectively mitigates the overestimation bias and improves the stability and accuracy of the policy.

(4). Optimization Effect of Different Approaches on Offloading Success Rate

Figure 4d shows the impact of different approaches on the offloading success rate. In terms of success rate comparison, the average values of different methods are utilized to ensure the credibility of the proposed approaches. From the experimental analysis, the GIVC-TD3 method in this study demonstrates the highest offloading success rate. Compared to the NC-TD3 and K-TD3 methods, the success rate after convergence improves by approximately 23.58% and 33.77%, respectively. The improvement can be attributed to the adoption of the clustering algorithm based on the gravitational model. This algorithm, with the assistance of DT, efficiently aggregates the optimal task vehicles, service vehicles, and edge servers into a group, thereby reducing the decision space and mitigating task failures caused by unstable links. When compared to the GIVC-DDPG method, the proposed GIVC-TD3 method yields a success rate improvement of about 16.58%. This enhancement is due to the introduction of the TD3 algorithm, which decreases overestimation of Q-values through dual-value networks, thereby improving the stability and accuracy of decision-making. In comparison to the GIVC-NF-TD3 method, the success rate of GIVC-TD3 increases by 9.95%, which can be attributed to the incorporation of a feedback mechanism in this study, ensuring robust performance in the dynamic and complex vehicular network environment. Furthermore, compared to the GIVC-PPO method, the success rate of GIVC-TD3 improves by 27.89%, confirming that the use of the TD3 algorithm as the decision-making approach is highly suitable for the experimental environment in this study.

5.3.2. Approach Adaptability Analysis

(1). Adaptability of the approach under different task sizes

Figure 5a compares the total computation cost of four approaches under different task sizes. The x-axis represents task size, and the y-axis represents total cost. As the task size increases, the total cost of all approaches rises. However, among the four approaches, the proposed GIVC-TD3 approach has the lowest total cost, while the GIVC-LOCAL approach has the highest total cost. The reason for this is that, as the task size increases, the GIVC-TD3 approach, with limited computational resources at the edge layer, first employs the GIVC algorithm to obtain the optimal aggregation group and then utilizes the TD3 algorithm to make optimal offloading decisions, including whether to offload, the best offloading ratio and the optimal offloading location. It is really worth noting that for the GIVC-LOCAL approach, the total task cost remains almost unchanged when the task size is greater than or equal to 1 Mbits. This is because the delay in local task computation exceeds the maximum tolerable delay, causing the penalty to reach its maximum, thereby keeping the total cost constant.

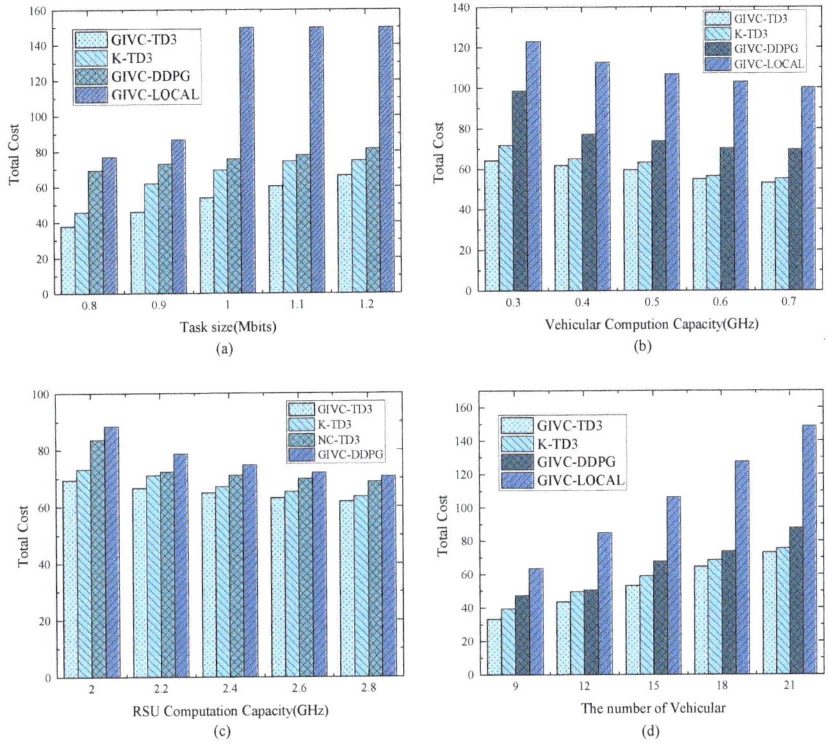

Figure 5. (**a**) The impact of different task sizes on the total cost of different approaches. (**b**) The impact of vehicle computing resources on the total cost of different approaches. (**c**) The impact of RSU computing resources on the total cost of different approaches. (**d**) The impact of the number of vehicles on the total cost of different approaches.

(2). Adaptability of the approach under different vehicle computational capacities

Figure 5b analyzes the impact of vehicle computational capacity on computation cost. The results show that as vehicle computational resources increase, the total computation cost of all approaches gradually decreases. This is because, with increased vehicle computational capacity, more task vehicles can obtain sufficient computational resources, which reduces both the energy consumption and transmission delay when offloading tasks to SVs or ES, as well as the high delay and energy losses caused by offloading failures. At the same time, among the four approaches, the proposed approach in this study consistently achieves the lowest total computation cost, followed by the K-TD3 approach and the GIVC-DDPG approach. This can be attributed to the fact that the algorithm in this study combines vehicle clustering algorithms with the TD3 deep reinforcement learning algorithm and ensures the robustness of the clustering algorithm through a feedback mechanism. In terms of performance, the approach introduced in this study surpasses the others.

(3). Adaptability of the approach under different RSU computational capacities

Figure 5c shows the impact of RSU computational capacity on the total computation cost of the four approaches. The results show that as the RSU computational capacity increases, the total computation cost of the approaches gradually decreases, indicating that an increase in RSU computational capacity enhances the overall system performance. It is worth noting that the proposed approach in this study consistently incurs the lowest total computation cost under different RSU computational capacities, while the local computation approach incurs the highest total computation cost. The main reason is that the proposed approach in this study makes full use of idle computational resources, combines an improved clustering algorithm to obtain the optimal aggregation group, and uses the TD3 algorithm to determine the best offloading location and task offloading ratio. Therefore, the final offloading decision minimizes the total computation cost.

(4). Adaptability of the approach under different vehicle counts

Figure 5d examines the impact of the number of vehicles on total computation cost. The experimental results show that as the number of vehicles increases, the total computation cost of the various approaches continues to rise. Among them, the proposed approach in this study has the lowest total computation cost. The main reason is that, first, this study uses the GIVC algorithm, which takes into account the distance, computational resources, and social trust values between vehicles. Even with an increase in the number of vehicles, the algorithm still achieves excellent aggregation groups, significantly reducing the size of the decision space. At the same time, the link quality between vehicles within the aggregation group is good, avoiding high delays and energy consumption caused by link interruptions. Furthermore, the feedback mechanism in this study enhances the robustness of the clustering algorithm as the number of vehicles increases. Meanwhile, the TD3 algorithm can quickly obtain optimal offloading decisions in complex environments with a large number of vehicles. The proposed approach in this study performs well in continuous action spaces, and as the number of vehicles increases, it still maintains the lowest total computation cost, demonstrating the good scalability of the approach.

6. Conclusions

This paper proposes a DTAITO task offloading approach for VEC systems, which comprehensively considers both delay and energy consumption, and defines it as a combinatorial optimization problem. The approach aims to provide an efficient and intelligent task offloading solution for dynamic and heterogeneous vehicular network environments, ensuring the smooth execution of user tasks. First, DT technology and the GIVC algorithm are used to cluster the vehicles on the road, obtaining the optimal decision space and ensuring the stability of vehicle links within the same aggregation group. Next, a partial task offloading method based on the TD3 algorithm is proposed. This method trains the offloading policy through the TD3 algorithm to obtain the best offloading decision. Finally, to ensure the stability of the clustering algorithm in different scenarios, a feedback mechanism is employed to adaptively tune the parameters of the GIVC algorithm according to offloading outcomes, thereby improving clustering performance in the subsequent round. Simulation results show that the proposed DTAITO approach outperforms other offloading approaches in terms of total delay, total cost, total energy consumption, and success rate. Although this study has made notable progress in both methodology and experimentation, several limitations remain to be addressed. First, in terms of digital twin technology, only a simplified version of the core functionalities was implemented, without constructing a comprehensive digital twin system that encompasses modeling, real-time interaction, and feedback mechanisms. This limitation may restrict the generalizability and applicability of this work. Second, due to space constraints, privacy preservation and secure communication during data transmission among vehicles were not sufficiently considered, which could pose potential risks in real vehicular networks.

Future work can be carried out in several directions. (1) Integrating resource allocation with task offloading to achieve more efficient system scheduling in multi-user competitive environments, thereby reducing resource wastage and improving overall performance; (2) developing advanced privacy-preserving mechanisms, such as differential privacy, to ensure data security while maintaining offloading efficiency; (3) exploring the feasibility of coordinating multiple edge servers within aggregation groups, aiming to enhance system adaptability and robustness in dynamic and complex scenarios; and (4) deploying a full-scale digital twin system and validating it in representative smart transportation scenarios, in order to assess its feasibility and practical value. By pursuing these directions, future studies are expected to better align with real-world requirements and provide both theoretical insights and practical support for the deep integration of edge computing and digital twin technologies.

Author Contributions: Conceptualization, Y.W., H.X. and M.Z.; methodology, Y.W., H.X. and M.Z.; software, H.X. and Y.W.; validation, H.X. and M.Z.; formal analysis, H.X.; investigation, H.X. and Y.W.; resources, H.X. and Y.W.; writing—original draft preparation, H.X. and Y.W.; writing—review and editing, Y.W. and H.X.; visualization, Y.W.; supervision, Y.W. All authors have read and agreed to the published version of the manuscript.

Funding: This work was supported by National Natural Science Foundation of China (62472147).

Data Availability Statement: Data are contained within the article.

Conflicts of Interest: The authors declare no conflicts of interest.

References

1. Kong, X.; Wang, K.; Hou, M.; Hao, X.; Shen, G.; Chen, X.; Xia, F. A federated learning-based license plate recognition scheme for 5G-enabled internet of vehicles. *IEEE Trans. Ind. Inform.* **2021**, *17*, 8523–8530. [CrossRef]
2. Zhang, K.; Cao, J.; Zhang, Y. Adaptive digital twin and multiagent deep reinforcement learning for vehicular edge computing and networks. *IEEE Trans. Ind. Inform.* **2021**, *18*, 1405–1413. [CrossRef]
3. Wang, S.; Song, X.; Xu, H.; Song, T.; Zhang, G.; Yang, Y. Joint offloading decision and resource allocation in vehicular edge computing networks. *Digit. Commun. Netw.* **2025**, *11*, 71–82. [CrossRef]
4. Liu, L.; Feng, J.; Pei, Q.; Chen, C.; Ming, Y.; Shang, B.; Dong, M. Blockchain-enabled secure data sharing scheme in mobile-edge computing: An asynchronous advantage actor–critic learning approach. *IEEE Internet Things J.* **2020**, *8*, 2342–2353. [CrossRef]
5. Chen, C.; Zeng, Y.; Li, H.; Liu, Y.; Wan, S. A multihop task offloading decision model in MEC-enabled internet of vehicles. *IEEE Internet Things J.* **2022**, *10*, 3215–3230. [CrossRef]
6. Wu, Q.; Zhao, Y.; Fan, Q.; Fan, P.; Wang, J.; Zhang, C. Mobility-aware cooperative caching in vehicular edge computing based on asynchronous federated and deep reinforcement learning. *IEEE J. Sel. Top. Signal Process.* **2022**, *17*, 66–81. [CrossRef]
7. Wu, Q.; Wang, W.; Fan, P.; Fan, Q.; Wang, J.; Letaief, K.B. URLLC-awared resource allocation for heterogeneous vehicular edge computing. *IEEE Trans. Veh. Technol.* **2024**, *73*, 11789–11805. [CrossRef]
8. Cao, H.; Lin, Z.; Yang, L.; Wang, J.; Guizani, M. Dt-sfc-6g: Digital twins assisted service function chains in softwarized 6g networks for emerging v2 x. *IEEE Netw.* **2023**, *37*, 289–296. [CrossRef]
9. Lu, Y.; Maharjan, S.; Zhang, Y. Adaptive edge association for wireless digital twin networks in 6G. *IEEE Internet Things J.* **2021**, *8*, 16219–16230. [CrossRef]
10. Liu, T.; Tang, L.; Wang, W.; Chen, Q.; Zeng, X. Digital-twin-assisted task offloading based on edge collaboration in the digital twin edge network. *IEEE Internet Things J.* **2021**, *9*, 1427–1444. [CrossRef]
11. Zhang, E.; Zhao, L.; Lin, N.; Zhang, W.; Hawbani, A.; Min, G. Cooperative task offloading in cybertwin-assisted vehicular edge computing. In Proceedings of the 2022 IEEE 20th International Conference on Embedded and Ubiquitous Computing (EUC), Wuhan, China, 9–11 December 2022; pp. 66–73.
12. Zheng, J.; Zhang, Y.; Luan, T.H.; Mu, P.K.; Li, G.; Dong, M.; Wu, Y. Digital twin enabled task offloading for IoVs: A learning-based approach. *IEEE Trans. Netw. Sci. Eng.* **2023**, *11*, 659–672. [CrossRef]
13. Yuan, X.; Zhang, W.; Yang, J.; Xu, M.; Niyato, D.; Deng, Q.; Li, C. Efficient IoV resource management through enhanced clustering, matching, and offloading in DT-enabled edge computing. *IEEE Internet Things J.* **2024**, *11*, 30172–30186. [CrossRef]
14. Sun, K.; Wu, J.; Pan, Q.; Zheng, X.; Li, J.; Yu, S. Leveraging digital twin and DRL for collaborative context offloading in C-V2X autonomous driving. *IEEE Trans. Veh. Technol.* **2023**, *73*, 5020–5035. [CrossRef]

15. Cao, H.; Garg, S.; Kaddoum, G.; Alrashoud, M.; Yang, L. Efficient resource allocation of slicing services in softwarized space-aerial-ground integrated networks for seamless and open access services. *IEEE Trans. Veh. Technol.* **2023**, *73*, 9284–9295. [CrossRef]
16. Zhao, L.; Zhang, E.; Wan, S.; Hawbani, A.; Al-Dubai, A.Y.; Min, G.; Zomaya, A.Y. MESON: A mobility-aware dependent task offloading scheme for urban vehicular edge computing. *IEEE Trans. Mob. Comput.* **2023**, *23*, 4259–4272. [CrossRef]
17. Li, M.; Gao, J.; Zhao, L.; Shen, X. Deep reinforcement learning for collaborative edge computing in vehicular networks. *IEEE Trans. Cogn. Commun. Netw.* **2020**, *6*, 1122–1135. [CrossRef]
18. Wu, H.; Ji, B.; Ma, H.; Zhang, X.; Xing, L.; Gao, J. R-MDDQN: A V2V-Based Secure Computation Offloading Algorithm for Video Analytics in Vehicle Edge Networks. *IEEE Trans. Veh. Technol.* **2025**, *74*, 10209–10224. [CrossRef]
19. Chen, C.; Zhang, Y.; Wang, Z.; Wan, S.; Pei, Q. Distributed computation offloading method based on deep reinforcement learning in ICV. *Appl. Soft Comput.* **2021**, *103*, 107108. [CrossRef]
20. Cong, Y.; Sun, W.; Xue, K.; Qian, Z.; Chen, M. Research on task offloading strategy of Internet of vehicles based on improved hybrid genetic algorithm. *J. Commun.* **2022**, *43*, 9.
21. Chen, F.; Li, L.; Zhang, R. Task offloading scheme of Internet of Vehicles based on improved immune genetic algorithm. *Appl. Res. Comput.* **2024**, *41*, 558–562.
22. Shi, J.; Du, J.; Shen, Y.; Wang, J.; Yuan, J.; Han, Z. DRL-based V2V computation offloading for blockchain-enabled vehicular networks. *IEEE Trans. Mob. Comput.* **2022**, *22*, 3882–3897. [CrossRef]
23. Yao, L.; Xu, X.; Bilal, M.; Wang, H. Dynamic edge computation offloading for internet of vehicles with deep reinforcement learning. *IEEE Trans. Intell. Transp. Syst.* **2022**, *24*, 12991–12999. [CrossRef]
24. Huang, J.; Wan, J.; Lv, B.; Ye, Q.; Chen, Y. Joint computation offloading and resource allocation for edge-cloud collaboration in internet of vehicles via deep reinforcement learning. *IEEE Syst. J.* **2023**, *17*, 2500–2511. [CrossRef]
25. Gao, A.; Geng, T.; Ng, S.X.; Liang, W. A continuous policy learning approach for hybrid offloading in backscatter communication. *IEEE Commun. Lett.* **2020**, *25*, 523–527. [CrossRef]
26. Liao, H.; Zhou, Z.; Liu, N.; Zhang, Y.; Xu, G.; Wang, Z.; Mumtaz, S. Cloud-edge-device collaborative reliable and communication-efficient digital twin for low-carbon electrical equipment management. *IEEE Trans. Ind. Inform.* **2022**, *19*, 1715–1724. [CrossRef]
27. Zhao, L.; Bi, Z.; Hawbani, A.; Yu, K.; Zhang, Y.; Guizani, M. ELITE: An intelligent digital twin-based hierarchical routing scheme for softwarized vehicular networks. *IEEE Trans. Mob. Comput.* **2022**, *22*, 5231–5247. [CrossRef]
28. Dai, Y.; Zhang, Y. Adaptive digital twin for vehicular edge computing and networks. *J. Commun. Inf. Netw.* **2022**, *7*, 48–59. [CrossRef]
29. Cao, B.; Li, Z.; Liu, X.; Lv, Z.; He, H. Mobility-aware multiobjective task offloading for vehicular edge computing in digital twin environment. *IEEE J. Sel. Areas Commun.* **2023**, *41*, 3046–3055. [CrossRef]
30. Sun, W.; Zhang, H.; Wang, R.; Zhang, Y. Reducing offloading latency for digital twin edge networks in 6G. *IEEE Trans. Veh. Technol.* **2020**, *69*, 12240–12251. [CrossRef]
31. Cao, H.; Kumar, N.; Yang, L.; Guizani, M.; Yu, F.R. Resource orchestration and allocation of E2E slices in softwarized UAVs-assisted 6G terrestrial networks. *IEEE Trans. Netw. Serv. Manag.* **2023**, *21*, 1032–1047. [CrossRef]
32. Bozorgchenani, A.; Mashhadi, F.; Tarchi, D.; Monroy, S.A.S. Multi-objective computation sharing in energy and delay constrained mobile edge computing environments. *IEEE Trans. Mob. Comput.* **2020**, *20*, 2992–3005. [CrossRef]
33. Zhao, L.; Li, T.; Zhang, E.; Lin, Y.; Wan, S.; Hawbani, A.; Guizani, M. Adaptive swarm intelligent offloading based on digital twin-assisted prediction in VEC. *IEEE Trans. Mob. Comput.* **2023**, *23*, 8158–8174. [CrossRef]
34. Feng, W.; Zhang, N.; Li, S.; Lin, S.; Ning, R.; Yang, S.; Gao, Y. Latency minimization of reverse offloading in vehicular edge computing. *IEEE Trans. Veh. Technol.* **2022**, *71*, 5343–5357. [CrossRef]
35. Cao, H.; Yang, L.; Garg, S.; Alrashoud, M.; Guizani, M. Softwarized resource allocation of tailored services with zero security trust in 6G networks. *IEEE Wirel. Commun.* **2024**, *31*, 58–65. [CrossRef]
36. Kuang, Z.; Chen, Q.; Li, L.; Deng, X.; Chen, Z. Multi-user Edge Computing Task offloading Scheduling and Resource Allocation Based on Deep Reinforcement Learning. *Chin. J. Comput.* **2022**, *45*, 13.
37. Son, D.B.; Binh, T.H.; Vo, H.K.; Nguyen, B.M.; Binh, H.T.T.; Yu, S. Value-based reinforcement learning approaches for task offloading in delay constrained vehicular edge computing. *Eng. Appl. Artif. Intell.* **2022**, *113*, 104898. [CrossRef]
38. Moon, S.; Lim, Y. Federated deep reinforcement learning based task offloading with power control in vehicular edge computing. *Sensors* **2022**, *22*, 9595. [CrossRef]

electronics

MDPI

Article

Spatially Adaptive and Distillation-Enhanced Mini-Patch Attacks for Remote Sensing Image Object Detection

Zhihan Yang, Xiaohui Li *, Linchao Zhang and Yingjie Xu

Information Science Academy, China Electronics Technology Group Corporation, Beijing 100846, China; zhihanyangzn@163.com (Z.Y.); hune213@163.com (L.Z.); yjiexu0518@163.com (Y.X.);
* Correspondence: lxh330@163.com

Abstract

Despite the remarkable success of Deep Neural Networks (DNNs) in Remote Sensing Image (RSI) object detection, they remain vulnerable to adversarial attacks. Numerous adversarial attack methods have been proposed for RSI; however, adding a single large-scale adversarial patch to certain high-value targets, which are typically large in physical scale and irregular in shape, is both costly and inflexible. To address this issue, we propose a strategy of using multiple compact patches. This approach introduces two fundamental challenges: (1) how to optimize patch placement for a synergistic attack effect, and (2) how to retain strong adversarial potency within size-constrained mini-patches. To overcome these challenges, we introduce the Spatially Adaptive and Distillation-Enhanced Mini-Patch Attack (SDMPA) framework, which consists of two key modules: (1) an Adaptive Sensitivity-Aware Positioning (ASAP) module, which resolves the placement challenge by fusing the model's attention maps from both an explainable and an adversarial perspective to identify optimal patch locations, and (2) a Distillation-based Mini-Patch Generation (DMPG) module, which tackles the potency challenge by leveraging knowledge distillation to transfer adversarial information from large teacher patches to small student patches. Extensive experiments on the RSOD and MAR20 datasets demonstrate that SDMPA significantly outperforms existing patch-based attack methods. For example, against YOLOv5n on the RSOD dataset, SDMPA achieves an Attack Success Rate (ASR) of 88.3% using only three small patches, surpassing other patch attack methods.

Keywords: adversarial attack; object detection; remote sensing image; knowledge distillation; adversarial robustness

1. Introduction

Remote sensing image (RSI) object detection plays a critical role in numerous real-world applications, including land resource monitoring, urban planning, environmental change detection, precision agriculture, and military surveillance. Deep learning techniques have significantly advanced in accuracy and robustness of object detection models in remote sensing scenes. Models such as YOLO, R-CNN, RetinaNet, DETR, and Swin Transformer have been widely applied to extract semantic information from high-resolution RSI, enabling accurate identification and localization of small, sparse, and densely distributed objects such as aircraft, vehicles, ships, and buildings.

Despite these advances, recent studies have shown that DNN-based object detectors are inherently vulnerable to adversarial attacks [1]. Among these, adversarial patch attacks have emerged as a particularly alarming threat. Unlike traditional pixel-level [2] attacks that

https://doi.org/10.3390/electronics14173433

introduce subtle perturbations across the entire image, adversarial patches are localized, designed to deceive a neural network's prediction [3,4].

An adversarial patch attack typically involves crafting a region of noise or texture that, when overlaid onto an image [5,6], can mislead the detector into ignoring objects, as illustrated in Figure 1, misclassifying them, or detecting false positives. Compared to noise-based attacks, patch-based attacks are highly efficient and deployment-friendly, especially when full-image perturbation is infeasible.

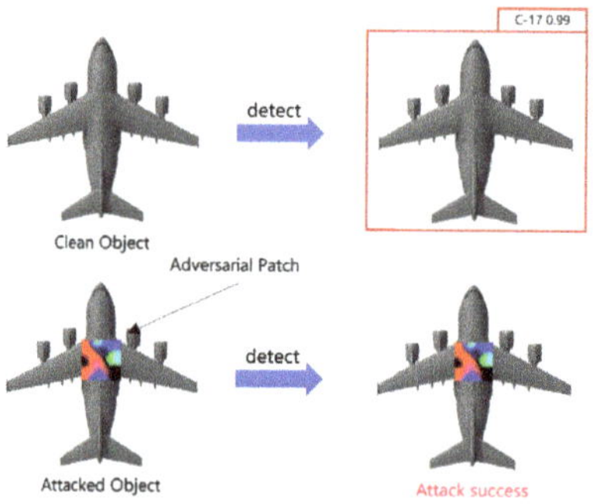

Figure 1. The effect of an adversarial patch attack. The top row shows the model correctly detecting the clean object, indicated by the red box. The bottom row demonstrates that after applying the adversarial patch, the attack is successful, causing the model to fail the detection.

Compared to general object detection scenarios, RSIs exhibit a significant span in target scales, which not only poses certain difficulties for conventional object detection but also introduces unique challenges for adversarial attacks—targets of different scales often lead to specific issues. Dong et al. [7] defined the target scales in RSI scenes as large, medium, and small, and conducted relevant statistical analyses. According to their research, small targets can account for approximately 60% in RSI. Although small targets dominate in RSI scenes, high-value large-scale targets (such as aircraft, oil tanks, and ships) are typically larger in physical dimensions. These large-scale targets are equally worthy of in-depth investigation, as deploying a single large-scale patch attack on them is often costly, conspicuous, and operationally inflexible, thereby limiting practical applications.

A straightforward solution is to reduce the patch size. However, simply downsizing the patch leads to weakened attack strength because the limited perturbation region may not inject sufficient adversarial signals into the network's high-level feature representations.

To overcome the limitations of single, large patches, a promising direction is to employ multiple compact patches. To the best of our knowledge, our work is the first to systematically investigate this multi-mini-patch strategy for the complex task of object detection. This pioneering approach, however, introduces two fundamental challenges: optimizing patch placement for synergistic effects, and retaining adversarial potency within size-constrained patches.

In light of these issues, we propose the Spatially Adaptive and Distillation-Enhanced Mini-Patch Attack (SDMPA) framework. To solve the placement problem, we design the Adaptive Sensitivity-Aware Positioning (ASAP) module, which leverages a novel fusion of explainable and adversarial signals. To solve the potency problem, we use knowledge distillation for adversarial content generation, realized through our Distillation-based Mini-Patch Generation (DMPG) module. This is, to our knowledge, the first work to repurpose knowledge distillation as an offensive tool to enhance the attack strength of compact patches. The contributions of our work can be summarized as follows:

- We propose a novel attack framework SDMPA for RSI object detection. To overcomes the impracticality of deploying a single, large-scale patch, we propose to generate multiple patches for adversarial attack.
- We design the Adaptive Sensitivity-Aware Positioning (ASAP) module, which intelligently selects optimal patch locations by fusing the model's explainable attention map with an adversarial gradient map. This synergistic approach ensures both effective placement and high attack potency.
- We develop the Distillation-based Mini-Patch Generation (DMPG) module, which utilizes knowledge distillation to transfer adversarial knowledge from large teacher patches to smaller student patches. This mechanism effectively enhances the adversarial potency of the compact patches.
- We conducted extensive experiments on the RSOD and MAR20 datasets. The results demonstrate that our SDMPA framework significantly outperforms existing patch-based attack methods by achieving a higher Attack Success Rate (ASR) with smaller adversarial patches.

2. Related Work

2.1. Adversarial Attack for Remote Sensing Image

Adversarial attacks have become a widely studied topic in the field of deep learning security [8]. Broadly speaking, these attacks can be categorized into two main types: pixel-level attacks [9], which apply imperceptible perturbations across an image to mislead the model's prediction, and patch-level attacks [10], which introduce a localized and visually perceptible adversarial patch designed to disrupt object detection or classification [11]. In particular, patch-level attacks such as DPatch [12] and Natural Patch [13] have demonstrated significant effectiveness in general computer vision scenarios, posing realistic threats even in physical-world settings [14]. These approaches typically aim to craft universal or targeted patches that can be deployed without requiring image-specific tuning, thereby offering high flexibility and practicality [15].

However, most of these patch-based methods [16–18] are developed for natural image benchmarks such as COCO or Pascal VOC. When transferred to RSI, they exhibit substantial limitations. Unlike natural images, RSIs feature densely distributed small objects, complex background textures, high viewpoint variability, and varying spatial resolutions. These characteristics pose unique challenges to adversarial attack design [19]. As a result, there has been a growing body of research that focuses specifically on adversarial attacks tailored to remote sensing applications.

To address the specific demands of RSIs, a range of specialized attack strategies have been proposed [20]. These include noise-based attacks that introduce pixel-level perturbations optimized for satellite or aerial imagery, background-based attacks such as the Contextual Background Attack (CBA) [21], which manipulate the semantic surroundings of target objects, and patch-based methods like the Adversarial Patch Positioning Attack (APPA) [22]. Additionally, the Environmental Masking Attack (EMA) [23] integrates scene priors and environmental factors to boost patch stealth and robustness under remote sensing conditions. Li [24] proposed a physical adversarial patch attack against fine grained aircraft recognition.

Although these works have greatly advanced the study of adversarial attacks in remote sensing, they predominantly focus on a single-patch paradigm, which is often costly and inflexible for physical deployment [25,26]. However, early attempts revealed that effectively coordinating multiple patches in object detection is a non-trivial challenge. For instance, Tang et al. [27] explored multi-patch attacks in RSI object detection scenarios but failed to achieve stronger attack effectiveness compared to a single patch. This limitation was mainly due to their use of a random strategy for patch placement, which did not exploit the potential synergistic effects among patches.

A notable exception is the work by Huang et al. [28], who proposed a multi-mini-patch adversarial attack framework designed for remote sensing imagery. Their study represents an early and valuable attempt to move beyond single-patch strategies. Building upon their foundational work, we identify two key areas for further advancement.

First, their approach primarily focuses on image classification models, while the more complex and broadly applicable task of object detection remains an open challenge. Unlike classification, object detection involves both localization and classification, demanding more precise feature manipulation. Second, the methodology for generating adversarial content within compact patches was not the central focus of their study; while they introduced the concept of using multiple small patches, the challenge of retaining strong adversarial effects when downsizing the patch warrants deeper investigation. Our work aims to address these specific challenges by proposing a systematic approach to jointly optimize patch content and placement.

2.2. Knowledge Distillation

Since Hinton et al. [29] first proposed Knowledge distillation (KD), KD has emerged as a powerful paradigm for model compression and knowledge transfer. In recent years, KD has demonstrated remarkable success in a variety of computer vision tasks. For example, it has been used to compress large language–vision models [30], improve the precision of object detectors [31,32], and enhance performance in dense prediction tasks such as semantic segmentation [33].

More recently, researchers have begun to explore the integration of knowledge distillation into adversarial learning frameworks. In most of these efforts, KD is adopted as a defense mechanism. Specifically, robust teacher models—often trained on adversarial examples—are used to guide student models toward improved adversarial robustness [34]. By mimicking the teacher's resilient behavior under attack, the student model can inherit resistance to various adversarial perturbations, thereby enhancing the system's overall security. These methods have demonstrated significant gains in adversarial defense, especially in classification tasks.

However, the use of knowledge distillation in the context of adversarial attacks has only recently begun to be explored. Liu [35] leveraged KD to generate adversarial patches with enhanced visual concealment, aiming to make the perturbations less perceptible to human observers.

While they focus on improving patch stealth, our work addresses a different yet equally critical challenge: retaining strong adversarial potency within a severely limited pixel budget. To the best of our knowledge, our work is the first to systematically exploit knowledge distillation as a tool for generating multiple compact mini-patches that bridge the gap between deployability and attack strength, particularly for the complex task of remote sensing object detection. This strategic repurposing of KD not only enables improved attack efficiency but also opens up new possibilities for research in adversarial patch attacks.

3. Proposed Method

3.1. Overview

The Spatially Adaptive and Distillation-Enhanced Mini-Patch Attack (SDMPA) framework is designed to address the impracticality of deploying single, large adversarial patches against large-scale physical targets in RSI. As illustrated in Figure 2, our framework overcomes this by strategically using multiple compact patches, tackling the dual challenges of optimal patch placement and adversarial strength retention through two core components.

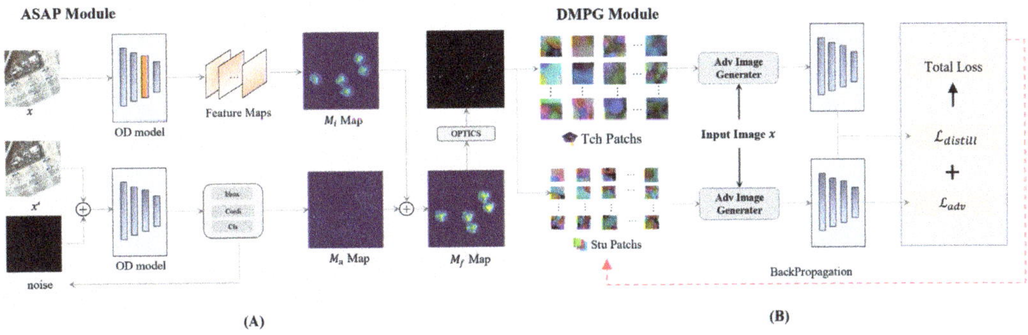

Figure 2. The overall framework of SDMPA. The ASAP module (Section (**A**)) facilitates effective selection of multiple patch locations by integrating information from both an explainable perspective and an adversarial perspective. In the generated attention maps, brighter colors indicate regions of higher model attention. The algorithm use the DMPG module (Section (**B**)) to generate multi-mini patches. The algorithm first generates teacher patches P_t with a larger size budget than the student patches. By constructing a distillation loss function, adversarial guidance is transferred from the teacher patch to the student patch.

First, the ASAP module solves the collaborative positioning problem. Rather than selecting vulnerable points individually, ASAP identifies a complementary set of locations that produce a synergistic attack effect. It achieves this by fusing two sources of information: a inner model attention map (M_i) for explainable view guidance and a adversarial view gradient map (M_a) for pinpointing adversarial weak spots within those regions. This fusion ensures that patch locations possess both global importance and local attack efficiency.

Second, after ASAP determines the optimal locations, the Distillation-based Mini-Patch Generation (DMPG) module addresses the challenge of retaining attack potency in small patches. It employs a knowledge distillation strategy where a larger, more powerful "teacher" patch is first optimized at each designated location. This teacher's adversarial knowledge is then transferred to a compact "student" patch via a specialized distillation loss function, guiding it to inherit potent attack characteristics despite its limited spatial budget. This combination of intelligent placement and guided generation allows SDMPA to achieve high attack success rates, making it a highly practical approach for real-world applications.

We provide a detailed description of the optimization procedures of the SDMPA approach in Algorithm 1. Specifically, given initial patch parameters, we first generate the explainable attention map M_i using LayerCAM and compute the adversarial gradient map M_a, fusing them into M_f to identify k optimal patch locations $\{L_1, \ldots, L_k\}$. Next, in Phase 1, we initialize the teacher patches P_t and sample mask M, placing the patches on the clean image x to form the adversarial image x_{adv}. Subsequently, we feed the adversarial image into the target detection model f, extract predictions *pred* via NMS, and use it as part of the teacher loss $\mathcal{L}_{tch}$. Then, we perform backpropagation to update the teacher patches P_t. Finally, we repeat the above steps until the end of the training process. In Phase 2, we use the distillation mechanism to transfer adversarial knowledge from the teacher patches to the student patches P_s, similarly generating x_{adv}, computing the student loss $\mathcal{L}_{stu}$ (including distillation loss), optimizing P_s, and repeating iterations to output the final adversarial image x_{adv}.

Algorithm 1: SDMPA.

Input: Target image x, detection model $f(\cdot)$, ground-truth label y, weights w_1, w_2, confidence thresholds T_c, T_i, number of patches k, patch size $s \times s$, maximum epoch N;
Output: Adversarial image x_{adv};
Generate explainable attention map $M_i \leftarrow \text{LayerCAM}(x, f)$;
Calculate adversarial gradient map $M_a \leftarrow 1_{S \times S} \otimes |\nabla_x \mathcal{L}_c(f(x), y)|$;
Create fused map $M_f \leftarrow w_1 \cdot M_i + w_2 \cdot M_a$;
Identify k optimal locations $\{L_1, \ldots, L_k\} \leftarrow \text{OPTICS}(M_f)$;
Phase 1: Generate optimized teacher patches;
Initialize teacher patches P_t;
Sample mask M with locations $\{L_1, \ldots, L_k\}$;
for *epoch = 1 to N* **do**
  Generate adversarial image $x_{adv} \leftarrow (1 - M) \odot x + M \odot P_t$;
  Obtain the output of detect model: $pred \leftarrow \text{NMS}(f(x_{adv}), T_c, T_i)$;
  Update the loss function min $\mathcal{L}_{tch}(pred)$;
  Optimize teacher patch P_t;
end
Store the final optimized teacher patch $\hat{P}_t \leftarrow P_t$;
Phase 2: Generate student patches via distillation;
Initialize student patch P_s;
Retrieve the final optimized teacher patch $\hat{P}_t$;
for *epoch = 1 to N* **do**
  Generate adversarial image $x_{adv} \leftarrow (1 - M) \odot x + M \odot P_s$;
  Obtain the output of detect model: $pred \leftarrow \text{NMS}(f(x_{adv}), T_c, T_i)$;
  Update the loss function min $\mathcal{L}_{stu}(pred)$;
  Optimize student patch P_s;
end
return x_{adv};

3.2. Adaptive Sensitivity-Aware Positioning (ASAP) Module

The Adaptive Sensitivity-Aware Positioning (ASAP) module is designed to precisely identify multiple, high-value locations on a target for our novel multi-mini-patch attack strategy. Its core idea is that the optimal attack points should simultaneously possess both semantic importance, reflecting the model's focus during normal recognition, and adversarial sensitivity, representing its vulnerabilities under attack. To this end, the ASAP module employs a dual-perspective fusion strategy to locate these critical regions.

First, we analyze the model's focus from a standard perspective by examining its behavior on unperturbed inputs. We use the LayerCAM [36] method to generate the model's internal attention map, denoted as M_i, while this map is rich in semantic information, highlighting the key regions the model relies on, it also has a low resolution and coarse granularity. Intuitively, perturbing these highly attended areas can most directly impact the model's decision-making process.

However, as shown by Wu et al. [37], a model's high-attention regions are not always equivalent to its adversarially vulnerable regions. Our multi-patch approach allows us to explore more complex attack patterns beyond targeting a single high-attention area. Adversarial perturbations can cause significant shifts in the model's attention, and these shifted feature points represent the model's sensitive areas from an adversarial perspective.

To capture these vulnerabilities from the adversarial perspective [38], we first generate an adversarial example by iteratively applying a small, imperceptible perturbation to the original sample. The number of iterations is empirically set to 10, with a step size α 0.001. The process for generating this adversarial example is defined as follows:

$$x_a^{(t+1)} = \mathrm{Clip}_{x_a,\epsilon}\left(x_a^{(t)} + \alpha \cdot \mathrm{sign}(\nabla_{x_a^{(t)}} J(x_a^{(t)}, y))\right) \tag{1}$$

Next, we obtain the model's attention map under adversarial conditions, which we define as the Adversarial Attention Map M_a. This map reveals the new, sensitive regions to which the model's attention shifts when under attack. To obtain a more fine-grained attention map, it is generated as follows:

$$M_a = 1_{S\times S} \otimes |\nabla_{x_a} \mathcal{L}_c(f(x_a), y)| \tag{2}$$

where ∇_{x_a} denotes the gradient of the loss function $\mathcal{L}_c$ with respect to the input image x_a, $1_{S\times S}$ is an all-one convolution kernel of size $S \times S$, and $\otimes$ represents the convolution operation. The kernel's side length, S, is equal to the patch's side length.

With these steps, we obtain two guidance maps that describe the model's behavior from complementary perspectives: M_i represents semantic importance, while M_a reveals adversarial vulnerability. The illustration of M_i and M_a is shown in Figure 3. To find optimal locations that possess both attributes, we combine them through a weighted fusion:

$$M_f = w_1 \cdot M_i + w_2 \cdot M_a \tag{3}$$

Here, w_1 and w_2 are hyperparameters that balance the contribution of the two perspectives. Through preliminary experiments, we determined that a weighting of $w_1 = 0.6$ and $w_2 = 0.4$ provides an effective balance between the model's standard attention and its adversarial sensitivities.

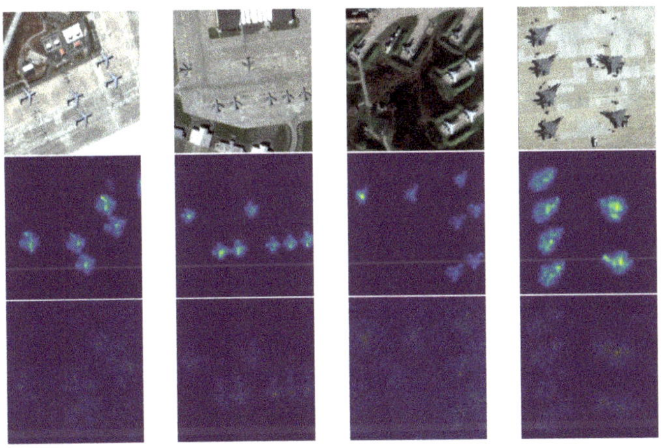

Figure 3. Feature map visualization: This figure shows the visualization results of feature maps at different levels. Specifically, M_i captures coarse semantic regions (second row), while M_a highlights fine-grained adversarially sensitive areas (third row), indicating that the selected features play an important role in the effectiveness of the attack.

Finally, to extract k discrete and spatially distinct attack points from the continuous fused map M_f, we employ the Ordering Points To Identify the Clustering Structure (OPTICS) algorithm. This approach is adept at identifying high-density core regions, which we designate as the final patch locations to maximize synergistic effects. Before applying the algorithm, we convert the map into a weighted point set, where each pixel's intensity determines its importance. To accommodate targets of varying scales, the algorithm's key parameter `max_eps` are dynamically adjusted based on the pixel count within the target area.

Specifically, we first construct weighted coordinate data based on pixel intensity values. The pixel intensities are normalized to the range of 1–5 and used as repetition counts, so that high-intensity pixels are assigned higher importance weights during clustering. Then, the key parameters of the OPTICS algorithm are dynamically adjusted according to the number of valid pixels within the target region: when the number of pixels is fewer than 50, we set `max_eps` = 30; when the number of pixels is between 50 and 200, we set `max_eps` = 40; and when the number of pixels exceeds 200, we set `max_eps` = 50.

For cluster identification, we utilize the xi-steep extraction method with $xi = 0.02$, a technique designed to automatically detect clusters by analyzing steep upward and downward shifts in the OPTICS reachability plot. Since this process yields cluster assignments rather than explicit centers, we then compute the weighted centroid C_i for each valid cluster i:

$$C_i = \frac{\sum_{p \in \text{Cluster}_i} I(p) \cdot p}{\sum_{p \in \text{Cluster}_i} I(p)} \tag{4}$$

where p represents the pixel coordinates and $I(p)$ is its intensity. To select the most potent locations, we score each centroid based on its cluster's total intensity and spatial compactness. In cases where the number of identified clusters is less than the required k, a supplementary strategy is activated. This strategy selects additional high-activation points from the remaining target area, ensuring that a sufficient number of spatially independent and optimally placed attack locations are always generated.

3.3. *Distillation-Based Mini Patch Generation (DMPG) Module*

Knowledge distillation is a well-known technique where a lightweight student model is trained by a more complex teacher model. Traditionally used for model compression, KD has been successfully applied in adversarial learning to enhance the robustness of models against adversarial perturbations. In the context of adversarial patch generation, we extend this concept to guide the optimization of compact patches. Instead of learning classification predictions, our goal is to offer a better training patch to compact patches by build the connection of strong adversarial patches. This allows the student patch to inherit the ability to perturb the model effectively while maintaining a small size, making it more deployable and harder to detect.

Figure 2 illustrates the core intuition behind the DMPG module: by leveraging a strong teacher patch as guidance, the student patch can obtain better attack information in the feature space, bridging the gap between weak and strong attacks while preserving compactness.

To implement this idea, we first generate larger teacher patches by optimization the teacher patch training loss $\mathcal{L}_{\text{tch}}$. These teacher patches serve as high-capacity ability of adversarial knowledge. We then distill the adversarial knowledge from teacher patches into smaller student patches through loss function $\mathcal{L}_{\text{distill}}$.

3.3.1. Teacher Patch Generation

The teacher patches, denoted as P_t, serve as a powerful knowledge source for the distillation process. Unlike the highly compact student patches, the teacher patches are generated with a larger size. The larger patch size not only means the bigger information capacity but also means it will be farther away from the ground truth in the high-dimensional space.

If the teacher patch is significantly larger than the student patch, the guidance effect may be weakened due to the substantial distribution gap between their feature representations in the high-dimensional space. The precise impact of the teacher–student size ratio will receive a detailed analysis in Section 4.4.3. The placement of these teacher patches follows the same spatial guidance as the student patches. Specifically, for each of the optimal locations identified by the ASAP module, we concurrently optimize a larger teacher patch and a smaller student patch. The optimization of the teacher patch is driven by three loss functions, each targeting a specific aspect of its performance:

- Detection Loss $\mathcal{L}_d$: This loss is designed to suppress the objectness confidence of predicted bounding boxes that correspond to ground-truth objects. To isolate relevant predictions from background noise that could hinder the optimization process, we first apply non-maximum suppression (NMS) to the detector's raw output. Specifically, we configure the NMS with a confidence threshold of 0.001 and an IoU threshold of 0.1. This pre-processing step ensures that the loss function focuses squarely on suppressing the most salient object predictions, thereby training the patch to diminish the detector's belief that a target is present.

$$\mathcal{L}_d = \frac{1}{N}\sum_{i=1}^{N} \mathrm{obj}(i) \tag{5}$$

  Here, $\mathrm{obj}(i)$ denotes the objectness score of the i-th predicted bounding box. Our goal is to directly minimize the detector's objectness confidence for true objects. Other scoring components (e.g., classification confidence) are not considered in this loss, since reducing objectness alone often suffices for successful suppression.
- Total Variation Loss $\mathcal{L}_{tv}$: This loss promotes spatial smoothness within the patch, reducing pixel-level artifacts that could make the patch detectable by human observers. This smoothness ensures that the perturbation remains subtle and stealthy, as described by:

$$\mathcal{L}_{tv} = \sum_{i,j}\left[(p_{i+1,j} - p_{i,j})^2 + (p_{i,j+1} - p_{i,j})^2\right] \tag{6}$$

- Saliency Loss $\mathcal{L}_{sal}$: The saliency loss reduces the perceptibility of the perturbation by discouraging overly bright or saturated colors. By controlling the color differences between the patch and surrounding pixels, this loss helps avoid detection by visual inspection, as defined by:

$$\begin{aligned} \mathrm{rg} &= R - G, \quad \mathrm{yb} = 0.5 \cdot (R + G) - B \\ \mathcal{L}_{\mathrm{sal}} &= \sqrt{\delta_{rg}^2 + \delta_{yb}^2} + 0.3 \cdot \sqrt{\mu_{rg}^2 + \mu_{yb}^2} \end{aligned} \tag{7}$$

The total loss for optimizing the teacher patch is the weighted sum of the three individual losses:

$$\mathcal{L}_{tch} = \alpha\mathcal{L}_d + \beta\mathcal{L}_{tv} + \eta\mathcal{L}_{sal} \tag{8}$$

3.3.2. Student Patch Generation

Once the high-capacity teacher patches P_t are optimized, the primary challenge shifts to generating the compact student patches P_s. In order to combine the information between student patches and teacher patches, we use the detection model's output layer to achieve this purpose.

The detection model provides three types of information: confidence scores, classification probabilities, and bounding box predictions. In the standard training phase, each type of information serves a distinct optimization objective. Similarly, during the adversarial distillation phase, these three types of information play complementary roles in guiding the optimization of student patches. The components of the distillation loss are illustrated in Figure 4.

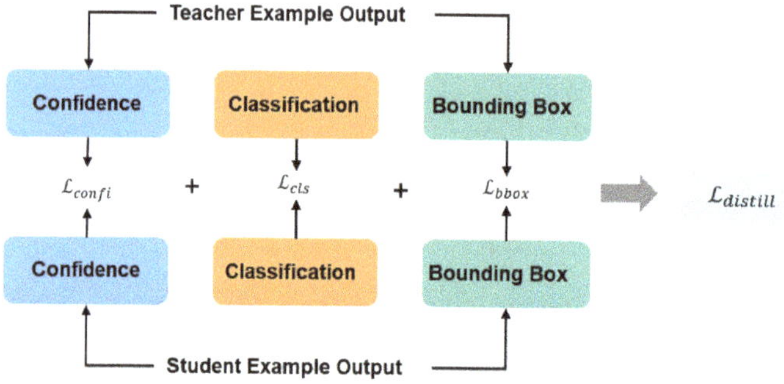

Figure 4. Illustration of the knowledge distillation loss function L_{distill} in the DMPG module.

Specifically, the distillation of bounding box predictions helps student patches learn the optimal spatial directions for perturbation, ensuring maximal disruption to object localization. The distillation of classification probabilities informs the student patches which categories are more susceptible to attack, enabling more targeted adversarial effects. Finally, the distillation of confidence scores indicates which targets are easier to suppress, guiding the student patches to focus on the most vulnerable objects. The distillation loss $\mathcal{L}_{\text{distill}}$ can be formulated as follows:

$$\mathcal{L}_{\text{distill}} = \lambda_{\text{conf}} \cdot \mathcal{L}_{\text{conf}} + \lambda_{\text{cls}} \cdot \mathcal{L}_{\text{cls}} + \lambda_{\text{bbox}} \cdot \mathcal{L}_{\text{bbox}} \tag{9}$$

Confidence Alignment Loss ($\mathcal{L}_{\text{conf}}$): The primary goal of the attack is to suppress object detections. This loss function is designed to efficiently transfer this capability from the teacher to the student:

$$\mathcal{L}_{\text{conf}} = \frac{1}{K}\sum_{k=1}^{K}\left|\sqrt{c_k^T} - \sqrt{c_k^S}\right| + \frac{1}{|\mathcal{U}|}\sum_{j\in\mathcal{U}} c_j^S \tag{10}$$

The design of this loss is principled, efficiently handling both matched and unmatched detections—where a pair is considered matched if their IoU exceeds 0.2.

- For matched detection pairs (indexed by k), we innovatively minimize the L1 distance of the square root of the confidence scores. The core objective is to amplify the otherwise faint discrepancies between the teacher and student models in the low-confidence regime (e.g., 0.1 vs. 0.05). This "amplification effect" provides a clearer, more potent guidance signal for the student's optimization.
- For unmatched boxes produced by the student patch ($\mathcal{U}$, indexed by j), where the teacher model detects nothing, the teacher provides an implicit "zero-confidence" target. In other words, the teacher's silence is itself a form of guidance, indicating these detections should not exist. Therefore, the term $\frac{1}{|\mathcal{U}|}\sum_{j\in\mathcal{U}} c_j^S$ is not a simple regularization penalty, but a direct distillation loss against this implicit zero-target, essentially minimizing $|c_j^S - 0|$.

Classification Alignment Loss ($\mathcal{L}_{\text{cls}}$): To ensure the student patch can induce the same misclassifications as the teacher, we align their probability distributions. Following standard practice in knowledge distillation, we employ the Kullback–Leibler (KL) divergence with a temperature scaling parameter $\tau = 2.0$:

$$\mathcal{L}_{\text{cls}} = \tau^2 \cdot \text{KL}\left(\text{softmax}\left(\frac{s^T}{\tau} \right) \parallel \text{softmax}\left(\frac{s^S}{\tau} \right) \right) \quad (11)$$

The temperature τ softens the probability distributions, allowing the student model to learn from the nuanced class relationships captured by the teacher's logits (s_k^T).

Bounding Box Alignment Loss ($\mathcal{L}_{\text{bbox}}$): The purpose of this loss is to extend the possible attack path. A bounding box predicted after the teacher's attack represents a successful adversarial state, where the model's internal features are likely severely corrupted. Thus, the true objective of $\mathcal{L}_{\text{bbox}}$ is to guide the student's predicted box locations toward the more adversarially potent directions established by the teacher, forcing it to predict in the most disruptive spatial state to study a more efficient attack knowledge. We employ the Generalized Intersection-over-Union (GIoU) loss to achieve this goal:

$$\mathcal{L}_{\text{bbox}} = \frac{1}{K} \sum_{k=1}^{K} \left(1 - \text{GIoU}(b_k^T, b_k^S) \right) \quad (12)$$

Here, K is the number of matched bounding box pairs between the teacher and student outputs. For the k-th matched pair, c^T, c^S are confidence scores, s^T, s^S are classification logits, and b^T, b^S are bounding box coordinates.

The final loss used to train the student patch integrates this distillation guidance with the fundamental attack objectives:

$$\mathcal{L}_{\text{stu}} = \alpha \mathcal{L}_d + \beta \mathcal{L}_{tv} + \eta \mathcal{L}_{sal} + \gamma \mathcal{L}_{\text{distill}} \quad (13)$$

where α, β, η, and γ are weighting coefficients. By jointly optimizing these components, the student patch is guided to inherit a rich and multi-faceted adversarial capability from its teacher, thereby achieving high attack efficacy despite its compact size.

4. Experiment

4.1. Experimental Settings

4.1.1. Dataset

We evaluate the effectiveness of our proposed method on two remote sensing object detection datasets: the Military Aircraft Recognition 20 dataset (MAR20) [39] and the Remote Sensing Object Detection dataset (RSOD) [40]. The MAR20 dataset comprises 3842 high-resolution remote sensing images collected from 60 military airports worldwide via Google Earth. It includes 22,341 annotated instances across 20 distinct military aircraft models. The RSOD dataset, released by Wuhan University, contains 976 images annotated for four object categories: aircraft, oil tanks, playgrounds, and overpasses. Specifically, it includes 446 images with 4993 aircraft instances, 165 images with 1586 oil tanks, 189 images with 191 playgrounds, and 176 images with 180 overpasses. In our experiments, we focus primarily on attacking the aircraft class. All images are resized to a uniform resolution of 640 × 640 pixels. Each dataset is split into training and validation sets using a 7:3 ratio. The object detection models are trained solely on the training set. During the adversarial attack phase, only the validation set is used for evaluation, ensuring no data leakage and a fair assessment of attack performance.

4.1.2. Evaluation Metrics

We evaluate attack performance using two complementary metrics: Attack Success Rate (ASR) and mean Average Precision (mAP). ASR measures the percentage of ground-truth objects that the detector fails to detect after the attack. It is defined as:

$$\text{ASR} = \frac{N_{\text{GT}} - N_{\text{TP}}}{N_{\text{GT}}} \times 100\% \tag{14}$$

where N_{GT} is the total number of ground-truth objects and N_{TP} is the number of true positives detected on the attacked images. A higher ASR signifies a more effective attack.

mAP is the standard metric for evaluating object detection performance, calculated as the mean of Average Precision (AP) over all object categories. In our context, a lower mAP indicates a more significant degradation of the detector's performance.

Together, these metrics provide a comprehensive assessment: ASR quantifies the attack's success in making objects disappear, while mAP reflects the performance degradation on the objects that remain detectable.

4.1.3. Implementation Details

All experiments are conducted on a workstation equipped with an Intel i5-14600KF CPU, 32 GB of RAM, and an NVIDIA RTX 4080 GPU. The implementation is based on PyTorch 2.4.1 and CUDA 12.4. For training adversarial patches, the learning rate is set to 0.1, and the maximum number of training epochs is fixed at 100. We use the Adam optimizer for gradient updates.

To enhance the visual naturalness and stealthiness of the generated adversarial patches, we incorporate the TV Loss and Sal Loss into the training objective. To enhance the robustness of adversarial patches under real-world lighting conditions, we apply a brightness adjustment during testing. During optimization, both the teacher and student patches are assigned identical weights for the TV and Sal losses to ensure appearance consistency and stable convergence. Meanwhile, the weights of other loss components are selectively adjusted according to different training objectives, such as detection suppression or knowledge distillation. The detailed parameter settings are provided in Table 1. A comprehensive summary of hyperparameters is provided in Appendix A.

Table 1. Loss function parameters configuration.

Parameters	Teacher Patches	Student Patches
Detect loss	1.0	0.3
TV loss	0.001	0.001
Sal loss	0.002	0.002
Distill loss	–	0.7

During the training phase, the confidence threshold is set to 0.001 to ensure sufficient gradient feedback from low-confidence predictions. In the validation (attack) phase, we adopt a confidence threshold of 0.4 and an IoU threshold of 0.45 to determine true positive matches. These settings are consistent with common object detection protocols.

4.2. Comparisons to SOTA Methods

To evaluate the effectiveness of our proposed method, we conduct comprehensive comparative experiments between SDMPA, APPA, NAP, and the method proposed by Thys et al. The baseline adversarial attack methods, APPA and Thys et al., are selected based on the recent survey by Mei et al. [41], which summarizes the state-of-the-art adversarial patch attacks in RSI object detection. Furthermore, NAP is a representative of natural patch attacks. To obtain a fair comparison in the experiment, we constrained the total perturbation area at 9% of the target bounding box area.

For SDMPA, we deploy three perturbation patches per target object, with each patch occupying approximately 3% of the target area. For the baseline methods, APPA, NAP, and Thys et al., we configured them according to their original design to generate a single, larger patch that covers the same total perturbation area of 9% of the target. This setup allows us to evaluate the effectiveness of our method. The attack results are visualized in Figure 5.

Figure 5. Visualization of adversarial attack results. Three adversarial patches are applied to each target, with each patch occupying 3% of the target's area. Green bounding boxes indicate detected objects.

The evaluations are performed on two widely used remote sensing object detection datasets, MAR20 and RSOD. Results are summarized in Table 2.

Table 2. Performance Comparison of Patch Attack Methods on ASR and mAP for Five Detection Models.

Datasets	Evaluation Metrics	Methods	YOLOv3	YOLOv5n	YOLOv5m	YOLOv5l	YOLOv8	Faster R-CNN
MAR20	ASR (%) ↑	Thys et al.	91.64	77.71	76.92	74.69	68.15	88.22
		APPA	88.94	82.29	83.58	72.31	74.55	91.95
		NAP	83.65	74.66	75.12	69.59	68.21	84.96
		SDMPA *	98.92	94.61	89.78	93.89	85.34	96.20
	mAP ↓	Thys et al.	0.494	0.473	0.681	0.594	0.641	0.273
		APPA	0.558	0.534	0.494	0.678	0.623	0.304
		NAP	0.578	0.584	0.523	0.629	0.682	0.382
		SDMPA *	0.232	0.269	0.273	0.318	0.404	0.151
RSOD	ASR (%) ↑	Thys et al.	78.32	66.09	68.07	73.24	63.38	78.80
		APPA	72.01	71.34	76.74	82.23	69.43	87.54
		NAP	74.46	63.21	73.89	78.34	67.66	76.65
		SDMPA *	93.23	88.30	85.40	82.37	79.83	93.32
	mAP ↓	Thys et al.	0.588	0.665	0.636	0.616	0.685	0.314
		APPA	0.553	0.531	0.504	0.609	0.749	0.373
		NAP	0.549	0.623	0.677	0.586	0.701	0.494
		SDMPA *	0.297	0.360	0.393	0.409	0.464	0.236

* Proposed methods; ↑: Higher is better; ↓: Lower is better.

As shown in Table 2, SDMPA consistently outperforms all baseline methods in terms of Attack Success Rate (ASR) across all models and datasets. For instance, on the MAR20 dataset, SDMPA achieves an ASR of 98.92% on YOLOv3, significantly higher than Thys et al. (91.64%), APPA (88.94%), and NAP (83.65%). The superiority is also evident against the more recent YOLOv8 model, where SDMPA achieves 85.34% ASR, far surpassing APPA (74.55%), NAP (68.21%), and Thys et al. (68.15%). Notably, when attacking the lightweight YOLOv5n model, SDMPA attains 94.61% ASR, demonstrating its robustness even on compact architectures. Similar trends are observed on other models, such as YOLOv5l and Faster R-CNN, where SDMPA maintains an ASR of above 93%, significantly outperforming prior approaches.

On the RSOD dataset, which contains smaller and more scattered objects, SDMPA remains superior. It achieves 93.23% ASR on YOLOv3 and 93.32% on Faster R-CNN, whereas APPA, Thys et al., and NAP show markedly lower performance, with ASRs often dropping below 80%. Against YOLOv8, SDMPA also shows a distinct advantage with an ASR of 79.83%, compared to baseline methods which fail to exceed 70%. This highlights SDMPA's advantage in handling fine-grained, real-world scenarios, where object distributions are more complex.

In terms of detection quality degradation, SDMPA also achieves the lowest mean Average Precision (mAP) across nearly all settings, indicating its strong ability to suppress correct detections. For example, on the MAR20 dataset, SDMPA reduces the mAP on YOLOv5l to 0.318, a sharp decline compared to APPA (0.678), NAP (0.629), and Thys et al. (0.594). Similarly, on RSOD, the mAP on YOLOv5n drops to 0.360 under SDMPA, significantly lower than APPA (0.531), NAP (0.623), and Thys et al. (0.665). The degradation effect is consistent on the YOLOv8 model, where SDMPA records the lowest mAP on both MAR20 (0.404) and RSOD (0.464) datasets.

The experimental results demonstrate the effectiveness of SDMPA, which achieves a favorable balance between attack performance and patch size. This improvement is primarily attributed to its adaptive patch placement strategy and distillation-based generation mechanism. The individual contribution of each of these components will be analyzed in the following sections.

To assess the generalization ability of SDMPA, we evaluate its transferability across different detection models. Patches are generated on a source detector (e.g., YOLOv5l) and applied directly to other target models. In order to obtain fair results, we constrained the perturbation rate to 8%, and each target received 4 mini patches.

As shown in Table 3, SDMPA achieves strong black-box performance. For example, patches trained on YOLOv5l yield an ASR of 92.8% on YOLOv3 and 97.7% on Faster R-CNN, indicating effective cross-model transfer. Even lightweight models like YOLOv5n produce transferable patches, reaching 89.3% ASR on YOLOv5m.These results demonstrate that SDMPA generates compact patches with strong transferability, benefiting from its distillation-based optimization strategy.

4.3. Ablation Study

To further validate the contributions of the proposed modules, this study conducted an ablation experiment, and the results are summarized in Table 4. The target model is YOLOv5L, and the dataset used is the MAR20 military aircraft remote sensing image dataset. The experiments in Table 2 are designed to evaluate the effectiveness of the ASAP and DMPG modules.

Table 3. Cross-model transferability of SDMPA. Diagonal entries (in bold) are white-box attacks.

Source	Metrics	YOLOv3	YOLOv5n	YOLOv5m	YOLOv5l	YOLOv8	Faster R-CNN
YOLOv3	ASR (%) mAP	**91.41** **0.270**	88.16 0.290	91.63 0.261	89.75 0.358	82.50 0.380	91.98 0.213
YOLOv5n	ASR (%) mAP	94.61 0.233	**90.76** **0.338**	89.38 0.208	85.68 0.326	78.20 0.420	91.53 0.220
YOLOv5m	ASR (%) mAP	91.67 0.204	90.42 0.320	**93.24** **0.250**	80.54 0.294	81.60 0.390	95.87 0.215
YOLOv5l	ASR (%) mAP	92.85 0.161	91.87 0.318	93.68 0.254	**89.23** **0.278**	84.70 0.360	97.78 0.213
YOLOv8	ASR (%) mAP	86.40 0.280	82.30 0.350	85.50 0.290	81.20 0.320	**82.34** **0.434**	92.60 0.240
Faster R-CNN	ASR (%) mAP	83.52 0.269	86.88 0.471	83.54 0.349	76.05 0.424	72.80 0.480	**95.83** **0.279**

Table 4. Ablation Study Results for ASAP and DMPG Modules.

ASAP	DMPG	Metric	Patch Number per Target				
			1	2	3	4	5
0	0	ASR (%) mAP	61.0 0.768	65.9 0.709	63.5 0.741	60.9 0.750	65.0 0.751
0	1	ASR (%) mAP	63.6 0.742	67.5 0.693	70.1 0.679	64.6 0.735	67.3 0.757
1	0	ASR (%) mAP	72.1 0.681	78.6 0.608	80.1 0.550	77.9 0.568	78.4 0.579
1	1	ASR (%) mAP	74.5 0.662	83.3 0.517	82.5 0.507	86.5 0.494	83.7 0.528

In addition, to assess the effectiveness of using multiple patches, we constrained the total perturbation rate to 5% per target and compared the attack results with different numbers of patches. For example, when the number of patches is one, the patch size is 5%; when the number of patches is five, each patch size is 1% of the target.

Table 4 summarizes the ablation results for the proposed ASAP and DMPG modules under varying patch counts. Several insights can be drawn from the results:

- Effect of Multi-Patch Strategy: As observed in the baseline setting (ASAP = 0, DMPG = 0), increasing the number of patches from one to five leads a rise in ASR from 61.0% to 65.0%. When both ASAP and DMPG are enabled (bottom row), ASR increases more significantly—from 74.5% with a single patch to 86.5% with four patches. This demonstrates the effectiveness of the multi-patch strategy when guided by adaptive placement and learning mechanisms.
- Effect of the ASAP Module: When comparing settings with ASAP = 0 and ASAP = 1 (with DMPG fixed), notable improvements are observed. For instance, under three patches, ASR increases from 63.5% to 80.1%, and mAP decreases from 0.741 to 0.550. This indicates that adaptive patch placement, guided by attention and gradient information, substantially enhances attack performance.
- Effect of the DMPG Module: Comparing the rows with and without DMPG under the same ASAP setting reveals the positive impact of DMPG. For example, with ASAP enabled and three patches applied, incorporating DMPG boosts ASR from 80.1% to 82.5%, while further reducing mAP from 0.550 to 0.507. These results confirm that DMPG improves attack strength by distilling patch effectiveness from a larger teacher patch.

An interesting phenomenon was observed in the configuration without the DMPG module, while the ASR generally increased when moving from one to three patches, it unexpectedly decreased when the patch count was raised to four.

A plausible explanation for this degradation is that as the number of patches increases, the dimensionality of the optimization space grows substantially. We hypothesize that without the regularizing guidance provided by a teacher model, the optimization process becomes easier to get stuck in a local best optimization. This phenomenon highlights the challenge of naive multi-patch attack strategies.

In stark contrast, the full SDMPA framework (with DMPG enabled) demonstrated improvement in performance as more patches were added. This suggests that the knowledge distillation mechanism serves as an effective guide for the optimization process, helping to navigate the complex search space and mitigate the instability observed in the baseline, thereby ensuring that additional patches contribute positively to the overall attack efficacy.

4.4. Discussions

4.4.1. Effectiveness of Multi-Patch Strategy

To further analyze the effectiveness of the multi-patch strategy in adversarial attacks, we investigated the impact of different placement strategies on attack performance. For this experiment, the DMPG module was disabled for all methods except for the final one (the full SDMPA framework). To isolate the effect of placement, we used identical base patches created by directly scaling a single APPA patch and only varied their spatial locations.

We established a comprehensive set of comparative experiments. First, we set a single-patch baseline using a conventional attack method. For the multi-patch attacks, we tested four distinct placement strategies: random placement, placement guided only by the Explainable Map (EM), placement guided only by the Adversarial Map (AM), and placement guided by the complete ASAP module, which fuses both EM and AM. Finally, to demonstrate the superiority of our complete attack framework, we included the performance of the full SDMPA for comparison. The experiment results are illustrated in Figure 6.

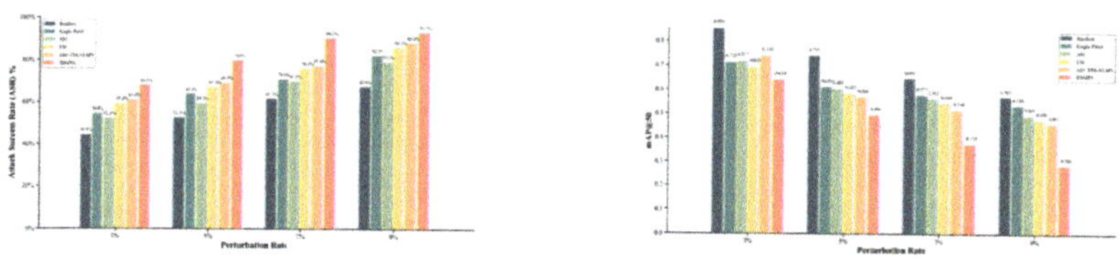

(a) (b)

Figure 6. Bar plots of ablation experiments under different multi-patch attack settings. (**a**) Attack success rate (ASR) results. (**b**) Mean Average Precision (mAP) results. These results indicate the superior effectiveness of multi-patch attack.

At a 9% total perturbation rate, the random placement strategy achieved an Attack Success Rate (ASR) of only 67.61%, which is significantly lower than the single-patch baseline's 82.29%. This indicates that blindly increasing the number of patches does not improve the attack success rate. On the contrary, guiding the placement using feature maps that represent the model's attention under different conditions enhances attack performance, demonstrating that the effectiveness of distributed perturbations relies on a valid placement strategy.

At the same 9% perturbation rate, using only EM or AM yielded ASRs of 86.1% and 79.3%, respectively. When fused, the complete ASAP module (EM+AM) further boosted the ASR to 88.2%. This clearly shows that the model's explainable features (EM) and adversarial sensitivities (AM) contain complementary information. Their fusion allows for a more precise localization of the target's vulnerable regions, leading to a stronger attack than either strategy alonc.

The complete SDMPA framework achieves optimal attack performance. Under all tested perturbation levels, the full SDMPA method consistently demonstrated the best results. This confirms that our proposed framework, by combining the multi-patch strategy with knowledge distillation, effectively enhances overall attack performance.

4.4.2. Effect of Distillation

We designed an experiment to explore the contribution of each patch. In this experiment, we fixed the size of each individual adversarial patch to 2% of the target object size and varied the total number of patches, thereby controlling the overall perturbation range from 2% to 10%. The corresponding Attack Success Rate (ASR) and mean Average Precision (mAP) are shown in Figure 7.

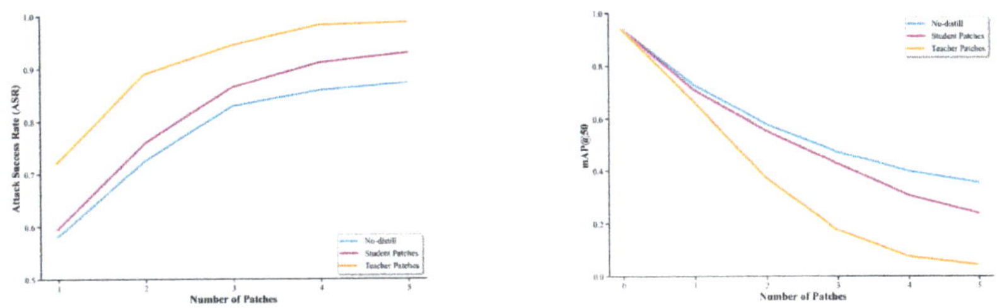

(a) (b)

Figure 7. Line plots showing ASR and mAP variations as the number of patches increases (student patches fixed perturbation per patch = 2%, teacher patches fixed perturbation per patch = 4%). (**a**) ASR variation with patch number. (**b**) mAP variation with patch number. The student patches guided by distillation outperform the non-distilled ones, especially when the optimization space becomes more complex.

As illustrated in Figure 7, the ASR and mAP curves exhibit that the attack performance does not increase linearly with the number of patches. Instead, as the search space for adversarial perturbations expands, the improvement in adversarial effectiveness follows a diminishing return pattern. This phenomenon suggests that simply increasing the number of patches leads to less significant performance gains after a certain threshold, likely due to overlapping perturbations and redundant interference.

Furthermore, by introducing Knowledge Distillation (KD) into the multi-patch strategy, the curves for both ASR and mAP show a more gradual decline compared to the non-distilled baseline. This indicates that knowledge distillation plays a crucial role in guiding the optimization process, helping the model focus on more effective regions and preventing performance degradation as additional patches are added. The distillation mechanism reduces the adverse effects caused by excessive patching, thus improving the overall attack success and preserving detection accuracy better than without distillation.

Additionally, we explored the impact of teacher patch size on the distillation performance of student patches. The size of the teacher patch directly influences the amount of adversarial information transferred to the student model. As shown in Figure 8, the perturbation introduced by the teacher patch varies based on its size, which in turn affects the student model's ability to learn adversarial patterns effectively.

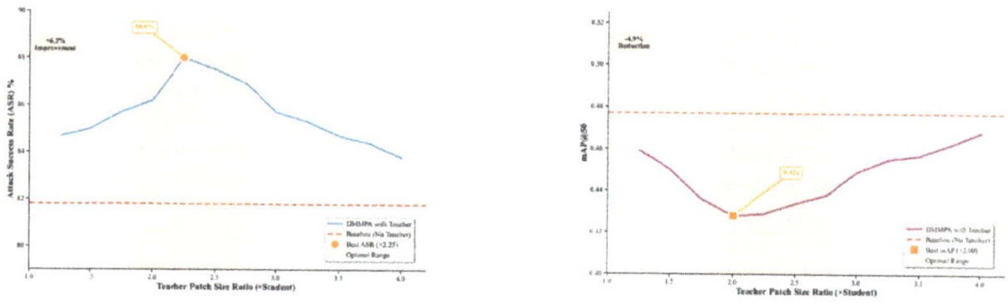

(a) (b)

Figure 8. Line plots showing variations in ASR and mAP as the ratio of teacher patch size to student patch size changes. We set the number of patches to 3 and the total perturbation rate to 6%. (**a**) ASR variation with different teacher-to-student patch size ratios. (**b**) mAP variation with different teacher-to-student patch size ratios. The best attack results achieved 88% ASR and 0.428 mAP.

The optimal teacher patch size balances the extent of perturbation with the specificity needed in the attack. In this study, we found that a teacher-to-student patch size ratio in the range of 1.75 to 2.75 yielded the best results in guiding the student model. Specifically, the highest mAP was observed at a ratio of 2.0, while the highest ASR was achieved at 2.25. These findings suggest that for multi-patch adversarial attacks, both the number of patches and the teacher patch size are critical factors for optimizing the distillation performance. This indicates that not only the number of patches but also the teacher patch size, plays a crucial role in determining the effectiveness of the distillation process.

When the teacher patch size is too small, the adversarial strength is insufficient, resulting in limited guidance for the student model. Conversely, when the teacher patch size is too large, the dimensional disparity between the teacher patch's high-dimensional space and the student patch's space becomes too significant, causing the guidance to lose its effectiveness. Therefore, to achieve optimal distillation performance, it is essential to control the ratio between the teacher patch and the student patch sizes.

To investigate the performance of each component within our proposed distillation loss, we conducted a comprehensive ablation study by testing all possible combinations of the three loss terms. The results are summarized in Table 5, from which we draw several key observations.

Table 5. Ablation study on the components of the distillation loss.

Method	ASR (%)	mAP	Method	ASR (%)	mAP
Non-distill (base)	81.8	0.477	Bbox	83.5	0.458
Confidence	84.8	0.448	Bbox + Confi	84.6	0.437
Confidence + Cls	88.0	0.428	Bbox + Confi + Cls	84.8	0.453
Cls	87.5	0.436	Bbox +Cls	86.8	0.438

First, the introduction of any single distillation component significantly outperforms the non-distillation baseline (ASR 81.8%, mAP 0.477). Specifically, the Classification Loss (cls) alone provides the most substantial improvement among the individual components, achieving an ASR of 87.5% and reducing the mAP to 0.436. This indicates that aligning the classification probability distributions is a powerful mechanism for transferring adversarial knowledge, which may also be attributed to the superior effectiveness of knowledge transfer through the classification loss.

Second, when combining two components, the confi+cls configuration demonstrates superior performance, achieving the highest ASR of 88.0% and the lowest mAP of 0.428. This synergistic effect highlights that guiding the student patch to simultaneously suppress object confidence and mimic the teacher's misclassification behavior is the most effective strategy.

Interestingly, the inclusion of the bounding box loss (bbox) does not consistently enhance attack performance and, in some cases, even degrades it. For instance, the combination of bbox+confi+cls yields a lower ASR (84.8%) compared to the confi+cls combination. This phenomenon suggests that while aligning bounding box predictions is intuitively plausible, it may introduce conflicting optimization objectives or noisy gradients within our framework, ultimately failing to effectively enhance the distillation process for attack generation.

The inclusion of the bounding box loss (L_{bbox}) does not consistently enhance attack performance, primarily due to a fundamental conflict in its optimization objective. The ultimate goal of the attack is detection suppression—eliminating the bounding box entirely. However, L_{bbox} inherently guides the student patch toward a suboptimal state of mimicking a teacher's damaged detection, an unstable and noisy signal. Unlike the classification loss (L_{cls}), which provides a clear, semantic-level directive for feature disruption, L_{bbox} only offers a vague spatial assessment without a clear optimization path. Consequently, the combination of confidence (L_{conf}) and classification (L_{cls}) alignment is more effective, as both synergistically target the core task with potent and unambiguous guidance.

4.4.3. Physical Experiment

To evaluate the deployability and physical-world effectiveness of the SDMPA framework, we conducted a set of real-world experiments involving printed adversarial patches. The objective was to assess whether adversarial patches generated digitally could retain their attack efficacy when physically printed, attached to remote sensing images, and recaptured via camera for inference by an object detector.

The experimental setup was as follows. Our test target was a 1:200 scale model of a C-17 transport aircraft (real-world dimensions: 53.04 m length, 51.81 m wingspan), featuring a length of 26.5 cm and a wingspan of 25.9 cm. The adversarial patches were printed at a resolution of 600 DPI to ensure high fidelity. The large single patch used for baseline comparison measured 7 cm × 7 cm, while the SDMPA mini-patches were 3 cm × 3 cm. To translate the digitally optimized patterns to their physical print dimensions, bilinear interpolation was employed for scaling. For the recapture process, a Redmi K70 Ultra with Sony IMX906 camera was used at a fixed distance of 3 m from the model.

The attack results against the YOLOv5L detector are presented in Figure 9. We evaluated six scenarios to benchmark our method against baselines and assess its rotational robustness. The results demonstrate that SDMPA-generated mini-patches exhibit superior real-world adversarial performance. In contrast, both the traditional large-patch method and a naive resizing of this patch placed at ASAP-identified locations failed to suppress detection, yielding confidence scores of 0.52 and 0.32, respectively. Notably, the SDMPA patches not only successfully evaded detection but also maintained their effectiveness under a $-45°$ rotation, showcasing a degree of robustness to viewpoint variations.

Furthermore, this experiment highlights the significant practical advantages of the multi-patch strategy for deployment on large-scale or irregularly shaped targets. Using the C-17 as an example, a proportionally scaled single large patch would require an impractically massive 14 m × 14 m pattern on a real aircraft. In contrast, our method utilizes multiple, far more manageable 6 m × 6 m patches. This size reduction offers two key benefits: enhanced convenience of physical application and greater flexibility in deployment. A vast 14 m × 14 m area might offer only a single placement option on the aircraft's fuselage—if any. Conversely, multiple smaller patches can be flexibly adapted to various surfaces like the wings, tail, and fuselage, conforming better to the target's complex geometry.

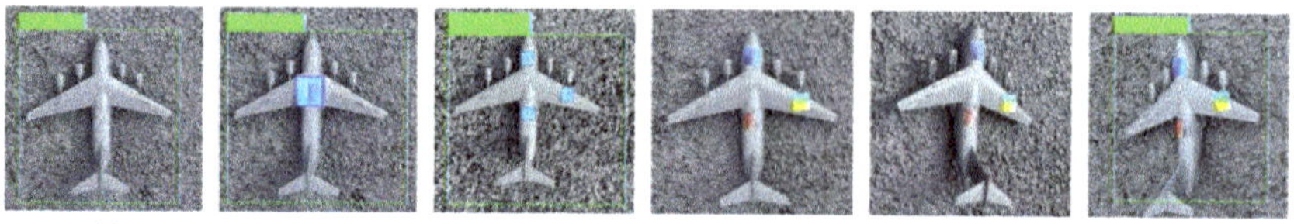

(1) (2) (3) (4) (5) (6)

Figure 9. Physical-world detection results under various patch settings: (1) clean image; (2) large single patch; (3) resized patch at SDMPA positions; (4) SDMPA mini patches; (5) SDMPA patches with -45° rotation; (6) SDMPA patches with $+45^\circ$ rotation. The green bounding boxes indicate the model's detection results with confidence scores.

In summary, the physical experiment confirms that the SDMPA framework not only achieves success in the digital domain but also possesses tangible physical-world applicability. Its robustness to rotation suggests strong potential for real-world deployment in aerial scenarios involving varying angles. Future work could integrate additional physical constraints, such as lighting variations and motion blur, to further enhance its generalization and reliability.

5. Conclusions

In this paper, we propose SDMPA, a novel framework for multi-mini-patch attacks for remote sensing object detection. Unlike traditional adversarial patch methods that rely on a single large patch, our approach strategically places multiple compact patches using the Adaptive Sensitivity-Aware Positioning (ASAP) module and enhances their adversarial potency through knowledge distillation in the Distillation-based Mini-Patch Generation (DMPG) module. Extensive experiments on the MAR20 and RSOD datasets demonstrate that SDMPA significantly improves the attack success rate (ASR) and reduces detection performance (mAP) while maintaining minimal patch size, while these results are promising, future work could further enhance the framework. Key directions include improving the keypoint localization accuracy in ASAP and exploring stronger feature associations among student patches within DMPG.

Author Contributions: Methodology, Z.Y.; validation, Z.Y. and Y.X.; writing—original draft, Z.Y.; supervision, X.L. and L.Z.; project administration, L.Z. AAll authors have read and agreed to the published version of the manuscript.

Funding: This research was funded by the National Natural Science Foundation of China (NSFC) under Grant No. U24B20175.

Data Availability Statement: The original contributions presented in this study are included in the article. Further inquiries can be directed to the corresponding author.

Acknowledgments: During the preparation of this manuscript, the authors used GPT-4o for the purpose of improving English language clarity. The authors have reviewed and edited the content and take full responsibility for the final version of the manuscript.

Conflicts of Interest: The authors declare no conflicts of interest. The funders had no role in the design of the study; in the collection, analyses, or interpretation of data; in the writing of the manuscript; or in the decision to publish the results.

Appendix A. Summary of Hyperparameters

To enhance the reproducibility of this paper, we have detailed the core hyperparameters used in our experiments below. These values were determined through a series of preliminary experiments and best practices from related literature to ensure a robust baseline for comparison.

The parameters are primarily divided into four sections, governing the key aspects of our framework: the overall optimization process (General Training), the physical constraints of the patches (Patch Geometry), the intelligent placement mechanism (ASAP Module), and the knowledge transfer process (DMPG Module). For example, in the General Training section, the learning rate was set to 0.1, while for the ASAP module, the fusion weights w_1 and w_2 were set to 0.6 and 0.4, respectively. the whole parameter of our experimental can be found in Table A1.

Table A1. Summary of Hyperparameters.

Parameter Category	Parameter Name	Value
General Training	Optimizer	Adam
	Learning Rate	0.1
	Max Epochs	100
	Random Seed	42
	Patch Initialization	Random Noise
	Brightness Adjustment	±20%
Patch Geometry	Patch Shape	Square
	Total Perturbation Area	5% (Ablation), 9% (SOTA Comp.)
	Patches per Target (k)	1–5 (Ablation), 3 (SOTA Comp.)
ASAP Module	Fusion Weight (w_1)	0.6
	Fusion Weight (w_2)	0.4
	iterations	10
	step size	0.001
	OPTICS xi	0.02
DMPG Module	NMS IoU Threshold	0.5
	NMS Score Threshold	0.01
	Temperature (τ)	2.0
	K-pair Match IoU	>0.2

References

1. Kurakin, A.; Goodfellow, I.J.; Bengio, S. Adversarial examples in the physical world. In *Artificial Intelligence Safety and Security*; Chapman and Hall/CRC: Boca Raton, FL, USA, 2018; pp. 99–112.
2. Wan, X.; Liu, W.; Niu, C.; Lu, W.; Li, Y. Fast sparse adversarial attack for synthetic aperture radar target recognition. *J. Appl. Remote Sens.* **2025**, *19*, 016502. [CrossRef]
3. Den Hollander, R.; Adhikari, A.; Tolios, I.; van Bekkum, M.; Bal, A.; Hendriks, S.; Kruithof, M.; Gross, D.; Jansen, N.; Perez, G.; et al. Adversarial patch camouflage against aerial detection. In *Artificial Intelligence and Machine Learning in Defense Applications II*; SPIE: Bellingham, WA, USA, 2020; Volume 11543, pp. 77–86.
4. Goodfellow, I.J.; Shlens, J.; Szegedy, C. Explaining and harnessing adversarial examples. *arXiv* **2014**, arXiv:1412.6572.
5. Yufeng, L.; Fengyu, Y.; Qi, L.; Jiangtao, L.; Chenhong, C. Light can be dangerous: Stealthy and effective physical-world adversarial attack by spot light. *Comput. Secur.* **2023**, *132*, 103345. [CrossRef]
6. Zhong, Y.; Liu, X.; Zhai, D.; Jiang, J.; Ji, X. Shadows can be dangerous: Stealthy and effective physical-world adversarial attack by natural phenomenon. In Proceedings of the IEEE/CVF Conference on Computer Vision and Pattern Recognition, New Orleans, LA, USA, 18–24 June 2022; pp. 15345–15354.
7. Dong, Q.; Han, T.; Wu, G.; Qiao, B.; Sun, L. Rsnet: Compact-align detection head embedded lightweight network for small object detection in remote sensing. *Remote Sen.* **2025**, *17*, 1965. [CrossRef]
8. Madry, A.; Makelov, A.; Schmidt, L.; Tsipras, D.; Vladu, A. Towards deep learning models resistant to adversarial attacks. *arXiv* **2017**, arXiv:1706.06083.
9. Dong, Y.; Liao, F.; Pang, T.; Su, H.; Zhu, J.; Hu, X.; Li, J. Boosting adversarial attacks with momentum. In Proceedings of the IEEE Conference on Computer Vision and Pattern Recognition, Salt Lake City, UT, USA, 18–22 June 2018; pp. 9185–9193.
10. Peng, X.; Zhou, J.; Wu, X. Distillation-based cross-model transferable adversarial attack for remote sensing image classification. *Remote Sens.* **2025**, *17*, 1700. [CrossRef]

11. Xie, C.; Wang, J.; Zhang, Z.; Zhou, Y.; Xie, L.; Yuille, A. Adversarial examples for semantic segmentation and object detection. In Proceedings of the IEEE International Conference on Computer Vision, Venice, Italy, 22–29 October 2017; pp. 1369–1378.
12. Liu, X.; Yang, H.; Liu, Z.; Song, L.; Li, H.; Chen, Y. Dpatch: An adversarial patch attack on object detectors. *arXiv* **2018**, arXiv:1806.02299.
13. Hu, Y.C.T.; Kung, B.H.; Tan, D.S.; Chen, J.C.; Hua, K.L.; Cheng, W.H. Naturalistic physical adversarial patch for object detectors. In Proceedings of the IEEE/CVF International Conference on Computer Vision, Montreal, BC, Canada, 11–17 October 2021; pp. 7848–7857.
14. Chow, K.H.; Liu, L.; Gursoy, M.E.; Truex, S.; Wei, W.; Wu, Y. Tog: Targeted adversarial objectness gradient attacks on real-time object detection systems. *arXiv* **2020**, arXiv:2004.04320. [CrossRef]
15. Ding, X.; Chen, J.; Yu, H.; Shang, Y.; Qin, Y.; Ma, H. Transferable adversarial attacks for object detection using object-aware significant feature distortion. In Proceedings of the AAAI Conference on Artificial Intelligence, Philadelphia, PA, USA, 25 February–4 March 2024; Volume 38, pp. 1546–1554.
16. Brown, T.B.; Mané, D.; Roy, A.; Abadi, M.; Gilmer, J. Adversarial patch. *arXiv* **2017**, arXiv:1712.09665.
17. Lee, M.; Kolter, Z. On physical adversarial patches for object detection. *arXiv* **2019**, arXiv:1906.11897. [CrossRef]
18. Thys, S.; Van Ranst, W.; Goedemé, T. Fooling automated surveillance cameras: Adversarial patches to attack person detection. In Proceedings of the IEEE/CVF Conference on Computer Vision and Pattern Recognition Workshops, Long Beach, CA, USA, 16–20 June 2019.
19. Zhang, Y.; Gong, Z.; Wen, H.; Hu, X.; Xia, X.; Jiang, H.; Zhong, P. Pattern corruption-assisted physical attacks against object detection in uav remote sensing. *IEEE J. Sel. Top. Appl. Earth Obs. Remote Sens.* **2024**, *17*, 12931–12944. [CrossRef]
20. Zhu, R.; Ma, S.; Lian, J.; He, L.; Mei, S. Generating adversarial examples against remote sensing scene classification via feature approximation. *IEEE J. Sel. Top. Appl. Earth Obs. Remote Sens.* **2024**, *17*, 10174–10187. [CrossRef]
21. Wang, X.; Mei, S.; Lian, J.; Lu, Y. Fooling aerial detectors by background attack via dual-adversarial-induced error identification. *IEEE Trans. Geosci. Remote Sens.* **2024**, *62*, 1–16. [CrossRef]
22. Lian, J.; Mei, S.; Zhang, S.; Ma, M. Benchmarking adversarial patch against aerial detection. *IEEE Trans. Geosci. Remote Sens.* **2022**, *60*, 1–16. [CrossRef]
23. Kong, D.; Liang, S.; Ren, W. Environmental matching attack against unmanned aerial vehicles object detection. *arXiv* **2024**, arXiv:2405.07595. [CrossRef]
24. Li, K.; Wang, D.; Zhu, W.; Li, S.; Wang, Q.; Gao, X. Physical adversarial patch attack for optical fine-grained aircraft recognition. *IEEE Trans. Inf. Forensics Secur.* **2024**, *20*, 436–448. [CrossRef]
25. Shrestha, S.; Pathak, S.; Viegas, E.K. Towards a robust adversarial patch attack against unmanned aerial vehicles object detection. In Proceedings of the 2023 IEEE/RSJ International Conference on Intelligent Robots and Systems (IROS), Detroit, MI, USA, 1–5 October 2023; pp. 3256–3263.
26. Bai, T.; Cao, Y.; Xu, Y.; Wen, B. Stealthy adversarial examples for semantic segmentation in remote sensing. *IEEE Trans. Geosci. Remote Sens.* **2024**, *62*, 1–17. [CrossRef]
27. Tang, G.; Jiang, T.; Zhou, W.; Li, C.; Yao, W.; Zhao, Y. Adversarial patch attacks against aerial imagery object detectors. *Neurocomputing* **2023**, *537*, 128–140. [CrossRef]
28. Huang, J.J.; Wang, Z.; Liu, T.; Luo, W.; Chen, Z.; Zhao, W.; Wang, M. Dempaa: Deployable multi-mini-patch adversarial attack for remote sensing image classification. *IEEE Trans. Geosci. Remote Sens.* **2024**, *62*, 1–13. [CrossRef]
29. Hinton, G.; Vinyals, O.; Dean, J. Distilling the knowledge in a neural network. *arXiv* **2015**, arXiv:1503.02531. [CrossRef]
30. Wang, S.; Yang, Y.; Liu, Z.; Sun, C.; Hu, X.; He, C.; Zhang, L. Dataset distillation with neural characteristic function: A minmax perspective. In Proceedings of the Computer Vision and Pattern Recognition Conference, Nashville TN, USA, 11–15 June 2025; pp. 25570–25580.
31. Chen, G.; Choi, W.; Yu, X.; Han, T.; Chandraker, M. Learning efficient object detection models with knowledge distillation. In *Advances in Neural Information Processing Systems*; Curran Associates, Inc.: Red Hook, NY, USA, 2017; Volume 30, pp. 742–751.
32. Zheng, Z.; Ye, R.; Wang, P.; Ren, D.; Zuo, W.; Hou, Q.; Cheng, M.M. Localization distillation for dense object detection. In Proceedings of the IEEE/CVF Conference on Computer Vision and Pattern Recognition, New Orleans, LA, USA, 18–24 June 2022; pp. 9407–9416.
33. Huang, T.; Zhang, Y.; You, S.; Wang, F.; Qian, C.; Cao, J.; Xu, C. Masked distillation with receptive tokens. *arXiv* **2022**, arXiv:2205.14589.
34. Lei, C.T.; Yam, H.M.; Guo, Z.; Qian, Y.; Lau, C.P. Instant adversarial purification with adversarial consistency distillation. In Proceedings of the Computer Vision and Pattern Recognition Conference, Nashville TN, USA, 11–15 June 2025; pp. 24331–24340.
35. Liu, W.; Wu, Y.; Li, C.; Liu, Z.; Yan, H. Distillation-enhanced physical adversarial attacks. *arXiv* **2025**, arXiv:2501.02232. [CrossRef]
36. Jiang, P.T.; Zhang, C.B.; Hou, Q.; Cheng, M.M.; Wei, Y. Layercam: Exploring hierarchical class activation maps for localization. *IEEE Trans. Image Process.* **2021**, *30*, 5875–5888. [CrossRef]

37. Wu, S.; Sang, J.; Xu, K.; Zhang, J.; Yu, J. Attention, please! adversarial defense via activation rectification and preservation. *ACM Trans. Multimed. Comput. Commun. Appl.* **2023**, *19*, 1–18. [CrossRef]
38. Smilkov, D.; Thorat, N.; Kim, B.; Viégas, F.; Wattenberg, M. Smoothgrad: Removing noise by adding noise. *arXiv* **2017**, arXiv:1706.03825. [CrossRef]
39. Wenqi, Y.; Gong, C.; Meijun, W.; Yanqing, Y.; Xingxing, X.; Xiwen, Y.; Junwei, H. Mar20: A benchmark for military aircraft recognition in remote sensing images. *Natl. Remote Sens. Bull.* **2024**, *27*, 2688–2696.
40. Long, Y.; Gong, Y.; Xiao, Z.; Liu, Q. Accurate object localization in remote sensing images based on convolutional neural networks. *IEEE Trans. Geosci. Remote Sens.* **2017**, *55*, 2486–2498. [CrossRef]
41. Mei, S.; Lian, J.; Wang, X.; Su, Y.; Ma, M.; Chau, L.P. A comprehensive study on the robustness of deep learning-based image classification and object detection in remote sensing: Surveying and benchmarking. *J. Remote Sens.* **2024**, *4*, 0219. [CrossRef]

electronics

MDPI

Article

Comparing CNN and ViT for Open-Set Face Recognition †

Ander Galván *, Mariví Higuero, Ane Sanz, Asier Atutxa, Eduardo Jacob and Mario Saavedra

Faculty of Engineering of Bilbao, Department of Communications Engineering, University of the Basque Country (UPV/EHU), Plaza Ingeniero Torres Quevedo, n. 1, 48013 Bilbao, Spain; marivi.higuero@ehu.eus (M.H.); ane.sanz@ehu.eus (A.S.); asier.atutxa@ehu.eus (A.A.); eduardo.jacob@ehu.eus (E.J.); msaavedra003@ikasle.ehu.eus (M.S.)

* Correspondence: ander.galvan@ehu.eus

† The figure in Section 2.1 of the manuscript was previously included in the following work, which was accepted and presented at the ICAISC 2025 conference, but has not been formally published: Higuero, M.; Galván, A.; Astorga, J.; Atutxa, A.; Jacob, E. Optimizing OpenMax Parameters for Open-Set Face Recognition. In Proceedings of the ICAISC 2025, Zakopane, Poland, 22–26 June 2025.

Abstract

At present, there is growing interest in automated biometric identification applications. For these, it is crucial to have a system capable of accurately identifying a specific group of people while also detecting individuals who do not belong to that group. In face identification models that use Deep Learning (DL) techniques, this context is referred to as Open-Set Recognition (OSR), which is the focus of this work. This scenario presents a substantial challenge for this type of system, as it involves the need to effectively identify unknown individuals who were not part of the system's training data. In this context, where the accuracy of this type of system is considered crucial, selecting the model to be used in each scenario becomes key. It is within this context that our work arises. Here, we present the results of a rigorous comparative analysis examining the precision of some of the most widely used models today for face identification, specifically some Convolutional Neural Network (CNN) models compared with a Vision Transformer (ViT) model. All models were pre-trained on the same large dataset and evaluated in an OSR scenario. The results show that ViT achieves the highest precision, outperforming CNN baselines and demonstrating better generalization for unknown identities. These findings support recent evidence that ViT is a promising alternative to CNN for this type of application.

Keywords: face recognition; open-set recognition; deep learning; convolutional neural network; vision transformer

1. Introduction

In recent years, advances in Artificial Intelligence (AI), and especially in the field of Deep Learning (DL), have significantly impacted various sectors. One of the areas where these innovations have been particularly relevant is biometrics, with a prominent focus on face recognition. Based on DL models, these systems allow current solutions to carry out the complex tasks of person identification and verification, maintaining a high level of accuracy even under adverse conditions. Thanks to its high accuracy, face recognition has become a fundamental component in applications like access control for company premises and airport boarding lounges.

Beyond its influential role in key sectors, face recognition represents a booming technology. According to [1], its market revenue demonstrates a consistently growing trend, with an estimated Compound Annual Growth Rate (CAGR) of approximately 14%

over the forecast horizon. Initiating at USD 5 billion in 2022, the market is projected to expand to approximately USD 9 billion by 2026 and exceed USD 13 billion by 2029. As technological maturation progresses, revenue streams are expected to increase further, reaching USD 17 billion by 2031 and USD 19 billion by 2032. This growth trajectory is illustrated in Figure 1.

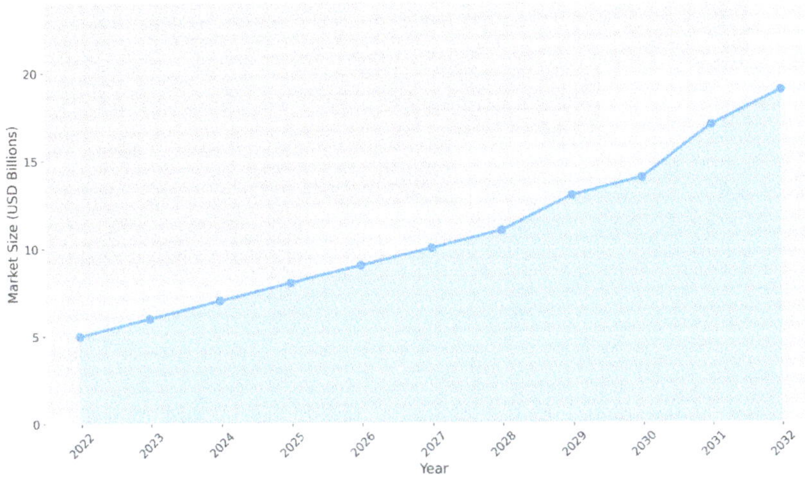

Figure 1. Estimated global revenue growth of the facial recognition market from 2022 to 2032 [1].

This rapid market growth underscores the growing reliance on face recognition systems across diverse sectors. However, despite their widespread adoption, current systems continue to encounter significant technical challenges when implemented in real-world scenarios. In these cases, most of these systems are implemented as Closed-Set Recognition (CSR) models and trained on a predefined set of labeled face images corresponding to known identities. Under this paradigm, the models are designed to assign each input face to one of the known identities, operating under the assumption that all faces to be observed during testing are part of the training set. However, in many real-world scenarios, it is common for the system to encounter people who were not involved during training. This situation, formerly known as Open-Set Recognition (OSR) [2,3], requires not only the correct identification of known identities but also the ability to detect unknown faces.

Furthermore, face recognition systems have traditionally relied on Convolutional Neural Networks (CNNs). However, due to their inherent limitations in capturing long-range dependencies and global context, recent research has explored alternative architectures with improved capabilities for modeling global representations. Among these, the Vision Transformer (ViT) [4], introduced in 2020, has garnered significant interest within the computer vision community, as it captures global relationships between different parts of an image rather than focusing solely on local patterns (as CNNs do).

In light of the above, the present study conducts a comparative analysis of CNN and ViT architectures for face recognition in OSR scenarios. The main objective is to compare the performance of both architectures in scenarios that require accurate facial recognition from known identities and the detection of unknown faces with high precision.

The rest of the document is structured as follows: Section 2 presents an overview of CNN, ViT, and OSR. Section 3 reviews relevant existing literature in the domain of face recognition. Sections 4 and 5, respectively, describe the models selected for comparison in this study and detail the experimental methodology employed. Section 6 offers a discussion of the results, along with an in-depth analysis, before finally, Section 7 summarizes the key conclusions.

2. Background

This section provides an overview of CNNs and ViTs, emphasizing their main features and suitability for biometric face recognition. Furthermore, the concept of OSR is introduced, as is the OpenMax algorithm used in this study to address the associated challenges.

2.1. Convolutional Neural Networks

CNNs are a type of DL architecture commonly utilized in computer vision applications. These networks operate through a sequence of layers that apply filters, also known as kernels, to input images [5], progressively extracting features ranging from basic elements such as edges, colors, and gradients to more complex, high-level representations that can distinguish specific objects or categories. The initial convolutional layers focus on feature extraction by scanning the image with filters, while subsequent pooling layers reduce the spatial dimensions of the data, emphasizing the most relevant features [6]. The final steps involve flattening the data and passing it through fully connected layers to perform the classification task. An overview of a typical CNN architecture for face recognition is illustrated in Figure 2.

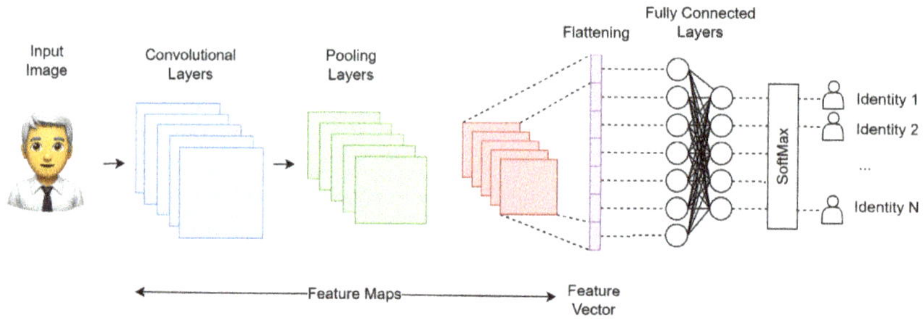

Figure 2. Schematic representation of a Convolutional Neural Network (CNN) architecture for face recognition tasks. The colors indicate different processing stages: blue for convolutional layers, green for pooling layers, red for flattened feature maps, and purple for the feature vector.

Despite their widespread success, CNNs have certain limitations. According to [7], a primary concern is their lack of interpretability, as these models often operate as black boxes with limited transparency regarding their decision-making processes. Additionally, CNNs are susceptible to domain shift, which can lead to performance deterioration when applied to data that differs from the original training set.

2.2. Vision Transformers

ViTs employ an entirely different methodology for image processing, dividing them into smaller patches, which are then flattened and converted into a sequence of tokens through linear projection. These tokens are subsequently processed through multiple transformer encoder layers, which are effective at capturing relationships across different image regions. This is achieved via the multi-head self-attention mechanism [5]. Figure 3 provides a visual representation of the ViT architecture for face recognition.

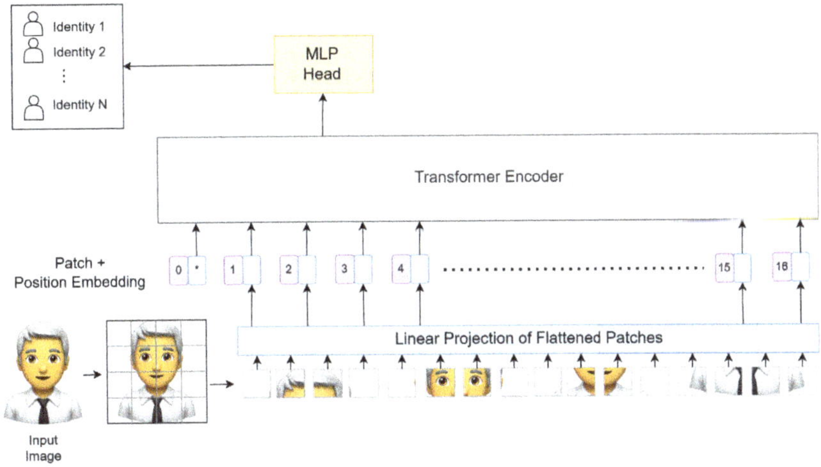

Figure 3. Schematic representation of the Vision Transformer (ViT) architecture for face recognition tasks. The colors indicate different components of the model: purple for the positional embeddings, blue for the linear projection of flattened patches (patch embeddings), grey for the transformer encoder, and yellow for the Multilayer Perceptron (MLP) head. The symbol * denotes the special classification token (CLS) added to the patch embeddings.

As reported by [7], ViTs have achieved state-of-the-art performance on several benchmark datasets, demonstrating excellent results on large-scale datasets such as ImageNet-21k [8] and JFT-300M [9] and outperforming many CNNs in terms of accuracy. For example, ViT has achieved accuracies of 88.55% on ImageNet and 94.55% on CIFAR-100 [4].

Nevertheless, it is important to consider some of the limitations associated with ViTs. They generally require larger training datasets compared to CNNs and tend to demand higher computational resources. Moreover, as a relatively newer architecture, there is less established knowledge and fewer best practices available for their implementation compared to CNNs [7].

2.3. Theoretical Analysis: Convolutional Neural Networks vs. Vision Transformers

Building upon the CNN and ViT architectures discussed in previous sections, the primary distinction between these models lies in their methods of processing spatial information within images. CNNs perform local, hierarchical analysis through convolutional layers, progressively extracting increasingly complex features from small, contiguous regions. Conversely, ViTs adopt a global processing approach by dividing images into patches and treating them as sequences of tokens. This methodology enables ViTs to model long-range dependencies across the image, overcoming the limitations inherent to local CNN operations.

As noted in [4], this fundamental difference influences their inductive biases. CNNs inherently incorporate biases such as locality, emphasizing the importance of nearby pixels, and translation equivariance, recognizing patterns regardless of their position (see Figure 4). These biases facilitate assumptions about image structure and enhance training efficiency, particularly when data resources are limited. In contrast, ViTs do not possess these domain-specific biases, providing greater flexibility to learn diverse spatial relationships. However, this lack of inherent biases necessitates larger volumes of training data to effectively learn image structures from scratch.

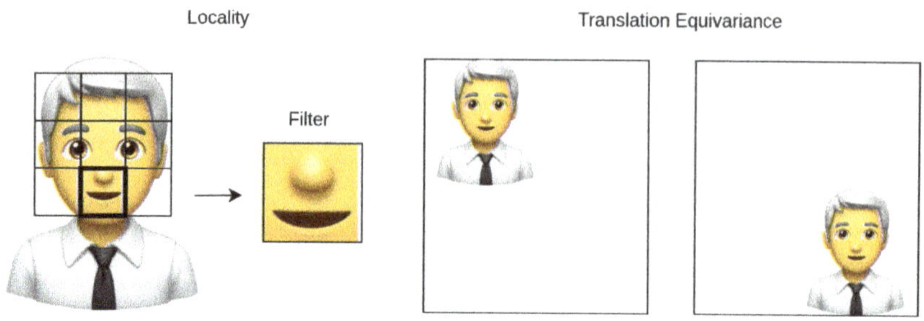

Figure 4. Illustration of inductive biases, locality, and translation equivariance present in CNNs for face recognition.

2.4. Open-Set Recognition and OpenMax

As previously mentioned, image classification models are typically trained within a CSR scenario. This means that the model is trained using images belonging to a predefined set of classes, referred to as known classes. Fundamentally, the training process for classification models relies on the assumption that all classes the model will encounter during testing have been previously observed during training.

However, during testing, images from unknown classes may be encountered in real-world applications. In such situations, the model incorrectly classifies these images as belonging to one of the known classes, since it lacks the ability to recognize images of unknown classes and does not consider the possibility that an image may not belong to any of the classes with which it was trained.

To address this issue, one potential solution involves applying a threshold to the maximum probability produced by the SoftMax layer. The concept is that when an image of unknown classes is introduced, the probabilities assigned to known classes would be low; implementing a threshold can help classify such images as unknown. However, this approach has been shown to be insufficient, as discussed in [10]. Their study demonstrates that even images entirely unrelated to known classes can sometimes produce high probabilities that surpass the threshold, resulting in misclassifications.

Consequently, methods such as OpenMax [10] have been developed to enable the model to classify images of known classes while effectively handling those from unknown classes, thereby enhancing performance in OSR scenarios. This method improves the capability of the SoftMax layer to include unknown class prediction. Specifically, the scores obtained from the fully connected layer preceding the SoftMax layer are utilized to determine whether an image is significantly different from the training data. These scores are referred to as the Activation Vector (AV).

The OpenMax algorithm accounts for the likelihood of errors within the recognition system, which is used to assess whether an image belongs to the unknown class. To facilitate this assessment, an adaptation of Meta-Recognition [11] is used, involving the evaluation of model scores to identify prediction errors and determine whether an image originates from the unknown class. Additionally, previous research on Meta-Recognition [11] examined the final scores utilizing Extreme Value Theory (EVT), establishing that these scores conform to Weibull distribution. In this context, such distribution is fitted for each known class, a fitting process that is described in detail below.

1. For each correctly classified image, obtain the AV.
2. For each known class, compute the Mean Activation Vector (MAV) by averaging the AVs of all correctly classified training samples belonging to that known class.
3. Calculate a Weibull distribution to the η largest distances (tail size) between the AVs and the MAV for each known class.

Once the Weibull distribution has been fitted for each known class, the OpenMax algorithm is employed during the testing phase to enhance the detection of images belonging to unknown individuals. When a new image is presented, its AV is computed, and the subsequent estimation process is carried out as described below.

1. Sort the known classes in the activation vector in descending order of their activation values.
2. Initialize the weights to 1 for all known classes.
3. For the α known classes (top classes to revise) with the highest activation values, compute a weight using the distance between the image and the MAV for that known class, along with the corresponding Weibull Cumulative Distribution Function (CDF) probability.
4. Modify the original AV by applying the weights to obtain a revised AV.
5. Calculate the activation value for the unknown class by computing a pseudo-activation.
6. Calculate the new OpenMax probabilities using the revised AV (including the unknown class).

To conclude, OpenMax classifies an image as belonging to the unknown class either when the highest probability corresponds to the unknown class or when the highest probability among the known classes does not exceed a predefined threshold ϵ.

3. Related Work

Until five years ago, CNNs dominated the field of computer vision. However, in 2020, the landscape began to change with the introduction of ViTs by the authors of [4]. This work demonstrated that ViTs can achieve high levels of accuracy in image classification tasks, provided that proper training is carried out. In particular, when ViTs are trained on small- to medium-sized datasets, such as ImageNet with 1000 classes and 1.3 M images, without applying significant regularization, they fail to outperform CNNs due to the lack of certain inductive biases, such as locality and translational equivariance. However, when ViTs are pre-trained with large-sized datasets, such as ImageNet-21k (a superset of ImageNet with 21,000 classes and 14 M images) or JFT-300M, before being fine-tuned to smaller datasets, they can match or even surpass the results of the CNNs. In summary, large-scale training tends to outperform reliance solely on inductive biases.

In order to justify the superior performance of ViTs over CNNs, a comparative analysis of the representations generated by both architectures was carried out in [12]. The study concludes that ViTs present more uniform representations across all layers, unlike CNNs, which exhibit a hierarchical structure in which extracted features are progressively more abstract with increasing depth. These differences are attributed to the self-attention mechanism—which allows for capturing global information from the first layers—as well as to residual connections, which facilitate the efficient propagation of features from lower to higher layers.

In the field of face recognition, the authors of [5] conducted a comparative analysis of different architectures, demonstrating that ViTs outperform CNNs in accuracy for face identification and verification tasks across five diverse datasets. Specifically, ViTs were evaluated against widely used CNN architectures, including EfficientNet [13], Inception [14], MobileNet [15], ResNet [16], and VGG [17]. The study also indicates that ViTs' inference speed is competitive: although approximately 24% slower than MobileNet, the fastest model tested, ViTs possess roughly seven times more parameters. Additionally, ViTs exhibit greater robustness to variations in image distance and are notably more effective in managing partial occlusions of the face, owing to their global receptive fields that are less impacted by local obstructions compared to CNNs. Overall, the results suggest that ViTs provide superior performance and enhanced adaptability under varying conditions.

Further studies [18] confirmed the advantage of transformer-based models, including ViT and Swin Transformer [19], in face recognition tasks involving masked faces. These models, pre-trained on ImageNet-21k, achieved accuracies above 90% for unmasked images and around 87% for masked images, illustrating the importance of large-scale pre-training in complex real-world scenarios. Similarly, the authors of [20] proposed the Sparse Vision Transformer (S-ViT) for face recognition, which incorporates relative positional encoding [21] to better capture spatial relationships. S-ViT outperformed conventional CNNs and standard ViTs, achieving up to 3.27% higher accuracy than ResNet50 using ArcFace loss [22]. ARTriViT [23], a ViT-based Siamese network with triplet loss, further demonstrated the effectiveness of ViTs in handling occlusions, pose variations, lighting changes, and limited sample sizes, achieving state-of-the-art performance on the Celeb-DF v2 dataset [24].

In addition, several hybrid architectures combining CNNs and ViTs have been proposed to capitalize on the strengths of both approaches. For example, the authors of [25] introduced EdgeFace, a lightweight face recognition model optimized for deployment on edge devices, achieving high accuracy on LFW [26], IJB-B [27], and IJB-C [28] datasets while maintaining low computational requirements. Similarly, ref. [29] developed MobileFaceFormer, which features parallel CNN and ViT branches with a feature fusion mechanism that retains both local and global facial features. Another approach, FaceLiVT [30], integrates a lightweight multi-head linear attention mechanism within a hybrid CNN-ViT architecture, delivering competitive performance across multiple benchmarks and enabling faster inference suitable for mobile applications. Lastly, ref. [31] proposed a hybrid model combining CNNs, ViTs, and Multi-Layer Perceptrons (MLPs) that utilizes CNNs for local feature extraction, ViTs for capturing global context, and an MLP classifier for decision-making, resulting in improved accuracy, robustness, and computational efficiency over pure architectures.

To date, no comprehensive comparison of CNNs and ViTs has been conducted in OSR scenarios for face recognition. This study therefore aims to evaluate the performance of pure CNN and pure ViT architectures in such a scenario, with hybrid models explicitly excluded from the scope of this research.

4. Features of the CNN and ViT Models

As noted earlier, this paper compares CNNs and ViTs for face recognition in OSR scenarios; these models are detailed in the following.

The selection of CNN architectures was guided by specific criteria: (i) historical significance, representing key milestones in the development of CNNs for computer vision; and (ii) architectural diversity, covering varying levels of complexity, connectivity patterns, and number of parameters. These criteria ensure that the comparison with ViTs captures a broad range of CNN models.

Based on these considerations, the following CNN models were selected, as summarized in Table 1: Inception-V3, ResNet50, DenseNet201, MobileNet-V3-Large, and EfficientNet-B0. These models have widespread use in the existing literature [5,31–34] and have been extensively validated across various computer vision applications [35–38], providing a relevant benchmark for comparing traditional CNNs with transformer-based architectures.

Since the introduction of CNN architectures, a series of increasingly advanced models have contributed to significant progress in the field of DL for computer vision. In 2015, the Inception-V3 model [14] introduced factorized convolutions and optimized module designs, improving both accuracy and computational efficiency. That same year, ResNet50 [16] revolutionized deep network training through residual connections, enabling significantly deeper architectures without compromising performance.

Table 1. Models, publication years, and number of parameters.

Model	Publication Year	Number of Parameters
Inception-V3 [14]	2015	≈22 M
ResNet50 [16]	2015	≈24 M
DenseNet201 [39]	2017	≈18 M
MobileNet-V3-Large [40]	2019	≈4 M
EfficientNet-B0 [13]	2019	≈4 M
ViT-B-16 [4]	2020	≈86 M

Later, DenseNet201 [39], published in 2017, proposed dense connectivity between layers to strengthen feature propagation and reduce parameter redundancy. In 2019, MobileNet-V3-Large [40] targeted efficient inference on mobile and embedded devices by combining neural architecture search with lightweight building blocks. EfficientNet-B0 [13], also released in 2019, achieved a balance between performance and efficiency through compound scaling and careful architecture design.

Finally, ViTs [4] (ViT-B-16), introduced in 2020, marked a paradigm shift by adapting Transformers [41] to computer vision, reaching competitive performance with CNNs when pre-trained on large-scale datasets.

5. Baseline Conditions for Analytical Comparison

This section provides a detailed account of the procedures followed in this study, which are divided into three main phases: pre-training, fine-tuning, and evaluation in an OSR scenario.

5.1. Pre-Training

All the models listed in Table 1 were initially pre-trained on a large-scale dataset to learn discriminative facial representations with strong generalization capabilities. For this pre-training phase, the VGGFace2 dataset [42] was employed, given its widespread adoption in the literature for its large volume of facial images. Developed by Oxford University, this dataset comprises a total of 3.3 M images representing 9131 individuals. The dataset is divided into two partitions: 8631 training classes containing 3.1 M images and 500 test classes containing 169,396 images. For this work, only the training split was used, which contains an average of 364 images per class. The distribution of the number of images per class in the training and testing splits, along with the total images across both splits, is illustrated in Figure 5.

Before pre-training the models, the images underwent a comprehensive pre-processing pipeline, including resizing, channel normalization and data augmentation techniques, with the aim of improving the generalization capacity and robustness of the model to variations in the capture conditions, such as changes in illumination or posture. The images were resized uniformly to 224 × 224 pixels, and normalization was applied using a mean and standard deviation of 0.5 per channel. In addition, various data augmentation techniques were incorporated, such as random horizontal flipping, rotations up to ±15 degrees, conversion to grayscale with a 10% probability, random adjustments in brightness, contrast, saturation, and hue, random cropping with scaling between 70% and 100% of the image area, and blurring. Each of these augmentations enhanced the models' robustness: flipping and rotations improved resilience to pose variations, grayscale conversion and color adjustments mitigated biases related to skin tone and lighting conditions, random cropping and scaling directed the models' attention to essential facial features rather than background details, and blurring increased resilience to low-quality or out-of-focus images. The application of these augmentations reduced overfitting, allowing the models to start the subsequent fine-tuning phase with weights that captured general facial representations.

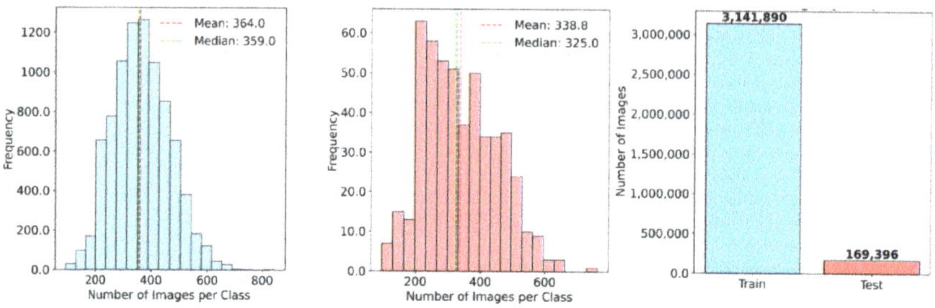

Figure 5. Overview of the image distribution across training and testing splits in the VGGFace2 dataset.

Furthermore, the set of images used was divided into 95% for training and 5% for validation in order to evaluate and monitor the generalizability of the models. The pre-training process was carried out over a maximum of 50 epochs, with both training and validation phases performed in each epoch. In addition, an early stopping strategy was implemented with a patience parameter of 5, so that if the accuracy of the validation set did not improve for 5 consecutive epochs, training was stopped early to prevent overfitting and optimize the use of computational resources.

In relation to learning rates, a uniform value of 5×10^{-4} was assigned, and a combined scheduler integrating a linear warm-up phase followed by a CosineAnnealingWarmRestarts readjustment was implemented to efficiently manage the learning rate during the pre-training process.

Finally, pre-training was performed using the CrossEntropyLoss loss function, and optimization was carried out using the AdamW algorithm [43], which combines the advantages of Adam with a weight decay regularization of 1×10^{-4}.

5.2. Fine-Tuning

After gaining a broad understanding of human faces through extensive pre-training on the large-scale VGGFace2 dataset, the models were subsequently fine-tuned using a smaller, more specific dataset containing a limited number of individuals. Specifically, the fine-tuning dataset consisted of exactly 100 people. This second phase aimed to adapt the models to the targeted dataset, thereby enhancing their performance within this particular group of people. During the fine-tuning phase, all parameters from the pre-trained models were preserved, except for the final classification layer, which was replaced and reinitialized to accommodate the change in the number of output classes from 8631 to 100.

For this second phase, 100 individuals from the CASIA-WebFace [44] dataset were used. CASIA-WebFace [44] is a face recognition dataset developed by the Chinese Academy of Sciences, comprising 494,414 images representing 10,575 individuals.

In this case, each of the 100 known individuals was represented by 70 training images and 10 validation images. Prior to fine-tuning, all images underwent a pre-processing procedure to ensure consistency with the pre-training phase. This process included face detection using Multi-task Cascaded Convolutional Networks (MTCNN) [45], which cropped the facial region by removing background noise. Subsequently, each cropped face was resized to 224×224 pixels and normalized using a mean and standard deviation of 0.5.

Once the training and validation images of the 100 known individuals were preprocessed, the fine-tuning phase was conducted over 40 epochs using the CrossEntropyLoss function and the Adam optimizer, with a learning rate of 7×10^{-5}. The final models were selected based on their validation set performance, specifically those with the highest classification accuracy.

5.3. Evaluation

After fine-tuning the models using images of 100 known individuals, their performance was first assessed in a CSR scenario to verify their ability to accurately identify these known individuals. In this scenario, the SoftMax function was used as the component responsible for converting the models' output scores into probability distributions over the 100 known classes. This allowed for the evaluation of the models' ability to differentiate and classify the previously mentioned 100 known people. For this purpose, 10 test images from each known person were used. These images were processed by applying MTCNN for face cropping, followed by resizing to 224 × 224 pixels and normalization using a mean and standard deviation of 0.5 in each channel.

Subsequently, the models were evaluated in an OSR scenario, which comprised both known and unknown individuals who were not part of the training set, neither during the pre-training nor the fine-tuning phases. For this scenario, the OpenMax algorithm was implemented, with the selected parameter values as summarized in Table 2.

Table 2. Selected parameter values for OpenMax.

Parameter	Value
Tail size (η)	5
Top classes to revise (α)	2
Distance type	Euclidean
Threshold (ϵ)	0.9

The selected OpenMax parameters ($\eta = 5$, $\alpha = 2$, $\epsilon = 0.9$) were adopted from [46], who focused on the optimization of OpenMax parameters for OSR scenarios. More precisely, the tail size η controls the number of extreme values used to fit the Weibull distributions, with larger values reducing sensitivity to unknown faces, while smaller values could make the model more sensitive to unknown faces but also more prone to false positives. The top classes to revise α specify the number of highest-scoring known classes to be adjusted by OpenMax; increasing α may distort the probability distribution, whereas decreasing α might leave some overconfident predictions uncorrected. The threshold ϵ was set to 0.9 to effectively balance the detection of unknown faces while maintaining high accuracy on known identities; raising ϵ would make the model more conservative in identifying known faces, while lowering it could increase the risk of misclassifying unknown faces as known.

To simulate images of unknown people, 1000 images were used, each representing individuals from the CASIA-WebFace dataset who were not included among the known people. These images were incorporated into the test set of known people and labeled as belonging to an unknown class. As in previous steps, all images were first cropped using MTCNN, then resized to 224 × 224 pixels and subsequently normalized using a mean and standard deviation of 0.5 in each channel.

6. Results and Discussion

This section presents the results of the study, beginning with an overview of the hardware and software environment employed. Subsequently, the models' learning behavior during the fine-tuning phase is examined through key metric training and validation curves, including loss, recall, and precision, providing insight into their performance evolution. Following this, the models' accuracy is evaluated in both a CSR scenario, involving known individuals, and an OSR scenario, which includes unknown identities. In order to isolate the effect of the OpenMax algorithm, an ablation study is conducted by applying a threshold to the probabilities generated by SoftMax rather than implementing the OpenMax mechanism, demonstrating that the observed performance differences between models are not solely attributable to the choice of mechanism for OSR scenarios. Finally, the discussion includes an analysis of the computational cost of the evaluated models, considering both FLOPs and inference time per image.

All results reported correspond to 10 independent runs with different seeds. For each metric, the mean, standard deviation, and 95% confidence interval were computed to ensure reliability and enable a robust comparison of the models.

6.1. Hardware and Software Environment

The experiments were conducted on a Dell PowerEdge R730 (Dell Inc., Round Rock, TX, USA) server equipped with 80-core Intel Xeon Silver 4416+ processors (Intel Corporation, Santa Clara, CA, USA), 128 GB of RAM, and two NVIDIA A40 GPUs (NVIDIA Corporation, Santa Clara, CA, USA), each with 48 GB of dedicated GPU memory. The software environment was based on Ubuntu 22.04.5 LTS (Canonical Ltd., London, UK), using the Python programming language, version 3.10.12. Moreover, Python libraries, as detailed in Table 3, played a key role in this study.

Table 3. Key Python libraries used, with versions and roles in the implementation.

Library	Version	Role
PyTorch [47]	2.2.2	Build and train DL models
Torchvision [48]	0.17.2	Implement models and image transformations
LibMR [11]	0.1.9	Fit Weibull distributions for OpenMax
Scikit-learn [49]	1.6.0	Metrics evaluation

6.2. Fine-Tuning Performance

Before delving into scenario-specific results, we should first examine how the models learned from the training images during the fine-tuning phase. Figure 6 illustrates the progression of loss, recall, and precision across epochs, with each plot corresponding to a specific metric and displaying both training and validation curves for all models. The curves represent the average performance across all runs of each model at each epoch, offering a comprehensive overview of the models' overall behavior during the fine-tuning phase.

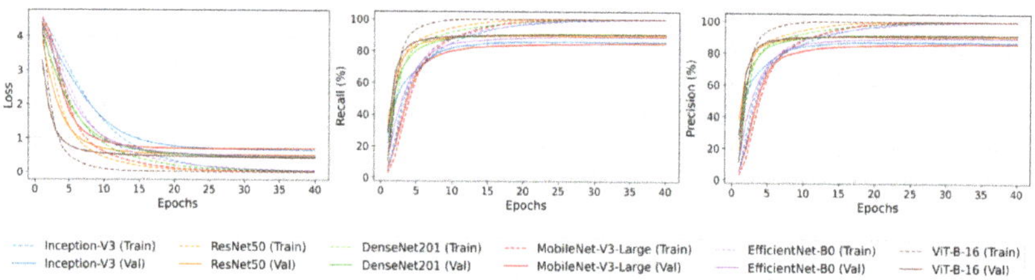

Figure 6. Training and validation curves of the fine-tuned models over epochs, showing loss (**left**), recall (**middle**), and precision (**right**).

The training curves demonstrate effective model learning, with loss decreasing and recall and precision steadily increasing. The validation curves exhibit a similar trend, expectedly slightly below the training performance. This pattern indicates that the models effectively classify and differentiate known individuals while demonstrating a suitable generalization to unseen face images.

6.3. Closed-Set Recognition Performance

Having observed the fine-tuning performance, the next step is to assess how well the models classify known individuals. In the CSR scenario, all models perform strongly, as indicated by the macro-averaged F1 score statistics presented in Table 4. Notably, DenseNet201 and ViT-B-16 achieve the highest mean macro-averaged F1 scores, showing a slight edge over the other CNN-based architectures. EfficientNet-B0 also performs well, with a mean macro-averaged F1 score close to these leading models. ResNet50 and Inception-V3 yield robust results, while MobileNet-V3-Large, designed for lightweight deployment, shows slightly lower performance relative to the other architectures.

Table 4. Macro-averaged F1 score statistics for models evaluated in the Closed-Set Recognition (CSR) scenario.

Model	Mean (%)	Std (%)	95% CI (%)
Inception-V3	89.96	0.41	89.67–90.25
ResNet50	91.43	0.35	91.18–91.68
DenseNet201	93.25	0.26	93.06–93.43
MobileNet-V3-Large	88.34	0.40	88.05–88.62
EfficientNet-B0	92.44	0.47	92.10–92.77
ViT-B-16	93.05	0.59	92.63–93.48

6.4. Open-Set Recognition Performance

Beyond known identities, it is critical to evaluate the models' ability to handle unfamiliar faces. Table 5 summarizes the macro-averaged F1 score statistics obtained by the evaluated models in the OSR scenario. In this context, the ViT-B-16 model attains the highest mean macro-averaged F1 score of 90.50%, accompanied by minimal standard deviation and a narrow 95% confidence interval, indicating consistent performance. MobileNet-V3-Large and EfficientNet-B0 also demonstrate strong results, with mean macro-averaged F1 scores of 87.32% and 87.65%, respectively, and relatively low variability across runs. ResNet50 and DenseNet201 exhibit moderate performance, while Inception-V3 achieves the lowest mean macro-averaged F1 score and shows greater variability, as reflected by its larger standard deviation and wider confidence interval.

Table 5. Macro-averaged F1 score statistics for models evaluated in the Open-Set Recognition (OSR) scenario.

Model	Mean (%)	Std (%)	95% CI (%)
Inception-V3	74.39	14.67	63.89–84.88
ResNet50	85.96	3.64	83.36–88.57
DenseNet201	84.78	5.45	80.89–88.68
MobileNet-V3-Large	87.32	0.52	86.95–87.69
EfficientNet-B0	87.65	2.94	85.54–89.75
ViT-B-16	90.50	0.41	90.21–90.80

To further evaluate how the models manage both known and unknown individuals, a detailed analysis of the False Positive (FPR), True Negative (TNR), True Positive (TPR), and False Negative (FNR) Rates was conducted. As detailed in Table 6, the ViT-B-16 model demonstrates a favorable balance, achieving a high TPR of 98.50% combined with a low FPR of 15.08%, indicating strong generalization capabilities. The EfficientNet-B0 model also performs interestingly, with a TPR of 98.42% and an FPR of 19.35%. MobileNet-V3-Large

Table 7. Macro-averaged F1 score statistics for models evaluated in the OSR scenario using SoftMax Thresholding.

Model	Mean (%)	Std (%)	95% CI (%)
Inception-V3	78.62	13.61	68.89–88.36
ResNet50	89.55	2.32	87.89–91.21
DenseNet201	87.88	4.95	84.34–91.42
MobileNet-V3-Large	88.54	0.48	88.20–88.89
EfficientNet-B0	89.22	3.56	86.68–91.77
ViT-B-16	92.60	0.38	92.33–92.87

The results clearly demonstrate that ViT-B-16 consistently surpasses all CNN architectures in the OSR scenario, independent of whether OpenMax or SoftMax Thresholding is employed. ViT-B-16 attains the highest mean macro-averaged F1 score with minimal variance, reflecting its enhanced capacity for identifying known and unknown identities. This finding indicates that the observed differences between models are not due to the choice of using OpenMax or another alternative but rather reflect the inherent robustness and accuracy of ViT-B-16.

6.6. Computational Cost and Inference Time Analysis

In addition to evaluating model accuracy, the deployment of DL models requires consideration of their computational cost. To this end, Figure 10 summarizes key metrics for all evaluated models, including floating-point operations (FLOPs) and inference time per image.

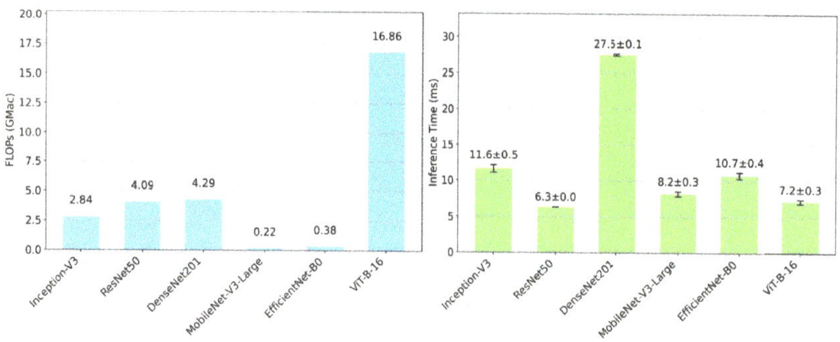

Figure 10. Analysis of the computational cost of the evaluated models, showing FLOPs (**left**) and inference time per image (**right**).

As illustrated in the graph on the left, the ViT-B-16 architecture has the highest computational cost at approximately 16.86 GFLOPs. This is mainly attributed to its attention-based design, which allows it to capture global relationships between all patches in the image, unlike CNNs, which focus on extracting local features through hierarchical convolutions. CNN architectures such as DenseNet-201 (4.29 GFLOPs), ResNet-50 (4.09 GFLOPs) and Inception-V3 (2.84 GFLOPs) offer a balance between depth and computational efficiency. Lighter models, such as MobileNet-V3-Large (0.22 GFLOPs) and EfficientNet-B0 (0.38 GFLOPs), significantly reduce the number of FLOPs, making them particularly suitable for resource-constrained environments.

The graph on the right shows the inference time per image, demonstrating that a higher number of FLOPs does not necessarily imply longer inference times. For example, the ViT-B-16 model requires an average of approximately 7.2 ms per image, remaining competitive thanks to the optimized parallelization of its attention mechanisms. Although DenseNet-201 has a lower FLOPs cost than ViT-B-16, it has a higher inference time. On the other hand, models such as ResNet-50, Inception-V3, EfficientNet-B0, and MobileNet-V3-Large show moderate inference times, indicating a balance between architectural depth and computational efficiency.

In summary, these results highlight the trade-offs between model accuracy and computational efficiency. While ViT-B-16 offers greater accuracy and robustness in capturing global dependencies in images, its high FLOPs requirements may limit its implementation in resource-constrained scenarios. On the other hand, lightweight architectures such as MobileNet-V3-Large and EfficientNet-B0 represent an attractive option, achieving competitive performance at a significantly lower computational cost, making them ideal for real-time applications or environments with limited hardware.

7. Conclusions

This paper presents a comparison between CNN and ViT architectures for face recognition in an OSR scenario. Specifically, five CNN models—Inception-V3, ResNet50, DenseNet201, MobileNet-V3-Large and EfficientNet-B0—are compared to the base ViT model, ViT-B-16. For the classification of individuals in such a scenario, the OpenMax algorithm is implemented, allowing the models to identify and assign an unknown category instead of forcing classification into one of the known identities from the training phase.

The results show that ViT-B-16 achieves the strongest performance in handling both known and unknown individuals, attaining a mean macro-averaged F1 score of 90.50% across multiple runs. These results are in line with the findings reported in related works, which demonstrate that ViTs constitute an emerging architecture capable of outperforming traditional CNNs when pre-trained on large-scale image datasets. In this work, the strong results achieved by ViT-B-16 can be attributed to such pre-training.

However, it is important to note that while the implemented VGGFace2 and CASIA-WebFace datasets are commonly used in face recognition research, they may not comprehensively represent the demographic diversity found in real-world populations. Variations in age, gender, and ethnicity can impact model performance, particularly in OSR scenarios, and may influence the overall identification accuracy of the evaluated models.

In practical applications such as surveillance and access control, the primary objective is typically to identify a specific group of individuals, rather than incorporating external individuals during training. Therefore, it is crucial to develop models that can reliably differentiate between known and unknown people, enhancing system robustness, security, and operational reliability. This work represents a further step in the development and deployment of such systems for real-world applications, where accuracy is a key requirement. As a result of the conducted study, we showed that ViTs emerge as a particularly promising alternative in OSR scenarios, especially when appropriate model pre-training is performed. Nonetheless, it is important to mention that CNNs remain highly effective and extensively utilized, especially in scenarios with limited training data, and therefore continue to serve a vital function in numerous practical applications.

In terms of future research directions, we propose conducting a comparative evaluation of different variants of ViTs, including Swin Transformers. In addition, researchers could explore hybrid models that take advantage of the complementary advantages of both approaches.

Author Contributions: Conceptualization, A.G. and M.H.; methodology, A.G. and M.H.; software, A.G. and M.S.; validation, A.G. and M.H.; investigation, A.G. and M.H.; writing—original draft preparation, A.G. and M.H.; writing—review and editing, M.H., A.S. and A.A.; supervision, M.H. and E.J.; project administration, M.H. and E.J.; funding acquisition, E.J. All authors have read and agreed to the published version of the manuscript.

Funding: This work has been funded by the Spanish Ministry of Science project through the AIBioSurv-Tech project—Biosurveillance through Artificial Intelligence (AI) in the post-COVID era: Implications for architecture and cybersecurity—under reference TED2021-129975B-C22AEI/AEI/10.13039/501100011033/Unión Europea NextGenerationEU/PRTR.

Data Availability Statement: Data is available in a publicly accessible repository: https://github.com/andergalvan/paper4_cnn_vit_comparison (accessed on 1 September 2025).

Conflicts of Interest: The authors declare no conflicts of interest.

References

1. Scoop Market.US. Facial Recognition Statistics and Market Trends. 2025. Available online: https://scoop.market.us/facial-recognition-statistics/ (accessed on 9 July 2025).
2. Scheirer, W.J.; de Rezende Rocha, A.; Sapkota, A.; Boult, T.E. Toward Open Set Recognition. *IEEE Trans. Pattern Anal. Mach. Intell.* **2013**, *35*, 1757–1772. [CrossRef]
3. Geng, C.; Huang, S.J.; Chen, S. Recent Advances in Open Set Recognition: A Survey. *IEEE Trans. Pattern Anal. Mach. Intell.* **2020**, *43*, 3614–3631. [CrossRef]
4. Dosovitskiy, A.; Beyer, L.; Kolesnikov, A.; Weissenborn, D.; Zhai, X.; Unterthiner, T.; Dehghani, M.; Minderer, M.; Heigold, G.; Gelly, S.; et al. An Image is Worth 16x16 Words: Transformers for Image Recognition at Scale. *arXiv* **2020**, arXiv:2010.11929.
5. Rodrigo, M.; Cuevas, C.; García, N. Comprehensive Comparison Between Vision Transformers and Convolutional Neural Networks for Face Recognition Tasks. *Sci. Rep.* **2024**, *14*, 12345. [CrossRef]
6. Maurício, J.; Domingues, I.; Bernardino, J. Comparing Vision Transformers and Convolutional Neural Networks for Image Classification: A Literature Review. *Appl. Sci.* **2023**, *13*, 5521. [CrossRef]
7. Takahashi, S.; Sakaguchi, Y.; Kouno, N.; Takasawa, K.; Ishizu, K.; Akagi, Y.; Aoyama, R.; Teraya, N.; Bolatkan, A.; Shinkai, N.; et al. Comparison of Vision Transformers and Convolutional Neural Networks in Medical Image Analysis: A Systematic Review. *J. Med. Syst.* **2024**, *48*, 84. [CrossRef]
8. Deng, J.; Dong, W.; Socher, R.; Li, L.J.; Li, K.; Li, F.-F. ImageNet: A Large-Scale Hierarchical Image Database. In Proceedings of the 2009 IEEE Conference on Computer Vision and Pattern Recognition (CVPR), Miami, FL, USA, 20–25 June 2009; pp. 248–255. [CrossRef]
9. Sun, C.; Shrivastava, A.; Singh, S.; Gupta, A. Revisiting Unreasonable Effectiveness of Data in Deep Learning Era. In Proceedings of the IEEE International Conference on Computer Vision, Venice, Italy, 22–29 October 2017; pp. 843–852.
10. Bendale, A.; Boult, T.E. Towards Open Set Deep Networks. In Proceedings of the 2016 IEEE Conference on Computer Vision and Pattern Recognition (CVPR), Las Vegas, NV, USA, 27–30 June 2016; pp. 1563–1572.
11. Scheirer, W.J.; Rocha, A.; Micheals, R.J.; Boult, T.E. Meta-Recognition: The Theory and Practice of Recognition Score Analysis. *IEEE Trans. Pattern Anal. Mach. Intell.* **2011**, *33*, 1689–1695. [CrossRef] [PubMed]
12. Raghu, M.; Unterthiner, T.; Kornblith, S.; Zhang, C.; Dosovitskiy, A. Do Vision Transformers See Like Convolutional Neural Networks? *Adv. Neural Inf. Process. Syst.* **2021**, *34*, 12116–12128.
13. Tan, M.; Le, Q. EfficientNet: Rethinking Model Scaling for Convolutional Neural Networks. In Proceedings of the International Conference on Machine Learning, Long Beach, CA, USA, 9–15 June 2019; pp. 6105–6114.
14. Szegedy, C.; Vanhoucke, V.; Ioffe, S.; Shlens, J.; Wojna, Z. Rethinking the Inception Architecture for Computer Vision. In Proceedings of the 2016 IEEE Conference on Computer Vision and Pattern Recognition (CVPR), Las Vegas, NV, USA, 27–30 June 2016; pp. 2818–2826.
15. Sandler, M.; Howard, A.; Zhu, M.; Zhmoginov, A.; Chen, L.C. MobileNetV2: Inverted Residuals and Linear Bottlenecks. In Proceedings of the 2018 IEEE Conference on Computer Vision and Pattern Recognition (CVPR), Salt Lake City, UT, USA, 18–23 June 2018; pp. 4510–4520.
16. He, K.; Zhang, X.; Ren, S.; Sun, J. Deep Residual Learning for Image Recognition. In Proceedings of the 2016 IEEE Conference on Computer Vision and Pattern Recognition (CVPR), Las Vegas, NV, USA, 27–30 June 2016; pp. 770–778.
17. Simonyan, K.; Zisserman, A. Very Deep Convolutional Networks for Large-Scale Image Recognition. *arXiv* **2014**, arXiv:1409.1556.
18. Tafur Acenjo, B.X.; Tello Pariona, M.A.; Escobedo Cárdenas, E.J. Comparativa entre RESNET-50, VGG-16, Vision Transformer y Swin Transformer para el reconocimiento facial con oclusión de una mascarilla. *Interfases* **2023**, *17*, 56–78. [CrossRef]
19. Liu, Z.; Lin, Y.; Cao, Y.; Hu, H.; Wei, Y.; Zhang, Z.; Lin, S.; Guo, B. Swin Transformer: Hierarchical Vision Transformer Using Shifted Windows. In Proceedings of the IEEE/CVF International Conference on Computer Vision, Montreal, QC, Canada, 10–17 October 2021; pp. 10012–10022.
20. Kim, G.; Park, G.; Kang, S.; Woo, S.S. S-ViT: Sparse Vision Transformer for Accurate Face Recognition. In Proceedings of the 38th ACM/SIGAPP Symposium on Applied Computing (SAC '23), New York, NY, USA, 27–31 March 2023; pp. 1130–1138. [CrossRef]

21. Wu, K.; Peng, H.; Chen, M.; Fu, J.; Chao, H. Rethinking and improving relative position encoding for vision transformer. In Proceedings of the IEEE/CVF International Conference on Computer Vision, Montreal, QC, Canada, 10–17 October 2021; pp. 10033–10041.
22. Deng, J.; Guo, J.; Xue, N.; Zafeiriou, S. ArcFace: Additive Angular Margin Loss for Deep Face Recognition. In Proceedings of the 2019 IEEE/CVF Conference on Computer Vision and Pattern Recognition (CVPR), Long Beach, CA, USA, 15–20 June 2019; pp. 4685–4694. [CrossRef]
23. Khan, M.; Saeed, M.; El Saddik, A.; Gueaieb, W. ARTriViT: Automatic Face Recognition System Using ViT-Based Siamese Neural Networks with a Triplet Loss. In Proceedings of the 2023 IEEE 32nd International Symposium on Industrial Electronics (ISIE), Helsinki, Finland, 19–21 June 2023; pp. 1–6. [CrossRef]
24. Li, Y.; Sun, P.; Qi, H.; Lyu, S. Celeb-DF: A Large-scale Challenging Dataset for DeepFake Forensics. In Proceedings of the IEEE Conference on Computer Vision and Patten Recognition (CVPR), Seattle, WA, USA, 13–19 June 2020.
25. George, A.; Ecabert, C.; Shahreza, H.O.; Kotwal, K.; Marcel, S. EdgeFace: Efficient Face Recognition Model for Edge Devices. *IEEE Trans. Biom. Behav. Identity Sci.* **2024**, *6*, 158–168. [CrossRef]
26. Huang, G.B.; Mattar, M.; Berg, T.; Learned-Miller, E. Labeled Faces in the Wild: A Database for Studying Face Recognition in Unconstrained Environments. In Proceedings of the Workshop on Faces in 'Real-Life' Images: Detection, Alignment, and Recognition, Marseille, France, 12–18 October 2008.
27. Whitelam, C.; Taborsky, E.; Blanton, A.; Maze, B.; Adams, J.; Miller, T.; Kalka, N.; Jain, A.K.; Duncan, J.A.; Allen, K.; et al. IARPA Janus Benchmark-B Face Dataset. In Proceedings of the 2017 IEEE Conference on Computer Vision and Pattern Recognition Workshops (CVPRW), Honolulu, HI, USA, 21–26 July 2017; pp. 592–600. [CrossRef]
28. Maze, B.; Adams, J.; Duncan, J.A.; Kalka, N.; Miller, T.; Otto, C.; Jain, A.K.; Niggel, W.T.; Anderson, J.; Cheney, J.; et al. IARPA Janus Benchmark—C: Face Dataset and Protocol. In Proceedings of the 2018 International Conference on Biometrics (ICB), Gold Coast, QLD, Australia, 20–23 February 2018; pp. 158–165. [CrossRef]
29. Li, J.; Zhou, L.; Chen, J. MobileFaceFormer: A lightweight face recognition model against face variations. *Multimed. Tools Appl.* **2024**, *83*, 12669–12685. [CrossRef]
30. Setyawan, N.; Sun, C.C.; Hsu, M.H.; Kuo, W.K.; Hsieh, J.W. FaceLiVT: Face Recognition using Linear Vision Transformer with Structural Reparameterization For Mobile Device. *arXiv* **2025**, arXiv:2506.10361.
31. Bharath, M. Advancing Face Recognition with Hybrid CNN-ViT-MLP: A Comparative Study. *Int. J. Res. Appl. Sci. Eng. Technol.* **2025**, *13*, 1106–1111. [CrossRef]
32. Nemavhola, A.; Chibaya, C.; Viriri, S. A Systematic Review of CNN Architectures, Databases, Performance Metrics, and Applications in Face Recognition. *Information* **2025**, *16*, 107. [CrossRef]
33. Lee, J.H.; Song, K.S. Comparison and Analysis of CNN Models to Improve a Facial Emotion Classification Accuracy for Koreans and East Asians. *Int. J. Adv. Sci. Eng. Inf. Technol.* **2024**, *14*, 811–817. [CrossRef]
34. Pinzón-Arenas, J.; Moreno, R.; Martínez Baquero, J. Comparison of convolutional neural network models for user's facial recognition. *Int. J. Electr. Comput. Eng. (IJECE)* **2024**, *14*, 192. [CrossRef]
35. Cuenat, S.; Couturier, R. Convolutional Neural Network (CNN) vs. Vision Transformer (ViT) for Digital Holography. In Proceedings of the 2022 2nd International Conference on Computer, Control and Robotics (ICCCR), Virtual, 18–20 March 2022; pp. 235–240. [CrossRef]
36. Reedha, R.; Dericquebourg, E.; Canals, R.; Hafiane, A. Transformer Neural Network for Weed and Crop Classification of High Resolution UAV Images. *Remote Sens.* **2022**, *14*, 592. [CrossRef]
37. Wu, Y.; Qi, S.; Sun, Y.; Xia, S.; Yao, Y.; Qian, W. A vision transformer for emphysema classification using CT images. *Phys. Med. Biol.* **2021**, *66*, 245016. [CrossRef]
38. Gheflati, B.; Rivaz, H. Vision Transformers for Classification of Breast Ultrasound Images. In Proceedings of the 2022 44th Annual International Conference of the IEEE Engineering in Medicine & Biology Society (EMBC), Scotland, UK, 11–15 July 2022; pp. 480–483. [CrossRef]
39. Huang, G.; Liu, Z.; Van Der Maaten, L.; Weinberger, K.Q. Densely Connected Convolutional Networks. In Proceedings of the 2017 IEEE Conference on Computer Vision and Pattern Recognition (CVPR), Honolulu, HI, USA, 21–26 July 2017; pp. 4700–4708.
40. Howard, A.; Sandler, M.; Chu, G.; Chen, L.C.; Chen, B.; Tan, M.; Wang, W.; Zhu, Y.; Pang, R.; Vasudevan, V.; et al. Searching for MobileNetV3. In Proceedings of the IEEE/CVF International Conference on Computer Vision, Seoul, Republic of Korea, 27 October–2 November 2019; pp. 1314–1324.
41. Vaswani, A.; Shazeer, N.; Parmar, N.; Uszkoreit, J.; Jones, L.; Gomez, A.N.; Kaiser, Ł.; Polosukhin, I. Attention Is All You Need. *Adv. Neural Inf. Process. Syst.* **2017**, *30*, 6000–6010.
42. Cao, Q.; Shen, L.; Xie, W.; Parkhi, O.M.; Zisserman, A. VGGFace2: A Dataset for Recognising Faces Across Pose and Age. In Proceedings of the 2018 13th IEEE International Conference on Automatic Face & Gesture Recognition (FG 2018), Xi'an, China, 15–19 May 2018; pp. 67–74. [CrossRef]
43. Loshchilov, I.; Hutter, F. Decoupled Weight Decay Regularization. *arXiv* **2017**, arXiv:1711.05101.

44. Yi, D.; Lei, Z.; Liao, S.; Li, S.Z. Learning Face Representation from Scratch. *arXiv* **2014**, arXiv:1411.7923. [CrossRef]
45. Zhang, K.; Zhang, Z.; Li, Z.; Qiao, Y. Joint Face Detection and Alignment using Multi-task Cascaded Convolutional Networks. *IEEE Signal Process. Lett.* **2016**, *23*, 1499–1503. [CrossRef]
46. Higuero, M.; Galván, A.; Astorga, J.; Atutxa, A.; Jacob, E. Optimizing OpenMax Parameters for Open-Set Face Recognition. In Proceedings of the International Conference on Artificial Intelligence and Soft Computing (ICAISC 2025), Zakopane, Poland, 22–26 June 2025.
47. Paszke, A.; Gross, S.; Massa, F.; Lerer, A.; Bradbury, J.; Chanan, G.; Killeen, T.; Lin, Z.; Gimelshein, N.; Antiga, L.; et al. PyTorch: An Imperative Style, High-Performance Deep Learning Library. *Adv. Neural Inf. Process. Syst.* **2019**, *32*, 8026–8037.
48. Marcel, S.; Rodriguez, Y. Torchvision The Machine-Vision Package of Torch. In Proceedings of the 18th ACM International Conference on Multimedia, Firenze, Italy, 25–29 October 2010; Association for Computing Machinery: New York, NY, USA, 2010; pp. 1485–1488. [CrossRef]
49. Pedregosa, F.; Varoquaux, G.; Gramfort, A.; Michel, V.; Thirion, B.; Grisel, O.; Blondel, M.; Prettenhofer, P.; Weiss, R.; Dubourg, V.; et al. Scikit-learn: Machine Learning in Python. *J. Mach. Learn. Res.* **2011**, *12*, 2825–2830.
50. Lu, K.; Xu, Y.; Yang, Y. Comparison of the potential between transformer and CNN in image classification. In Proceedings of the 2nd International Conference on Machine Learning and Computer Application (ICMLCA 2021), Shenyang, China, 17–19 December 2021; pp. 1–6.

electronics

MDPI

Article

PestOOD: An AI-Enabled Solution for Advancing Grain Security via Out-of-Distribution Pest Detection

Jida Tian [1], Chuanyang Ma [1], Jiangtao Li [2] and Huiling Zhou [1,*]

1 School of Intelligent Engineering and Automation, Beijing University of Posts and Telecommunications, Beijing 100876, China; tianjida@bupt.edu.cn (J.T.); chuanyang.ma@bupt.edu.cn (C.M.)
2 School of Artificial Intelligence, Beijing University of Posts and Telecommunications, Beijing 100876, China; lijiangtao@bupt.edu.cn
* Correspondence: huiling@bupt.edu.cn

Abstract

Detecting stored-grain pests on the surface of the grain pile plays an important role in integrated pest management (IPM), which is crucial for grain security. Recently, numerous deep learning-based pest detection methods have been proposed. However, a critical limitation of existing methods is their inability to detect out-of-distribution (OOD) categories that are unseen during training. When encountering such objects, these methods often misclassify them as in-distribution (ID) categories. To address this challenge, we propose a one-stage framework named PestOOD for out-of-distribution stored-grain pest detection via flow-based feature reconstruction. Specifically, we propose a novel Flow-Based OOD Feature Generation (FOFG) module that generates OOD features for detector training via feature reconstruction. This helps the detector learn to recognize OOD objects more effectively. Additionally, to prevent network overfitting that may lead to an excessive focus on ID feature extraction, we propose a Noisy DropBlock (NDB) module and integrate it into the backbone network. Finally, to ensure effective network convergence, a Stage-Wise Training Strategy (STS) is proposed. We conducted extensive experiments on our previously established multi-class stored-grain pest dataset. The results show that our proposed PestOOD demonstrates superior performance over state-of-the-art methods, providing an effective AI-enabled solution to ensure grain security.

Keywords: stored-grain pests; pest detection; out-of-distribution object detection; flow-based module; grain security

1. Introduction

The proliferation and infestation of pests during grain storage can lead to the loss of both the quality and quantity of grain [1]. Therefore, integrated pest management (IPM) systems, which aim to detect and control pest infestations, are crucial for grain security [2]. Since pests are often found on the surfaces of grain piles, robust vision-based detection is critical for effective IPM. Recently, numerous deep learning-based pest detection methods have been proposed [3,4], but they still face limitations, particularly in the detection of unknown pest categories. Specifically, existing methods are restricted to detecting in-distribution (ID) categories. This means that detectors can only recognize the categories present in the training set. When faced with out-of-distribution (OOD) categories, detectors are prone to making overconfident predictions for ID categories or missing detections altogether [5]. In IPM, differential treatment strategies are required for distinct pest categories, and newly emerging pest categories often require immediate intervention. Thus, addressing the OOD problem is a critical challenge in pest detection to ensure robust grain security.

To detect OOD categories, a straightforward approach is to incorporate samples of these categories into the training data. However, since such categories are often relatively rare and highly diverse, this incorporation leads to a long-tailed data distribution [6]. Furthermore, expanding the training data with additional OOD categories can divert the detector's attention away from ID categories, ultimately leading to the degradation of detection accuracy [7]. A more practical approach is to leverage the out-of-distribution object detection (OOD-OD) technique, which is designed to classify and locate ID categories while identifying unseen categories as OOD [8]. Some studies have attempted to identify OOD objects by comparing the differences in intermediate features between ID and OOD objects [9,10]. However, in pest detection tasks, the intra-class similarity of pest features often causes overlap in the feature space [11], making it challenging to distinguish between ID and OOD objects. Other methods address this by estimating the detector's input uncertainty, where high uncertainty indicates the potential presence of OOD data [12,13]. Unfortunately, the precision of this uncertainty estimation approach is highly sensitive to the network architecture, training data, and parameter settings, which can lead to misjudgments.

Recently, a novel approach has emerged that utilizes generative models to generate OOD features for training detectors, enabling the detection of OOD categories [14,15]. The strength of this approach lies in the creation of diverse synthetic OOD samples. This allows detectors to capture a wider range of unknown distributions and improves their ability to distinguish between ID and OOD objects. However, for pest detection tasks, OOD detection faces two main challenges: (1) The small size of pests poses challenges for robust feature representation, increasing the susceptibility of generative models to mode collapse. (2) Pest detection involves fine-grained classification among pest categories, making it particularly difficult to define clear decision boundaries between ID and OOD features.

Previous studies have demonstrated that flow-based generative models [16] excel in generation and density estimation due to their reversibility [17], a property crucial for OOD feature generation. Thus, inspired by FFS [18], we propose a one-stage framework named PestOOD to address the above challenges in stored-grain pest detection, as shown in Figure 1. Specifically, we first propose a Flow-Based OOD Feature Generation (FOFG) module. This module is optimized using ID feature vectors via maximum likelihood estimation (MLE). This training paradigm enables the FOFG module to estimate the actual distribution of ID features by transforming them into a simple probability distribution within a latent variable space during its forward process. Subsequently, during the inverse process, we reconstruct the latent variables into feature vectors that closely approximate the original ID feature distribution. These reconstructed features exhibit distinctiveness from the ID features and thus serve as generated OOD features. Finally, these OOD features are incorporated into detector training, enabling the detector to identify OOD objects. Furthermore, we propose a Noisy DropBlock (NDB) module and introduce it into the backbone. NDB randomly selects contiguous regions on the original feature maps and replaces them with random Gaussian noise, thereby preventing the backbone network from overfitting and reducing its excessive reliance on ID features. Finally, in conjunction with our framework, we propose a Stage-Wise Training Strategy (STS) to facilitate effective network convergence. The results of extensive experiments demonstrate that PestOOD achieves good performance, outperforming SOTA methods in OOD stored-grain pest detection.

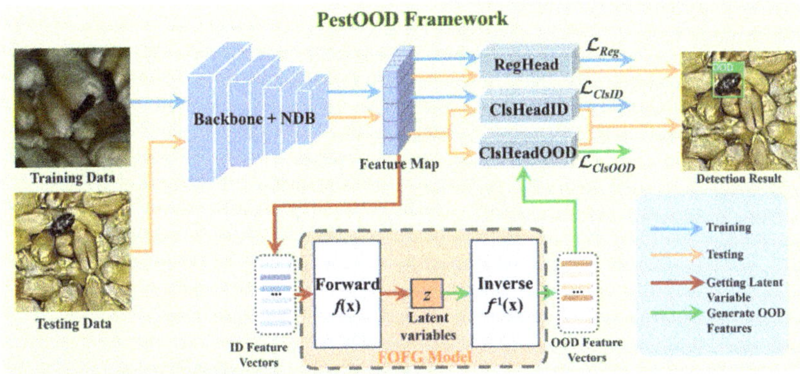

Figure 1. Overall PestOOD framework. The FOFG module is first trained on ID features. After this, OOD features are generated by feature reconstruction. Finally, these generated OOD features are fed into the classification head of the PestOOD detector for training.

We summarize our contributions as follows:

- We propose PestOOD, a framework for out-of-distribution stored-grain pest detection via flow-based feature reconstruction to achieve robust grain security.
- We propose FOFG to generate OOD features for detector training. NDB is introduced into the backbone network to prevent overfitting. Additionally, we propose an STS for effective network convergence.
- Extensive experiments demonstrate that PestOOD can effectively detect OOD objects, outperforming other SOTA methods in OOD stored-grain pest detection.

2. Related Work

2.1. Research on Pest Detection

With advances in artificial intelligence and computer vision, numerous object detection frameworks have been developed, achieving remarkable performance [19]. Recent research has shown increasing interest in the application of these technologies to pest detection. Some studies have employed image optimization techniques to address the challenges posed by small sizes and low resolution in pest identification. For example, Zhou et al. [20] proposed the combination of a generative model with a classifier to effectively enhance the classification performance of low-resolution insect images, providing a novel approach for automated stored-grain insect identification. Other approaches improve detection accuracy by enhancing detector representation abilities. For example, Li et al. [21] proposed a data augmentation strategy for CNN-based pest detection. They diversified the training data by generating multi-pose samples through image rotation and by cropping images into grids of varying sizes to simulate multi-scale features. Hu et al. [22] proposed the MACNet model based on YOLOv8s, which incorporates CARMF modules and DSConv technology. By optimizing feature sampling and convolution operations, it improves both the accuracy of agricultural pest detection and the model's lightweight design, making it more suitable for deployment in real-world environments. Amrani et al. [23] proposed a Bayesian-based multi-task learning model. By integrating a joint loss function combining classification and a customized size loss, the model significantly improves detection and estimation accuracy, while the Bayesian approach effectively quantifies prediction uncertainties. Duan et al. [24] proposed a multimodal framework integrating tiny-BERT with R-CNN. Their innovation leverages ensemble learning to optimally fuse text and image modalities, overcoming the limitations of single-modality approaches. Nevertheless, the inability of these methods to detect OOD categories limits their practical application in complex detection scenarios.

2.2. Out-of-Distribution Object Detection

To enhance the adaptability of deep learning methods in practical applications, recent studies have increasingly focused on the OOD-OD task [5,8,25]. Most research distinguishes between ID and OOD objects by applying specific rules in the feature space. For example, Yang et al. [9] proposed a OneRing method, which uses a Cls+1-way classifier to achieve OOD detection. They devised a dual cross-entropy loss training strategy based on source data to enable the effective recognition of unknown classes. Additionally, the method adopts a weighted entropy minimization strategy for target-domain adaptation without requiring access to source data. Wilson et al. proposed a method named SAFE [10], which detects OOD samples by identifying sensitive residual convolutional and batch normalization layers in object detectors. It extracts object-specific SAFE vectors and trains an auxiliary MLP to differentiate between normal ID detections and OOD ones. Wu et al. [13] proposed leveraging PCA decomposition to generate supervisory information for OOD categories and employed dynamic prototypes extracted from residual principal components to help the detector distinguish OOD objects. However, these methods exhibit performance limitations when the detector's representation ability is insufficient or when features overlap in the feature space. Therefore, recent research has started to focus on employing generative models, such as diffusion models [26], to generate OOD features. For example, Liu et al. [15] proposed using a diffusion model to fit the ID data distribution and generate samples, combined with a K-Nearest Neighbors-based filtering strategy to select low-density OOD samples for training the OOD object detector. Kumar et al. [18] used flow models to synthesize OOD features. In this method, features from ID categories are first mapped into the latent space. Then, random sampling is conducted in the latent space to generate OOD features via the inverse process of the flow model. In our research, we also adopt this OOD feature generation approach and focus on addressing challenges in OOD feature synthesis and decision boundary definition.

3. Methodology

3.1. Preliminaries

Figure 2 shows a schematic of our proposed AI-enabled solution, PestOOD, for detecting stored-grain pests. The camera devices installed in the granaries capture images of the surfaces of the grain piles. These images are transmitted to a computer that runs an object detector, which identifies and classifies the pests present in the captured images.

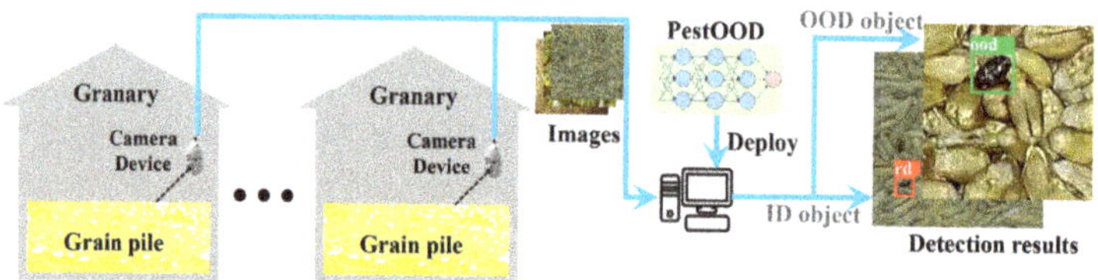

Figure 2. A schematic of PestOOD for detecting stored-grain pests.

To enhance the practical adaptability of the detector to ensure grain security, we propose a flow-based feature reconstruction method for out-of-distribution pest detection. We are given a training dataset $\mathcal{D}_{Train}$ containing only ID categories $\mathcal{C} = \{c_1, c_2, \ldots, c_n\}$, where n is the number of ID categories. Our goal is to train a detector that, given input images I containing both ID and OOD pest objects, can localize a set of bounding boxes $\mathcal{B} = \{b_1, b_2, \ldots, b_m\}$ to identify objects in I while correctly classifying ID categories and labeling unseen categories as "ood". To achieve this, we leverage flow-based feature reconstruction to generate OOD features for detector training, enabling the detector to effectively identify OOD objects. In addition, a Noisy DropBlock module is introduced to prevent overfitting, and a Stage-Wise Training Strategy is proposed to ensure effective network convergence. The mathematical notations used throughout this paper are summarized in Table 1.

Table 1. Summary of mathematical notations.

Notations	Descriptions	Notations	Descriptions
x	Original features	Φ_{Θ_1}	Backbone of detector
z	Latent variable	h_{Θ_2}	Detection head of detector
$p_\theta(z)$	Distribution of latent variable	$\mathcal{L}(\mathcal{D})$	Objective function of FOFG
$f_K(x)$	Flow block	$\mathcal{L}_{det}$	Objective function of detector
$\mathcal{D}_{Train}$	Training data	$\mathcal{Z}$	Latent variable space
$\mathcal{T}$	Temperature	$f_\theta(x)$	FOFG module
$\mathcal{B}$	Bounding boxes	$\mathcal{C}$	ID categories
$\mathbf{M}$	Feature maps		

3.2. *Flow-Based OOD Feature Generation (FOFG)*

3.2.1. Objective of the FOFG

Similar to conventional flow-based generative models, our proposed FOFG module consists of two processes: A forward process and an inverse process. The forward process transforms original features into latent variables following a simple distribution, which are used to estimate the complex original distribution in the latent space. Conversely, the inverse process not only enables random sampling from the latent space to generate random features but also reconstructs the original features using the latent variables obtained during the forward pass. These two processes are described as follows:

$$z = f_\theta(x) = f_K \circ f_{K-1} \circ \cdots \circ f_1(x) \tag{1}$$

$$x = g_\theta(z) = g_1 \circ g_2 \circ \cdots \circ g_K(z) \tag{2}$$

For the pest detection task, the variable x in the aforementioned formula represents a pest feature that follows a complex and highly dimensional distribution. The latent variable z is associated with a simple density $p_\theta(z)$, such as a Gaussian distribution: $p_\theta(z) = \mathcal{N}(z; 0, I)$. The function $f_\theta(x)$ is invertible; therefore, given x, the corresponding z is computed as $z = f_\theta(x) = g_\theta^{-1}(x)$. The entire FOFG module is composed of a sequence of invertible transformation blocks $f_1, f_2, \ldots, f_k$. The objective of the FOFG module is to minimize the negative log-likelihood over the given dataset $\mathcal{D}$, which contains only ID categories, as follows:

$$\mathcal{L}(\mathcal{D}) = \frac{1}{N}\sum_{i=1}^{N} -\log f_\theta\left(\mathbf{x}^{(i)}\right) \tag{3}$$

The OOD pest feature can be generated by reconstructing the latent variable z, which is derived from the forward process, using the inverse process of the FOFG module.

3.2.2. Method of OOD Feature Generation

Figure 3a illustrates the architecture of the FOFG module and the OOD feature generation process. The design of the invertible transformation blocks in the flow model is based on Glow [16], as shown in Figure 3b. Each flow block in the FOFG module comprises an ActNorm layer, an invertible 1 × 1 convolution, and an affine transformation [27]. The FOFG module employs a multi-scale architecture with multiple layers, where each layer is composed of stacked flow blocks.

The generation of OOD features proceeds as follows: During detector training, input images are processed by the backbone network to extract feature maps $\mathbf{M} \in \mathbb{R}^{B \times C \times H \times W}$. Within the one-stage object detection framework, a portion of the feature vectors from the feature maps are labeled as positive samples by the label assignment strategy for classification and localization. These 1D positive samples, which contain only ID features and have a C-dimensional representation, are reshaped into 2D features with shape $\sqrt{C} \times \sqrt{C}$. These transformed features are then used to train the FOFG module by minimizing the objective function defined in Equation (3). After sufficient iterations, the FOFG module can estimate the ID feature distribution by a simple distribution $p_\theta(z)$ in the latent variable space $\mathcal{Z}$. When applying OOD feature generation, in contrast to random OOD feature generation methods [18], our method leverages the feature reconstruction approach. Specifically, the FOFG forward process first maps 2D ID features to the latent space $\mathcal{Z}$. Subsequently, the resulting latent variables are transformed back into 2D features through the FOFG module's inverse process. Finally, these 2D features are reshaped into 1D features that conform to the original feature distribution, thus obtaining the OOD pest features. We regulate the randomness of generated features via the temperature parameter $\mathcal{T}$, producing features that are semantically similar to but distributionally distinct from the original pest features. These generated features with similarity below a predefined threshold to the original features are considered OOD features. Finally, these OOD features are fed into the detection head of the detector for training, allowing the detector to identify OOD objects.

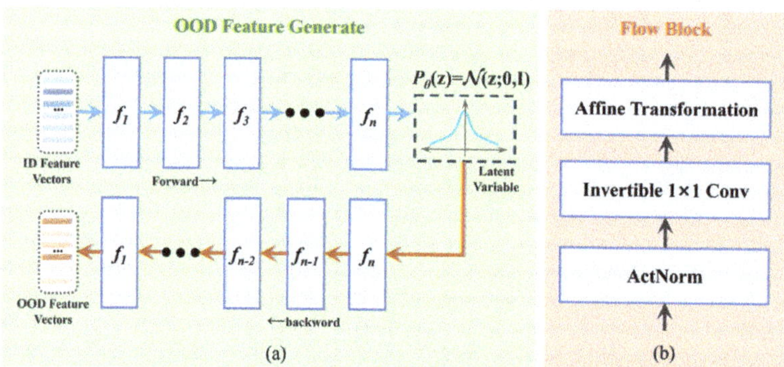

Figure 3. Flow-Based OOD Feature Generation (FOFG) module. (**a**) The process for OOD feature generation. (**b**) Structure of flow block.

3.3. Noisy DropBlock (NDB)

Due to the absence of OOD categories during training, the detector's backbone network often overemphasizes feature extraction for ID categories, resulting in overfitting to ID categories. Consequently, the detector may either fail to detect OOD objects or incorrectly classify them with high confidence as ID categories. To address the phenomenon of overfitting, traditional deep learning methods tend to introduce regularization techniques such as the dropout layer [28] to mitigate the issue. However, dropout's effectiveness in convolutional layers is limited [29]. Inspired by DropBlock [30], we propose Noisy DropBlock. Specifically, Noisy DropBlock first randomly selects contiguous regions on the original feature map as mask blocks, as shown in Figure 4b,c. Then, it replaces the feature activations within these mask blocks with random Gaussian noise, as shown in Figure 4d. The size of the block serves as a configurable hyperparameter.

Compared to methods that simply drop contiguous regions in feature maps, our method injects random Gaussian noise into mask blocks. This approach strategically integrates regularization techniques with feature-based data augmentation, thereby compelling the backbone network to learn more generalizable pest representations beyond ID characteristics. In addition, given that shallow features contain more fine-grained information and that deep features are rich in semantic information, to avoid damaging the fine-grained information of pest objects, the NDB module should be applied to deep features. Furthermore, empirical evidence also demonstrates that augmenting deep features enhances detector robustness [31]; therefore, we apply the NDB module to the outputs of Stages 2, 3, and 4 of the backbone, as shown in Figure 4a.

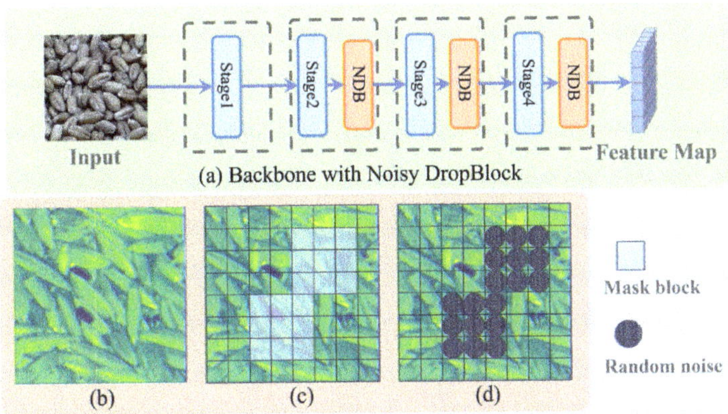

Figure 4. Operational mechanism of Noisy DropBlock (NDB). (**a**) Implementation location of NDB in the backbone. (**b**) Original feature map. (**c**) Mask block selection. (**d**) Addition of Gaussian noise. NDB randomly selects contiguous regions as mask blocks and replaces their activations with Gaussian noise to achieve dropout and data augmentation. It is applied in the shallow layers of the backbone to avoid disrupting semantic information.

3.4. Stage-Wise Training Strategy (STS)

PestOOD involves optimizing both the FOFG module and the object detector. Given their different optimization objectives, separate training is required to ensure effective convergence. To address this issue, we propose a Stage-Wise Training Strategy (STS) comprising three distinct phases: ID Feature Representation Learning, ID Feature Distribution Estimation, and Detector Fine-Tuning. We summarize the whole strategy in Algorithm 1; the detailed procedure is as follows:

(1) Stage One, ID Feature Representation Learning: In this stage, we train only the object detector to establish the fundamental representational capacity for ID pest features. The standard objective function shown in Equation (4) for the object detector is used, where $F_{cls}(\cdot)$ and $F_{reg}(\cdot)$ are the classification loss and bounding box regression loss, respectively. This stage continues until there is no improvement in detection performance over five consecutive epochs.

$$\mathcal{L}_{det} = \lambda_{\text{cls}} \cdot F_{cls}(c_p, c_{gt}) + \lambda_{\text{reg}} \cdot F_{reg}(b_p, b_{gt}) \tag{4}$$

(2) Stage Two, ID Feature Distribution Estimation: In this stage, we freeze the parameters of the detector backbone network Φ_{Θ_1} and train the FOFG module f_θ using the ID features extracted by Φ_{Θ_1}. This enables the FOFG module to estimate the original feature distribution in the latent space by minimizing the flow model's objective function in Equation (3). This stage continues until the loss computed by Equation (3) plateaus below 5% of its initial value.

(3) Stage Three, Detector Fine-Tuning: In this stage, the FOFG module f_θ generates OOD features via feature reconstruction. These generated features are then used to fine-tune the detection head h_{Θ_2}, allowing the detector to detect OOD objects.

Algorithm 1: Stage-Wise Training Strategy (STS) for PestOOD.

Input: Training data with only ID categories $C = \{c_1, c_2,...,c_n\}$. Object detector $h_{\Theta_2}(\Phi_{\Theta_1}(.))$ with parameter Θ_1 and Θ_2, FOFG module f_θ with parameter $\boldsymbol{\theta}$. The hyperparameter of temperature $\mathcal{T}$, the blocksize.

Output: The trained object detector $h_{\Theta_2}(\Phi_{\Theta_1}(.))$.

Initialize Θ_1, Θ_2 and $\boldsymbol{\theta}$;

while train **do**
- 1.Input training data to detector $h_{\Theta_2}(\Phi_{\Theta_1}(.))$.
- **if** *Stage* = *1* **then**
  - 2.Update the parameters Θ_1 and Θ_2.
- **else if** *Stage* = *2* **then**
  - 3.Freeze backbone network Φ_{Θ_1}.
  - 4.Get ID features from Φ_{Θ_1} and input to FOFG f_θ.
  - 5.Update the parameter $\boldsymbol{\theta}$ using ID features by minimizing the objective function shown in Equation (3).
- **else if** *Stage* = *3* **then**
  - 6.Get OOD features from f_θ.
  - 7.Fine-tune h_{Θ_2} using OOD features.

while val **do**
- Calau FPR95, AUROC and mAP(ID).

This Stage-Wise Training approach prevents interference between the FOFG module and object detector optimization. In addition, during the Detector Fine-Tuning Stage, the backbone network remains frozen with only the classification head being optimized. This approach preserves robust ID feature representation while equipping the detector with the OOD detection ability, thereby ensuring effective convergence of the overall framework.

4. Experiments

4.1. Datasets and Preprocessing

The training dataset used in this study is our previously established pest dataset, GrainPest [32]. Taking into account pest occurrence frequency and economic impact [1], we select five in-distribution (ID) categories: *Cryptolestes ferrugineus* (Stephens) "cf", *Rhizopertha dominica* (Fabricius) "rd", *Sitophilus zeamais* (Linnaeus)/*Sitophilus oryzae* Motschulsky "sz", *Tribolium castaneum* (Herbst) "tc", and *Oryzaephilus surinamensis* (Linnaeus) "os". The terms in double quotations following each scientific name are the corresponding category labels of pests.

For out-of-distribution (OOD) categories, we select three less frequently occurring categories, namely, *Trogoderma variabile* (Ballion), *Alphitobius diaperinus* (Panzer), and *Lariophagus distinguendus* (Förster), all labeled as "ood". Example images of the ID and OOD pest categories are shown in Figure 5. To standardize image sizes, the original images from the GrainPest dataset are cropped to 512 × 512 pixels. The dataset is then split into training and testing sets in an 8:2 ratio, ensuring that only ID categories are present in the training set.

Figure 5. Example images of ID and OOD pest categories. (a) *Cryptolestes ferrugineus* (Stephens). (b) *Oryzaephilus surinamensis* (Linnaeus). (c) *Rhizopertha dominica* (Fabricius). (d) *Sitophilus zeamais* (Linnaeus)/*Sitophilus oryzae* Motschulsky. (e) *Tribolium castaneum* (Herbst). (f) *Trogoderma variabile* (Ballion). (g) *Alphitobius diaperinus* (Panzer). (h) *Lariophagus distinguendus* (Förster).

4.2. Implementation Details and Evaluation Metrics

We adopt UniRepLKNet-T [33] as the backbone. We use the YOLO Head [34] for classification and regression branches in conjunction with the one-stage framework. The FOFG module employs three layers with 16 flow blocks in each layer in our experiments. All experiments are conducted using the PyTorch 1.12.0 framework with two NVIDIA 3090 GPUs. We select SGD [35] as the optimizer. The evaluation metrics comprise the Mean Average Precision for ID categories (mAP(ID)) to assess OOD detection's impact on ID object detection performance; the False Positive Rate at 95% True Positive Rate (FPR95) [36] to measure the probability of the misdetection of OOD objects under high-recall conditions; and the Area Under the Receiver Operating Characteristic Curve (AUROC) [37] to evaluate the detector's discrimination ability between ID and OOD categories.

4.3. Comparison Experiments

We compare PestOOD with object detection baselines, including YOLOv10 [38] and RT-DETR [39], and previous SOTA OOD-OD methods: FFS [18] (generating OOD features via random sampling); DFDD [14] (using feature deblurring diffusion); and NAP [40]/CSI [41] (recognizing OOD objects through intermediate feature discrepancies). The detection performance is presented in Table 2. Additionally, we provide confusion matrices, as shown in Figure 6, for four frameworks (YOLOv10, NAP, FFS, and PestOOD), allowing for a visual comparison of their OOD detection abilities.

The results in Table 2 show that the object detection baselines completely fail to detect OOD objects. As a result, evaluation metrics such as the FPR95 and AUROC are not applicable to these baselines. This limitation is visually confirmed in Figure 6a, where YOLOv10 either fails to detect OOD objects or misclassifies them as ID categories. Compared to PestOOD, the methods that directly differentiate ID and OOD objects in the feature space (e.g., NAP and CSI) exhibit a higher FPR95 and lower AUROC. This performance gap highlights the limitation of relying solely on feature-level differences to distinguish OOD from ID objects in object detection tasks involving fine-grained inter-class variation, such as pest detection. This observation is clearly illustrated in the confusion matrix shown in Figure 6b. In addition, FFS generates OOD features by random sampling in the latent space. This approach has a high degree of randomness and yields suboptimal generation quality, which frequently results in false detections. Therefore, it tends to have a high FPR95. In contrast, our method reconstructs features that are similar to but distinct from ID features. This reconstruction process induces a low-density region between the ID feature space and negative samples, with features located in this transitional space designated as OOD features. As a result, our method shows a superior discriminative ability in identifying OOD objects. Figure 6c,d provide a visual comparison of how the two OOD feature generation strategies influence detection performance. Furthermore, flow-based models benefit from a more precise log-likelihood estimation of input data compared to diffusion models [42], enabling more accurate modeling of the pest feature distribution. This enhanced ability facilitates the superior generation of OOD features, which is reflected in PestOOD having superior performance metrics over DFDD.

Table 2. Comparative results of PestOOD with baseline method and SOTAs.

Method	Evaluation Metrics		
	FPR95 ↓	AUROC ↑	mAP(ID) ↑
YOLOv10	-	-	0.812
RT-DETR	-	-	0.768
FFS	0.979	0.162	0.653
DFDD	0.757	0.277	0.676
NAP	0.579	0.421	0.667
CSI	0.507	0.507	0.650
Ours	0.425	0.595	0.727

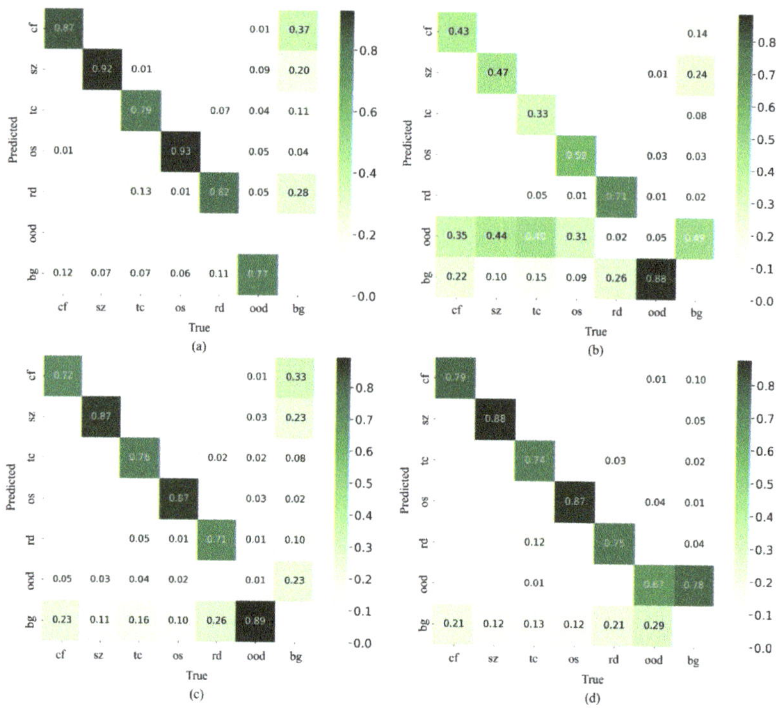

Figure 6. Confusion matrix. (**a**) YOLOv10. (**b**) NAP. (**c**) FFS. (**d**) PestOOD.

4.4. Ablation Studies of PestOOD

In the PestOOD framework, FOFG and STS are essential for out-of-distribution detection. Adjusting the temperature $\mathcal{T}$ in FOFG affects detection performance by modulating the randomness of feature generation. Furthermore, NDB enhances detection performance through regularization that mitigates overfitting. Therefore, we conduct ablation studies to evaluate the impact of temperature $\mathcal{T}$ and the contribution of NDB.

4.4.1. Impact of Temperature $\mathcal{T}$ on Detector Performance

Table 3 shows the impact of the temperature parameter $\mathcal{T}$ on detection performance. In addition, we provide Figure 7 to intuitively illustrate how $\mathcal{T}$ affects the feature distribution and discriminability in the feature space. Our findings demonstrate optimal detection performance at $\mathcal{T} = 1.1$. Higher temperature values introduce greater randomness into the FOFG process, causing the reconstructed features to lose essential pest-specific semantic information. This degradation results in confusion between the generated OOD features and background features, as illustrated in Figure 7b. Conversely, at lower $\mathcal{T}$ values, the reconstructed OOD features closely resemble ID features. This leads to confusion in the feature space and undermines the detector's ability to distinguish between ID and OOD objects, as shown in Figure 7c. Given the significant impact of $\mathcal{T}$ on detector performance and the task-dependent nature of its optimal value, empirical tuning of this parameter is critical for optimizing PestOOD's effectiveness.

Table 3. Impact of temperature $\mathcal{T}$ on detector performance.

$\mathcal{T}$ Value	Evaluation Metrics		
	FPR95 ↓	**AUROC** ↑	**mAP(ID)** ↑
0.9	0.878	0.298	0.302
1.1	0.422	0.595	0.727
1.3	0.763	0.480	0.711

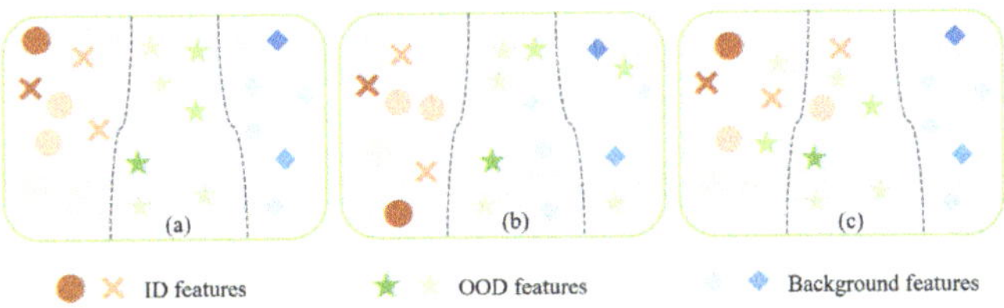

Figure 7. Effects of $\mathcal{T}$ on feature distribution and discrimination. (**a**) Feature distribution and decision boundaries at optimal $\mathcal{T} = 1.1$. (**b**) Feature distribution and boundaries at high $\mathcal{T}$. (**c**) Feature distribution and boundaries at low $\mathcal{T}$.

4.4.2. Ablative Study of Noisy DropBlock

We compare the impact of different NDB block sizes on detection performance and the implementation location of the NDB module in the backbone. Quantitative results are presented in Table 4. Specifically, a block size of 0 indicates that NDB is disabled. In our experiments, NDB modules are incorporated in Stages 2, 3, and 4 by default. The results show that, when the block size is 0, the detector exhibits a high FPR95, indicating a tendency to misclassify OOD objects as ID. In contrast, excessively large block sizes, such as 0.6, substantially reduce the AUROC. This shows that overly aggressive dropout regions hinder discriminative spatial feature learning, thereby compromising the detection accuracy of pest categories. Among all results, a block size of 0.4 achieves optimal overall performance by striking the best balance between ID and OOD detection abilities. Additionally, applying

NDB across all four backbone layers results in underperformance on all evaluation metrics, demonstrating that damaging shallow features degrades the representation ability, thus affecting detection performance.

Table 4. Impact of block size and implementation location of NDB on detector performance.

Block Size	Evaluation Metrics		
	FPR95 ↓	**AUROC** ↑	**mAP(ID)** ↑
0	0.853	0.196	0.291
0.2	0.448	0.526	0.740
0.4	0.422	0.595	0.727
0.4 [1]	0.412	0.527	0.713
0.6	0.413	0.552	0.753

[1] applying NDB across all four backbone layers.

4.5. Visualization and Analysis

Figure 8 shows the detection results of the object detection baselines YOLOv10 and RT-DETR, as well as those of our proposed PestOOD. The results indicate that the baseline methods tend to overlook OOD objects or misclassify them as ID objects. This failure arises from their fundamental inability to represent OOD features, leading to a complete failure in detecting OOD objects. In contrast, PestOOD successfully identifies OOD categories. Notably, our framework accurately localizes both ID and OOD objects, demonstrating its effectiveness in comprehensive pest detection. This distinction is particularly important in real-world pest monitoring scenarios.

Figure 8. Comparison of detection results between PestOOD and object detection baselines.

Figure 9 provides a comparative visualization of the detection results of the PestOOD and SOTA OOD-OD frameworks. Since NAP distinguishes ID and OOD objects solely based on feature discrepancies, its detection results exhibit significantly higher false detection rates. FFS shows both increased false positives and missed detections, which aligns with our previous analysis. The OOD features generated through random sampling are of suboptimal quality, and training detectors on such features compromises their accuracy in pest detection. In contrast, our proposed PestOOD significantly outperforms other frameworks in OOD object detection while maintaining a strong balance in detection accuracy in both ID and OOD instances. Thus, PestOOD demonstrates enhanced adaptability and robustness. Given the complexity of practical detection scenarios, a robust OOD detection ability is critical to ensure reliable pest detection. Therefore, PestOOD provides an effective AI-enabled solution to ensure grain security.

Figure 9. Comparison between detection results of PestOOD and SOTA methods.

5. Conclusions

In this paper, we propose PestOOD, a novel framework for OOD stored-grain pest detection. Our primary contribution is the introduction of an FOFG module, which generates OOD features for the detector's training, thus enabling the robust identification of OOD objects. Additionally, to prevent the backbone network from overfitting and to reduce its excessive reliance on ID features, we propose an NDB module and incorporate it into the backbone network. Finally, we further propose STS to facilitate effective network convergence. Experimental results show that PestOOD can effectively distinguish between ID and OOD pest objects and outperforms other SOTA methods. In future work, we will track emerging technologies in deep learning and computer vision with the aim of developing more adaptable pest detection frameworks. We hope that this work will contribute to the security of food and grain storage and improve the practicality of AI-enabled security in real-world applications.

Author Contributions: Conceptualization, J.T.; Methodology, J.T. and C.M.; Software, C.M.; Validation, C.M. and J.L.; Formal Analysis, H.Z.; Investigation, J.T. and C.M.; Resources, J.L.; Data Curation, H.Z.; Writing—Original Draft Preparation, J.T.; Writing—Review and Editing, H.Z.; Visualization, J.T. and C.M.; Supervision, H.Z.; Project Administration, H.Z.; Funding Acquisition, H.Z. All authors have read and agreed to the published version of the manuscript.

Funding: This research was funded by the Proof-of-Concept Program for University Research Achievements in Changping District, Beijing Municipal Science and Technology Commission. Project title: Sensor and Intelligent Analysis System for Grain Pest Occurrence Monitoring. Grant number: SHGNYZ202302.

Institutional Review Board Statement: Not applicable.

Informed Consent Statement: Not applicable.

Data Availability Statement: Data will be made available on request.

Conflicts of Interest: The authors declare no conflicts of interest.

References

1. Deshwal, R.; Vaibhav, V.; Kumar, N.; Kumar, A.; Singh, R. Stored grain insect pests and their management: An overview. *J. Entomol. Zool. Stud.* **2020**, *8*, 969–974.
2. Rustia, D.J.A.; Chiu, L.Y.; Lu, C.Y.; Wu, Y.F.; Chen, S.K.; Chung, J.Y.; Hsu, J.C.; Lin, T.T. Towards intelligent and integrated pest management through an AIoT-based monitoring system. *Pest Manag. Sci.* **2022**, *78*, 4288–4302. [CrossRef] [PubMed]
3. Chithambarathanu, M.; Jeyakumar, M. Survey on crop pest detection using deep learning and machine learning approaches. *Multimed. Tools Appl.* **2023**, *82*, 42277–42310. [CrossRef] [PubMed]
4. Guo, B.; Wang, J.; Guo, M.; Chen, M.; Chen, Y.; Miao, Y. Overview of pest detection and recognition algorithms. *Electronics* **2024**, *13*, 3008. [CrossRef]
5. Yang, J.; Zhou, K.; Li, Y.; Liu, Z. Generalized out-of-distribution detection: A survey. *Int. J. Comput. Vis.* **2024**, *132*, 5635–5662. [CrossRef]
6. Yu, W.; Yang, T.; Chen, C. Towards resolving the challenge of long-tail distribution in UAV images for object detection. In Proceedings of the IEEE/CVF Winter Conference on Applications of Computer Vision (WACV), Virtual, 5–9 January 2021; IEEE: Piscataway, NJ, USA, 2021; pp. 3258–3267.
7. Kennerley, M.; Wang, J.G.; Veeravalli, B.; Tan, R.T. Cat: Exploiting inter-class dynamics for domain adaptive object detection. In Proceedings of the IEEE/CVF Conference on Computer Vision and Pattern Recognition (CVPR), Nashville, TN, USA, 11–15 June 2025; IEEE: Seattle, WA, USA, 2024; pp. 16541–16550.
8. Cui, P.; Wang, J. Out-of-distribution (OOD) detection based on deep learning: A review. *Electronics* **2022**, *11*, 3500. [CrossRef]
9. Yang, S.; Wang, Y.; Wang, K.; Jui, S.; van de Weijer, J. OneRing: A simple method for source-free open-partial domain adaptation. *arXiv* **2022**, arXiv:2206.03600.
10. Wilson, S.; Fischer, T.; Dayoub, F.; Miller, D.; Sünderhauf, N. Safe: Sensitivity-aware features for out-of-distribution object detection. In Proceedings of the IEEE/CVF International Conference on Computer Vision (ICCV), Paris, France, 2–3 October 2023; IEEE: Paris, France, 2023; pp. 23565–23576.
11. Wu, X.; Zhan, C.; Lai, Y.K.; Cheng, M.M.; Yang, J. Ip102: A large-scale benchmark dataset for insect pest recognition. In Proceedings of the IEEE/CVF Conference on Computer Vision and Pattern Recognition (CVPR), Long Beach, CA, USA, 15–20 June 2019; IEEE: Long Beach, CA, USA, 2019; pp. 8787–8796.
12. Liu, W.; Wang, X.; Owens, J.; Li, Y. Energy-based out-of-distribution detection. In Proceedings of the Advances in Neural Information Processing Systems (NeurIPS), Virtual, 6–12 December 2020; pp. 21464–21475.
13. Wu, A.; Deng, C.; Liu, W. Unsupervised out-of-distribution object detection via PCA-driven dynamic prototype enhancement. *IEEE Trans. Image Process.* **2024**, *33*, 2431–2446. [CrossRef] [PubMed]
14. Wu, A.; Chen, D.; Deng, C. Deep feature deblurring diffusion for detecting out-of-distribution objects. In Proceedings of the IEEE/CVF International Conference on Computer Vision (ICCV), Paris, France, 1–6 October 2023; IEEE: Paris, France, 2023; pp. 13381–13391.

15. Liu, J.; Yu, X.; Zheng, A.; Sun, K.L.; Qi, X. Diffusion-based Data Generation for Out-of-Distribution Object Detection. In Proceedings of the International Conference on Learning Representations (ICLR), Vienna, Austria, 7–11 May 2024.
16. Kingma, D.P.; Dhariwal, P. Glow: Generative flow with invertible 1x1 convolutions. In Proceedings of the Advances in Neural Information Processing Systems (NeurIPS), Montréal, QC, Canada, 3–8 December 2018; pp. 10236–10245.
17. Liu, D.; Jain, M.; Dossou, B.F.; Shen, Q.; Lahlou, S.; Goyal, A.; Malkin, N.; Emezue, C.C.; Zhang, D.; Hassen, N.; et al. Gflowout: Dropout with generative flow networks. In Proceedings of the International Conference on Machine Learning (ICML), PMLR, Honolulu, HI, USA, 23–29 July 2023; pp. 21715–21729.
18. Kumar, N.; Šegvić, S.; Eslami, A.; Gumhold, S. Normalizing flow based feature synthesis for outlier-aware object detection. In Proceedings of the IEEE/CVF Conference on Computer Vision and Pattern Recognition (CVPR), Vancouver, BC, Canada, 17–24 June 2023; IEEE: Vancouver, BC, Canada, 2023; pp. 5156–5165.
19. Zou, Z.; Chen, K.; Shi, Z.; Guo, Y.; Ye, J. Object detection in 20 years: A survey. *Proc. IEEE* **2023**, *111*, 257–276. [CrossRef]
20. Zhou, H.; Miao, H.; Li, J.; Jian, F.; Jayas, D.S. A low-resolution image restoration classifier network to identify stored-grain insects from images of sticky boards. *Comput. Electron. Agric.* **2019**, *162*, 593–601. [CrossRef]
21. Li, R.; Wang, R.; Zhang, J.; Xie, C.; Liu, L.; Wang, F.; Chen, H.; Chen, T.; Hu, H.; Jia, X.; et al. An effective data augmentation strategy for CNN-based pest localization and recognition in the field. *IEEE Access* **2019**, *7*, 160274–160283. [CrossRef]
22. Hu, Y.; Wang, Q.; Wang, C.; Qian, Y.; Xue, Y.; Wang, H. MACNet: A more accurate and convenient pest detection network. *Electronics* **2024**, *13*, 1068. [CrossRef]
23. Amrani, A.; Diepeveen, D.; Murray, D.; Jones, M.G.; Sohel, F. Multi-task learning model for agricultural pest detection from crop-plant imagery: A Bayesian approach. *Comput. Electron. Agric.* **2024**, *218*, 108719. [CrossRef]
24. Duan, J.; Ding, H.; Kim, S. A multimodal approach for advanced pest detection and classification. *arXiv* **2023**, arXiv:2312.10948. [CrossRef]
25. Hsu, Y.C.; Shen, Y.; Jin, H.; Kira, Z. Generalized odin: Detecting out-of-distribution image without learning from out-of-distribution data. In Proceedings of the IEEE/CVF Conference on Computer Vision and Pattern Recognition (CVPR), Seattle, WA, USA, 13–19 June 2020; IEEE: Piscataway, NJ, USA, 2020; pp. 10951–10960.
26. Ho, J.; Jain, A.; Abbeel, P. Denoising diffusion probabilistic models. In Proceedings of the Advances in Neural Information Processing Systems (NeurIPS), Virtual, 6–12 December 2020; pp. 6840–6851.
27. Dinh, L.; Krueger, D.; Bengio, Y. Nice: Non-linear independent components estimation. *arXiv* **2014**, arXiv:1410.8516.
28. Srivastava, N.; Hinton, G.; Krizhevsky, A.; Sutskever, I.; Salakhutdinov, R. Dropout: A simple way to prevent neural networks from overfitting. *J. Mach. Learn. Res.* **2014**, *15*, 1929–1958.
29. Gal, Y.; Ghahramani, Z. Dropout as a bayesian approximation: Representing model uncertainty in deep learning. In Proceedings of the International Conference on Machine Learning (ICML), PMLR, New York, NY, USA, 19–24 June 2016; pp. 1050–1059.
30. Ghiasi, G.; Lin, T.Y.; Le, Q.V. Dropblock: A regularization method for convolutional networks. In Proceedings of the Advances in Neural Information Processing Systems (NeurIPS), Montréal, QC, Canada, 3–8 December 2018.
31. Wang, Y.; Qi, L.; Shi, Y.; Gao, Y. Feature-based style randomization for domain generalization. *IEEE Trans. Circuits Syst. Video Technol.* **2022**, *32*, 5495–5509. [CrossRef]
32. Li, D.; Tian, J.; Li, J.; Sun, M.; Zhou, H.; Zheng, Y. Establishment of a Dataset for Detecting Pests on the Surface of Grain Bulks. *Appl. Eng. Agric.* **2024**, *40*, 363–376. [CrossRef]
33. Ding, X.; Zhang, Y.; Ge, Y.; Zhao, S.; Song, L.; Yue, X.; Shan, Y. Unireplknet: A universal perception large-kernel convnet for audio video point cloud time-series and image recognition. In Proceedings of the IEEE/CVF Conference on Computer Vision and Pattern Recognition (CVPR), Seattle, WA, USA, 16–22 June 2024; IEEE: Seattle, WA, USA, 2024; pp. 5513–5524.
34. Varghese, R.; Sambath, M. Yolov8: A novel object detection algorithm with enhanced performance and robustness. In Proceedings of the Advances in Data Engineering and Intelligent Computing Systems (ADICS), Chennai, India, 18–19 April 2024; IEEE: Chennai, India, 2024; pp. 1–6.
35. Amari, S.i. Backpropagation and stochastic gradient descent method. *Neurocomputing* **1993**, *5*, 185–196. [CrossRef]
36. Aguilar, E.; Raducanu, B.; Radeva, P.; Van de Weijer, J. Continual evidential deep learning for out-of-distribution detection. In Proceedings of the IEEE/CVF International Conference on Computer Vision (ICCV), Paris, France, 1–6 October 2023; IEEE: Paris, France, 2023; pp. 3444–3454.
37. Wang, H.; Liu, W.; Bocchieri, A.; Li, Y. Can multi-label classification networks know what they don't know? In Proceedings of the Advances in Neural Information Processing Systems (NeurIPS), Virtual, 6–14 December 2021; pp. 29074–29087.
38. Wang, A.; Chen, H.; Liu, L.; Chen, K.; Lin, Z.; Han, J.; Ding, G. Yolov10: Real-time end-to-end object detection. In Proceedings of the Advances in Neural Information Processing Systems (NeurIPS), Vancouver, BC, Canada, 9–15 December 2024; pp. 107984–108011.
39. Zhao, Y.; Lv, W.; Xu, S.; Wei, J.; Wang, G.; Dang, Q.; Liu, Y.; Chen, J. Detrs beat yolos on real-time object detection. In Proceedings of the IEEE/CVF Conference on Computer Vision and Pattern Recognition (CVPR), Seattle, WA, USA, 16–22 June 2024; IEEE: Seattle, WA, USA, 2024; pp. 16965–16974.

40. Olber, B.; Radlak, K.; Chachuła, K.; Łyskawa, J.; Frątczak, P. Detecting Out-of-Distribution Objects Using Neuron Activation Patterns. In *European Conference on Artificial Intelligence (ECAI)*; IOS Press: Kraków, Poland, 2023; pp. 1803–1810.
41. Tack, J.; Mo, S.; Jeong, J.; Shin, J. Csi: Novelty detection via contrastive learning on distributionally shifted instances. *Adv. Neural Inf. Process. Syst.* **2020**, *33*, 11839–11852.
42. Papamakarios, G.; Nalisnick, E.; Rezende, D.J.; Mohamed, S.; Lakshminarayanan, B. Normalizing flows for probabilistic modeling and inference. *J. Mach. Learn. Res.* **2021**, *22*, 1–64.

electronics

MDPI

Article

Robust Federated Learning Against Data Poisoning Attacks: Prevention and Detection of Attacked Nodes

Pretom Roy Ovi [1,*] **and Aryya Gangopadhyay** [2]

[1] Department of Data Science, University of North Texas, Denton, TX 76205, USA
[2] Department of Information Systems, University of Maryland Baltimore County, Baltimore, MD 21250, USA; gangopad@umbc.edu
* Correspondence: pretomroy.ovi@unt.edu

Abstract

Federated learning (FL) enables collaborative model building among a large number of participants without sharing sensitive data to the central server. Because of its distributed nature, FL has limited control over local data and the corresponding training process. Therefore, it is susceptible to data poisoning attacks where malicious workers use malicious training data to train the model. Furthermore, attackers on the worker side can easily manipulate local data by swapping the labels of training instances, adding noise to training instances, and adding out-of-distribution training instances in the local data to initiate data poisoning attacks. And local workers under such attacks carry incorrect information to the server, poison the global model, and cause misclassifications. So, the prevention and detection of such data poisoning attacks is crucial to build a robust federated training framework. To address this, we propose a prevention strategy in federated learning, namely confident federated learning, to protect workers from such data poisoning attacks. Our proposed prevention strategy at first validates the label quality of local training samples by characterizing and identifying label errors in the local training data, and then excludes the detected mislabeled samples from the local training. To this aim, we experiment with our proposed approach on both the image and audio domains, and our experimental results validated the robustness of our proposed confident federated learning in preventing the data poisoning attacks. Our proposed method can successfully detect the mislabeled training samples with above 85% accuracy and exclude those detected samples from the training set to prevent data poisoning attacks on the local workers. However, our prevention strategy can successfully prevent the attack locally in the presence of a certain percentage of poisonous samples. Beyond that percentage, the prevention strategy may not be effective in preventing attacks. In such cases, detection of the attacked workers is needed. So, in addition to the prevention strategy, we propose a novel detection strategy in the federated learning framework to detect the malicious workers under attack. We propose to create a class-wise cluster representation for every participating worker by utilizing the neuron activation maps of local models and analyze the resulting clusters to filter out the workers under attack before model aggregation. We experimentally demonstrated the efficacy of our proposed detection strategy in detecting workers affected by data poisoning attacks, along with the attack types, e.g., label-flipping or dirty labeling. In addition, our experimental results suggest that the global model could not converge even after a large number of training rounds in the presence of malicious workers, whereas after detecting the malicious workers with our proposed detection method and discarding them from model aggregation, we ensured that the global model achieved convergence within very few training rounds. Furthermore, our proposed approach stays robust under different data distributions and model sizes and does not require prior knowledge about the number of attackers in the system.

Keywords: federated learning; data poisoning attack; label-flipping; confident learning

1. Introduction

Distributed machine learning has been a topic of interest for many years. Distributed machine learning offers the advantage of processing large amounts of data by distributing the workload among multiple machines [1,2]. It can train models faster and more efficiently, mainly when dealing with large-scale datasets. However, it raises data privacy concerns and requires additional resources for data management and coordination. So, maintaining use privacy and data security is always a critical research problem to solve, and research in this area has been accelerated significantly with the advent of federated learning [3–5]. With the rapid increase in the computational capacity of edge devices and advancements in efficient communication technologies with low power consumption, FL is being applied nowadays in many fields [6,7].

The concept of federated machine learning involves collaborative machine learning model building across multiple workers while ensuring data privacy, where the raw data remain locally across numerous local devices. Despite recent progress in federated learning on privacy preservation, FL is still vulnerable to poisoning attacks. Based on the attacker's goal, it has been possible to categorize the attacks into targeted poisoning attacks [8,9] and an untargeted poisoning attacks [10,11]. A targeted attack is a deliberate attempt by the client to manipulate a model's behavior by altering classification decisions or data. Targeted attacks affect only the subset of classes that are under attack, while having no impact on the remaining classes. In data poisoning attacks, a malicious FL participant alters their training data by adding poison to the instances or changing existing instances in an adversarial manner. Moreover, attackers can dominate a certain number of participants and inject poisonous data directly into the model's training data to degrade the model's performance. Also, due to the server's limited authority over the activities and local data of each client involved in the process, any of them can deflect from normal behavior and poison the global model.

Existing prevention methods of data poisoning attacks are primarily designed for centralized data collection scenarios, and their effectiveness in federated learning settings needs further investigation. Recent research on poisoning attacks and their defense strategies in FL often relies on unfeasible assumptions. In particular, these assumptions encompass aspects such as the percentage of compromised clients, the proportion of poisoned samples, the number of manipulated labels, prior knowledge about the number of adversaries, and the type of FL system. Therefore, there is a need for further research to make federated learning more resistant to poisoning attacks, specifically to data poisoning attacks. The authors in [12] pointed out that dirty-label data poisoning attacks tend to cause a lot of misclassifications, up to 90%, when an attacker adds a small number of dirty-label samples to the training dataset. And the authors in [13] pointed out data poisoning attacks in FL as an issue that needs immediate addressing. This severe issue can compromise the accuracy and reliability of the machine learning model.

To address the issues mentioned above, we first focus on the vulnerability of FL systems to malicious participants who aim to poison the global model. We attempt to analyze the effect of data poisoning attacks in federated training. In data poisoning attacks, it is assumed that attackers/malicious participants manipulate the local training data on their local devices. The label-flipping attack is the most attractive among all data poisoning attacks due to its simplicity and significant impact. It allows even non-expert attackers to carry out data poisoning attacks without knowing the model type, parameters, or FL process. Label-flipping attacks are already shown to be effective against traditional, centralized ML models [14]. This paper focuses on the targeted label-flipping attack, where the adversaries maliciously alter the true labels of training samples with the chosen class labels.

In this paper, we first focus on developing a prevention strategy utilizing the concept of confident learning [15] to validate the quality of the data label and propose a *confident federated learning (CFL)* framework to prevent label-flipped data poisoning attacks. We also demonstrate the potential of our proposed approach in preventing workers from label-flipped data poisoning attacks. Secondly, we found that our prevention strategy can prevent the attack when the percentage of label-flipped samples is under a certain threshold. In certain cases, the prevention strategy may not be effective. So in addition to the prevention strategy, we also propose a clustering-based detection strategy to detect the attacked poisonous workers. So, we divided this paper into two parts: the first part is on developing a prevention strategy against attacks (Section 2) and the second part is on developing a detection strategy (Section 3).

2. Prevention Strategy of Data Poisoning Attacks

We first conduct experiments to showcase the effect of label-flipped data poisoning attacks in the federated learning setup. Our findings reveal that the effectiveness of the attack, measured by the decrease in model utility, depends on the percentage of malicious users involved. Even when only a small percentage of users are malicious, the attack can still be effective. Additionally, we found that such attacks are targeted, which means that attacks have a significantly negative impact on the subset of classes which are under attack while having little to no impact on the remaining classes. This is advantageous for adversaries who want to poison only a specific subset of classes while avoiding the detection of a completely corrupted global model. Finally, we utilize the concept of confident learning [15] to validate the label quality of the data and propose a *confident federated learning (CFL)* framework to prevent label-flipped data poisoning attacks. We also demonstrate the potential of our proposed approach in protecting workers from label-flipped data poisoning attacks. Our approach typically involves estimating label noise probabilities and a confidence threshold to identify potentially mislabeled instances and then excluding them from the local training on the workers' side.

The major contributions we have included in this section are as follows:

- *Effect of Compromised Workers on Performance:* In the federated training setup, we first showed how compromised clients under data poisoning attacks affect the performance of the global model. Experimental results suggested that data poisoning attacks could be targeted, and even a small number of malicious clients cause the global model to misclassify instances belonging to targeted classes while other classes remain relatively intact.
- *Proposed Prevention Approach Against Data Poisoning Attacks:* We propose a confident federated learning (CFL) framework to prevent data poisoning attacks during local training on the workers' side. Along with ensuring data privacy and confidentiality, our proposed approach can successfully detect mislabeled samples, discard them from local training, and ensure prevention against data poisoning attacks.

2.1. Background Literature

By nature, deep learning models necessitate a substantial amount of data to make good predictions. This specific requirement gives rise to the potential problem of a data breach. Moreover, numerous adversarial attacks have been launched to target machine learning and deep learning models. However, most research has focused on poisoning the models in the traditional setting, where a centralized party collects the training data. So, many of the attacks and defenses designed for traditional machine learning do not apply to FL because the server only observes local updates from FL participants, not their instances.

The growing usage of federated learning has prompted research into different types of attacks, such as backdoor attacks [16,17], gradient leakage attacks [18–22], poisoning attacks [8,23–25], and membership inference attacks [26]. The type of attack that is relevant to this chapter is poisoning attacks, which can be classified into two categories: model poisoning and data poisoning. Model poisoning can be effective in specific scenarios, whereas data poisoning may be preferable due to the fact that it does not require malicious manipulation of the model learning software on participant devices, making it efficient and accessible for non-expert poisoning participants. Our research explicitly investigates data poisoning attacks in the context of federated learning. The authors in [12] launched targeted backdoor attacks using data poisoning and pointed out that using only a small number of poisonous samples achieves an attack success rate of above 90%. A backdoor poisoning attack was proposed in [16,27], in which the attacker injects backdoored inputs into local data to modify specific features of training data and implant backdoors in the global model. An aggregation-agnostic attack, which continuously adds noises to the model parameters to introduce backdoors and restrict the global model from converging, was developed in [28]. Data poisoning attacks can cause substantial drops in classification [8]. In data poisoning attacks [8], the adversary can introduce a number of data samples it wishes to misclassify with the desired target label into the training set. This data-centric poisoning can be of two types: label-flipping [29] and dirty labeling. An attacker can easily manipulate its local data by directly swapping the labels of honest training instances of one class (the source class) to a specific target class while keeping the features of the training data unchanged. This is known as a label-flipping attack [30], which can cause significant drops in the performance of the global model even with a small percentage of malicious clients [8]. And in dirty labeling, the attacker aims to add some out-of-box samples (irrelevant samples for training) to the training dataset and mislabels them. For example, the server wants the global model to be trained on handwritten digits, but the attacker adds some samples to the training set which are not even digits (e.g., animal images, but labeled as the digit class). This type of labeling is known as dirty labeling.

Several methods have been suggested to address poisoning attacks in FL [31–34]. These defense strategies are designed to identify malicious updates that deviate from benign updates. For instance, Auror [31] attempts to cluster model updates into two classes, in which the smaller class will be identified as the malicious class and filtered out. Furthermore, other researchers have introduced Byzantine-robust FL methods: Krum [32], in which the client with the smallest sum of distances to other clients will be selected as the global model. However, in the presence of a large number of malicious participants, these approaches were found to be ineffective in defending against the attacks. The authors in [8] presented a defense mechanism that leverages parameter extraction combined with PCA for dimensionality reduction to differentiate malicious and legitimate participants in model updates.

Researchers have introduced an adaptive federated aggregation technique [35], which involved comparing gradients against medians and adjusting their weights accordingly.

This method is particularly effective in detecting and mitigating malicious gradients. Their experiments, focusing on label flipping and backdoor attacks with a network of 51 clients, demonstrated efficacy, especially in scenarios where less than 50% of the participants were malicious. Researchers have also advocated the defense mechanism CONTRA in FL [36]. This system employs cosine similarity, an adaptive learning rate, and a reputation-based scheme. It works by assessing the credibility of clients, adjusting local learning rates, and evaluating client contributions based on their historical contribution, irrespective of the data distribution being IID or non-IID. In [37], the authors introduced a novel defense approach which involves extracting and clustering the parameter gradients from the output layer's neurons during local updates. This method enables the identification and removal of undesirable updates within the clusters. In [38], the authors proposed an enhanced defense mechanism, building upon previous work [8]. Their approach uses an improved variant of the dimensionality reduction algorithm, PCA, and subsequently applied k-means clustering on IID data. The authors in [39] evaluated the impact of unreliable clients on the system by deriving a convergence upper bound on the loss function based on the gradient descent updates.

Moreover, these defenses are designed for untargeted model poisoning attacks. In contrast, in respect to data poisoning attacks, a very few research studies have [12,24] pointed out the effect of data poisoning on the performance of the global model. However, the research gap lies in developing prevention strategies for data poisoning attacks that can effectively prevent such data manipulation on the training set.

2.2. Methodology: Proposed Prevention Strategy

In this section, we describe the detailed architecture and work flow of our proposed federated training. Our proposed framework is built on top of the FedAvg [3] algorithm, where some of the notations used in this description are $\mathcal{N} = \{1, \ldots, N\}$, which signifies the set of N clients, each of which has its own dataset $D_{k\in\mathcal{N}}$. Each client trains a local model on its local dataset and only shares the weight updates of local model with the server. Then, the global model formation, $\mathbf{w}_G$, takes place with all the local model updates, which can denoted by $\mathbf{w} = \cup_{k\in\mathcal{N}}\mathbf{w}_k$. The proposed federated framework is depicted in Figure 1. The process based on the workload of the server and the client is described below:

(1) **Executed in server**

- *Weight initialization:* The server determines the type of application and how the user will be trained. Based on the application, the global model is built in the server. The server then distributes the global model $\mathbf{w}_G^0$ to selected clients.
- *Aggregation and global update:* The server aggregates the local model updates from the participants and then sends the updated global model $\mathbf{w}_G^{t+1}$ back to the clients. The server wants to minimize the global loss function [13] $L(\mathbf{w}_G^t)$, i.e.,

$$L(\mathbf{w}_G^t) = \frac{1}{N}\sum_{k=1}^{N} L(\mathbf{w}_k^t) \quad (1)$$

This process is repeated until the global loss function converges or a desirable training accuracy is achieved. The Global Updater function runs on the SGD [40] formula for weight updates. The formal equation of the global loss minimization formula by the averaged aggregation at the tth iteration is given below:

$$\mathbf{w}_G^t = \frac{1}{\sum_{k\in\mathcal{N}} D_k}\sum_{k=1}^{N} D_k\mathbf{w}_i^t \quad (2)$$

(2) **Executed at the client level**

- *Validate label quality:* Each client will first validate the label quality of local dataset after receiving the global model $\mathbf{w}_G^0$ from the server. To detect the mislabeled samples in the local dataset, every participant needs to compute the out-of-sample predictions for every data point of its local dataset. Then, the out-of-sample prediction and the given labels will be utilized to estimate the joint distribution of the given and latent true labels. Finally, the label errors for each pair of true and noisy classes are estimated, with details given in Section 2.3. After validating the class labels of every data point in the local dataset, the overall health score for the local dataset can be calculated to track label quality.
- *Local training:* Each client will utilize $\mathbf{w}_G^t$ from the server, where t stands for each iteration index, to start local training on the verified local training samples, where detected mislabeled samples are discarded from the local training. The client tries to minimize the loss function [13] $L(\mathbf{w}_k^t)$ and searches for optimal parameters $\mathbf{w}_k^t$.

$$\mathbf{w}_k^{t^*} = \arg\min_{\mathbf{w}_k^t} L(\mathbf{w}_k^t) \quad (3)$$

- *Local updates transmission:* After each round of training, updated local model weights are sent to the server. In addition, each client may send the health score of local data so that the server may monitor the label validation process by tracking the health score.

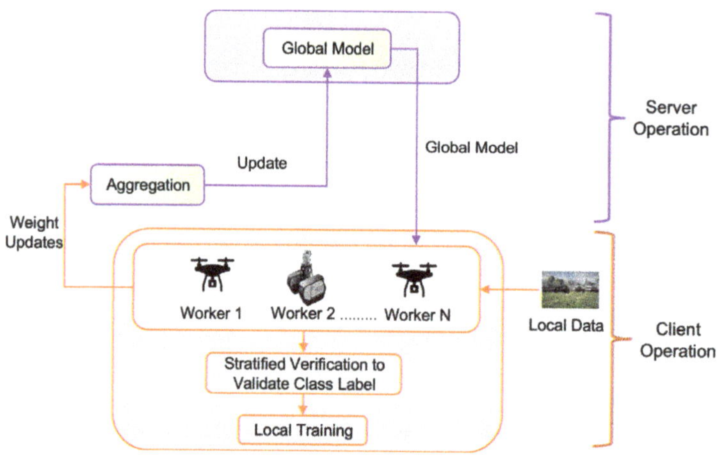

Figure 1. Proposed confident federated learning.

2.3. *Stratified Training to Validate Label Quality*

To identify label errors across the local dataset, out-of-sample predicted probabilities for each data point needs to be computed first with K-fold cross-validation. Out-of-sample predicted probabilities refer to the model's probabilistic predictions made only on data points not shown to the model during training. For example, in a traditional train–test split of the data, the predicted probabilities generated for the test set can thus be considered out-of-sample. K-fold cross-validation can be used to generate out-of-sample predicted probabilities for every data point in the training set.

The diagram in Figure 2 depicts K-fold cross-validation with K = 5. K independent copies of our model are trained, where for each model copy, one fold of the data is held out from its training (the data in this fold may be viewed as a validation set for this copy of the model). Each copy of the model has a different validation set for which we can obtain out-of-sample predicted probabilities from this copy of the model. Since each data point is held-out from one copy of the model, this process allows us to obtain out-of-sample predicted probabilities for every data point. We recommend applying stratified cross-validation, which tries to ensure the proportions of data from each class match across different folds. Then the out-of-sample predicted probabilities and noisy (given) labels will be used to estimate the joint distribution of noisy (given) and true labels, and find the incorrectly labeled samples in the local dataset, following the steps described below:

Threshold calculation for label validation: The first step in the label validation process involves calculating a confidence threshold for each class, as described in Equation (4). This threshold, denoted as t_j, represents the average self-confidence of the model for samples with a given label j. It is computed by averaging the predicted probabilities assigned to the observed class label j across all instances labeled as j:

$$t_j = \frac{1}{|\mathbf{X}_{\tilde{y}=j}|} \sum_{x \in \mathbf{X}_{\tilde{y}=j}} \hat{p}(\tilde{y} = j; \boldsymbol{x}, \boldsymbol{\theta}) \tag{4}$$

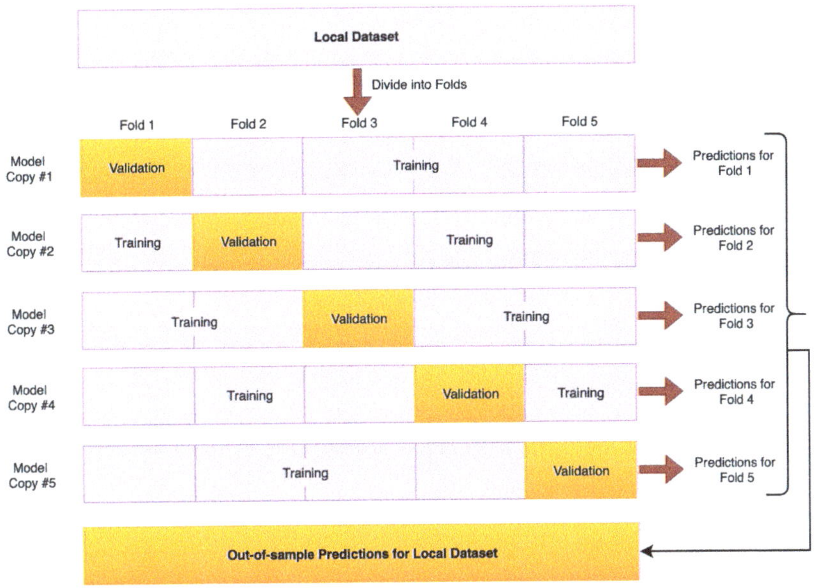

Figure 2. Out-of-sample predictions for local dataset with K-fold cross validation.

Confident joint estimation and label error identification: Once the class-wise confidence thresholds t_j are computed, the next step in confident learning is to estimate the joint distribution between noisy labels $\tilde{y}$ and the unknown true labels y^*. This is achieved by identifying instances that are likely mislabeled, i.e., those whose model predictions strongly indicate a different class than their observed label. And we define the set $\hat{\mathbf{X}}_{\tilde{y}=i,y^*=j}$, as in Equation (5).

$$\hat{\mathbf{X}}_{\tilde{y}=i,y^*=j} = \{\boldsymbol{x} \in \mathbf{X}_{\tilde{y}=i} : \hat{p}(\tilde{y} = j; \boldsymbol{x}, \boldsymbol{\theta}) \geq t_j\} \tag{5}$$

Here, $\tilde{y}$ is the discrete random variable which takes a given noisy label, y^* is the discrete random variable which takes the unknown, true latent label, the threshold t_j is the expected (average) self-confidence for each class, and $\hat{\boldsymbol{X}}_{\tilde{y}=i,y^*=j}$ is the set of examples of x labeled $\tilde{y} = i$ with large enough $\hat{p}(\tilde{y} = j; \boldsymbol{x}, \boldsymbol{\theta})$ to likely belong to class $y^* = j$, determined by a per-class threshold t_j. This set contains examples originally labeled as class i, but whose model-predicted class is j with a confidence greater than the threshold t_j for class j. Using these sets, we estimate the confident joint matrix $C_{\tilde{y},y^*}$, formally defined in Equation (6). The confident joint $C_{\tilde{y},y^*}$ estimates $\boldsymbol{X}_{\tilde{y}=i,y^*=j}$, the set of examples with the noisy label i that actually should have the true label j, by partitioning X into estimate bins $\hat{\boldsymbol{X}}_{\tilde{y}=i,y^*=j}$. When $\hat{\boldsymbol{X}}_{\tilde{y}=i,y^*=j} = \boldsymbol{X}_{\tilde{y}=i,y^*=j}$, then $C_{\tilde{y},y^*}$ exactly finds the label errors. This matrix approximates the count of samples that were labeled as class i, but whose true label is likely class j, based on the model's confident predictions. Diagonal entries (i.e., i=j) correspond to likely correctly labeled samples, while off-diagonal entries indicate potential label errors.

$$
\left.
\begin{aligned}
&C_{\tilde{y},y^*}[i][j] := \left|\hat{\boldsymbol{X}}_{\tilde{y}=i,y^*=j}\right|, \quad \text{where} \\
&\hat{\boldsymbol{X}}_{\tilde{y}=i,y^*=j} := \left\{\boldsymbol{x} \in \boldsymbol{X}_{\tilde{y}=i} : \hat{p}(\tilde{y} = j; \boldsymbol{x}, \boldsymbol{\theta}) \geq t_j, \right. \\
&\qquad\qquad j = \arg \max_{l \in [m],\, \hat{p}(\tilde{y}=l;\boldsymbol{x},\boldsymbol{\theta}) \geq t_l} \hat{p}(\tilde{y} = l; \boldsymbol{x}, \boldsymbol{\theta})
\end{aligned}
\right\} \tag{6}
$$

2.4. Experiment Setup and Results Analysis

This section will step through the detailed experiment setup and results analysis.

Federated Training Setup: Experiments were conducted on a system with an Intel(R) Core(TM) i9-11900K CPU (8 cores) and an NVIDIA GeForce RTX 3090 GPU. The federated learning framework was implemented using Keras with a TensorFlow backend. The server controlled the training pace, including the number of epochs per round and the overall number of rounds. The server sets the pace of the training, determines the number of epochs per round, and how many rounds of overall training are to be conducted. We utilized the LeNet-5 CNN architecture as the global model and simulated FL training with 15 clients. For each round, 1 epoch of local training is conducted on the client side. We used the SGD optimizer and set the learning rate η to 0.01 during training. And the datasets we used in this experiment are pre-divided into training and testing subsets. The test set is kept on the sever and used for model evaluation only and is therefore not included in any participants' local training data.

Datasets: To demonstrate the attack effect and evaluate the performance of our proposed approach, we conducted experiments on the MNIST, Fashion-MNIST, and CIFAR-10 datasets.

MNIST: This dataset comprises handwritten digit images showing individual digits (0 to 9). The training set has 60,000 samples and the test set has 10,000 samples, with images of size 28×28.

Fashion-MNIST: This dataset includes grayscale images of ten clothing categories, with 60,000 training set samples and 10,000 test set samples, all with an image size of 28×28.

CIFAR-10: This dataset encompasses color images of ten classes, each with 50,000 training set samples (5000 images per class) and 10,000 test set samples (1000 images per class) at a pixel resolution of 32×32.

Label-Flipping Process: We randomly chose $N \times m\%$ of the participants as malicious to explore the impact of a label-flipping attack on the federated learning system containing N participants, where a particular percentage ($m\%$) of them are malicious. The remaining participants are considered honest. To account for the impact of the random selection of malicious participants, we repeat the experiment multiple times and report the average results. We explore label-flipping attack scenarios for the MNIST, Fashion-MNIST, and CIFAR-10 datasets by flipping the label of the source class to a specific target class, denoted as a source class → target class pairing. For MNIST, we experiment with the following pairings: 0: digit_0 → 2: digit_2 and 1: digit_1 → 5: digit_5. For Fashion-MNIST, we evaluated the pairings of 1: trouser → 3: dress and 0: t-shirt/top → 4: coat. For CIFAR-10, we experiment with the following pairings: 6: frog → 7: horse and 1: automobile → 3: cat.

Attack Effects Analysis: Label flipping denoted by src → target class indicates that ground truth labels of the source class samples have been flipped with the target class label. If we train a machine learning model on a dataset in which the ground-truth labels of some examples from the source class have been flipped with those of the target class, some samples from the source class will be predicted as belonging to the target class during testing. This implies that the source class will have some false negatives, which will ultimately impact its recall. On the other hand, the target class will have some false positives, which will affect its precision. Label-flipping attacks are targeted attacks, meaning they have a significant negative impact on a subset of classes that are under attack while having no impact on the remaining classes. So, to evaluate the attack effects with varying percentages of malicious participants, we utilize recall for the source class and precision for the target class as the evaluation metrics.

Figure 3 illustrates the degradation of the recall of the source class and precision of the target class when the percentage of malicious participants (m) varies from 0% to 40%. The value 0% signifies that none of the participants are malicious, and therefore, there is no poisoning (NP) in the considered scenario. The findings reveal that with the increase in malicious participants, the global model's potential to predict the source and target classes declines. Even with a small percentage of malicious participants, both the source class recall and the target class precision deteriorate in comparison to a non-poisoned scenario (NP) for both MNIST and Fashion-MNIST, as depicted in Figure 3a and Figure 3b, respectively. For example, when malicious participants reach 40%, recall drops from 0.99 to 0.73 and precision drops from 0.98 to 0.78 for MNIST. A similar trend is observed for the Fashion-MNIST dataset as well.

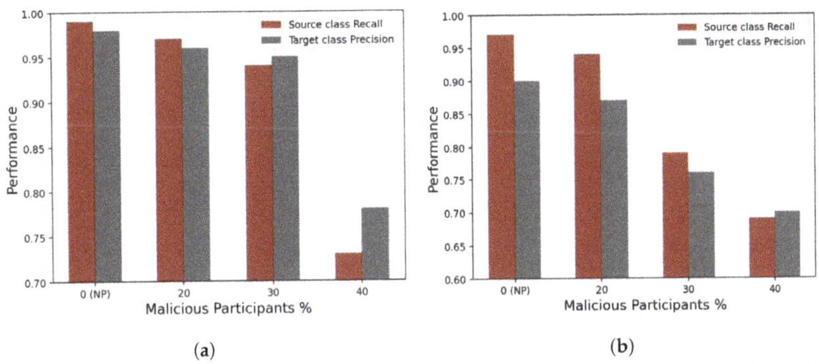

Figure 3. Impact of label-flipping attacks on targeted classes on (**a**) MNIST data and (**b**) Fashion-MNIST data.

Furthermore, in Figure 4, we depict the global model's performance drop (accuracy, source class recall, and target class precision) for the CIFAR-10 data with an increasing percentage of malicious participants. It is clear from the figure that the higher the percentage of malicious participants, the more the performance drop can be. In the experiments, once the malicious percentage reaches 50%, the precision and recall of the targeted classes drop around 0.24 and 0.65, respectively, while the overall accuracy of the global model declines only by 0.06. This result indicates the targeted nature of label-flipping attacks where the attack degrades the global model's potential in predicting the instances belonging to the source and target classes while the performance for other classes remains relatively the same. And so, the overall accuracy of the global model deteriorates less in comparison with the drop in precision and recall of the target and source class, respectively. Therefore, it is evident that an attacker who controls even a small proportion of the total participants can significantly affect the global model's utility.

Performance Evaluation of Proposed Approach: Based on the analysis presented above, it is clear that preventing data poisoning attacks is crucial in the context of federated training. Our proposed FL framework involves validating the local dataset of each client to identify label-flipped samples prior to the commencement of local training. To evaluate the effectiveness of our approach for detecting mislabeled training samples and preventing them from affecting the local training process, we conducted experiments wherein we deliberately manipulated the local dataset of a few clients to initiate data poisoning attacks. Specifically, we altered the class labels of a few samples in the MNIST dataset (digit 0 and digit 2 images were changed to class label 1). Similarly, in Fashion-MNIST, t-shirt/top images were assigned to class label 0, and ankle boot images were assigned to class label 9. We intentionally altered the label of some ankle boot samples to class label 0. Experimental results using both datasets demonstrate that our proposed approach can successfully detect the poisoned samples of local workers, shown in Figure 5, with an accuracy of over 88% for MNIST and 86% for Fashion-MNIST, albeit with a small number of false positives (approximately 5%).

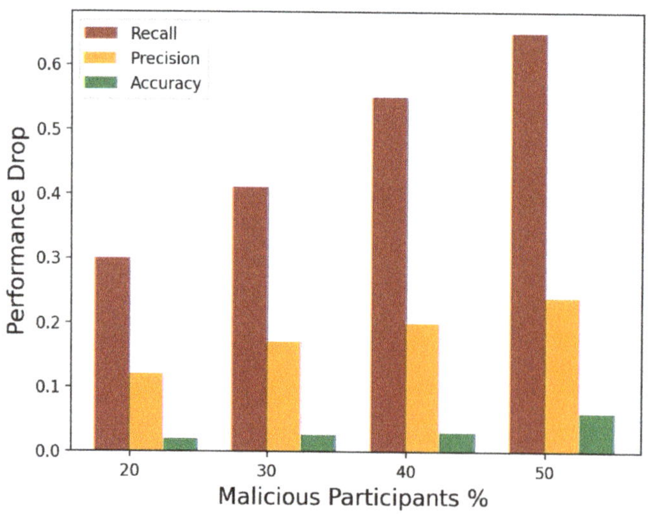

Figure 4. Impact of attacks on performance for CIFAR-10 data.

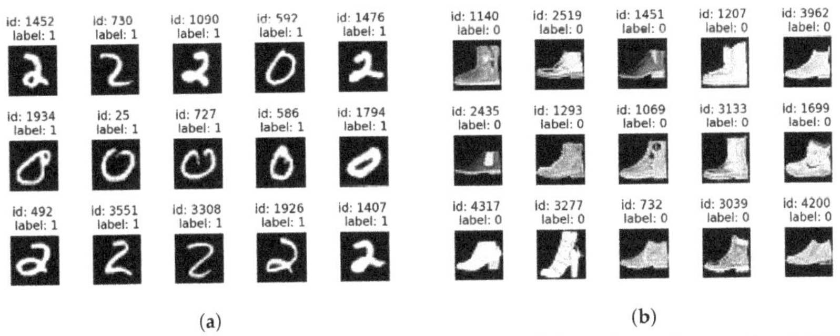

Figure 5. Detection of label-flipped samples. (**a**) Detected flipped samples on altered MNIST. (**b**) Detected flipped samples on altered Fashion-MNIST.

3. Detection Strategy of Data Poisoning Attacks

The proposed prevention strategy can prevent the attack when the percentage of label-flipped samples is under a certain threshold (around 35%). So, for any worker, if the incorrectly labeled samples are higher in percentage than the correctly labeled samples and/or the training set of a worker is entirely poisoned, the prevention strategy fails to prevent attacks. So, in addition to prevention, we propose a class-wise cluster-based detection strategy to detect the workers affected by data poisoning attacks.

This data poisoning can be of two types–label-flipping and dirty labeling. The label-flipping attack is swapping the source label with the target label while keeping the features of the training data unchanged. On the other hand, in dirty labeling, the attackers/poisoned workers add out-of-distribution samples as training instances and mislabel them. Numerous strategies have been developed to counteract poisoning attacks, particularly label flipping, yet they often fall short because they are either impractical or have strong assumptions regarding the distribution of local training data. For example, research study [41] assumes the server has some data examples representing the distribution of the workers' data, which is not always a realistic assumption in FL. Some of the defense approaches assume data to be independent and identically distributed (IID) among workers, which causes degradation in performance when the data are non-IID [36]. Some research studies [30,36] detect untrustworthy workers by auditing the model behavior, e.g., local gradient/weight updates. However, the existing approaches of auditing model behavior may be effective for detecting the worker affected by model poisoning attacks but cannot guarantee the detection of the worker affected by label-flipped data poisoning attacks because malicious workers under label-flipped attacks can have similar local updates as trustworthy local workers. Additionally, methods like multi-Krum (MKrum) [32] and trimmed mean (TMean) [42] require prior knowledge about the ratio of attackers in the system, which is impractical. Beyond data distribution or behavioral assumptions, model dimensionality plays a crucial role in these defense mechanisms. High-dimensional models are particularly susceptible to poisoning, as attackers can make minor yet impactful alterations in their local updates that go undetected [43].

Here, we introduce an innovative method to identify attacked workers by examining the activation of the neurons of second-last layer, which is linked to the neurons of the source and target classes in the SoftMax output layer. Specifically, we find that the discrepancies between the honest workers and compromised workers due to data poisoning attacks are reflected in the activation of the neurons of second-last layer, which is connected to the final output layer. And this activation serves as a more effective discriminative feature for attack detection. And so, our approach involves a cluster-based representation technique to create a distinct cluster representation for each worker that leverages the activation maps of the second-last layers for each of the local training samples and their associated class labels. This clustering-based strategy enables determining whether a worker has been attacked with data poisoning attacks. So, we propose to create a class-wise cluster representation for every worker by utilizing the activation maps of the neurons of the local model and analyze the resulting clusters to filter out the workers under attack before model aggregation.

3.1. Related Literature

The defenses proposed in the current literature to counter poisoning attacks (label-flipping attacks in particular) against FL are based on one of the following types:

- **Representative dataset based:** Approaches within this category exclude or penalize a local update if it has a negative impact on the evaluation metrics of the validation dataset of the global model, e.g., accuracy metrics. Specifically, studies [41,44] have used a validation dataset on the server to compute the loss on a designated metric caused by the local updates of each worker. Subsequently, updates that detrimentally influence this metric are omitted from the aggregation process of the global model. However, the efficacy of this method hinges on the availability of realistic validation data, which implies a necessity for the server to have insights into the distribution of workers' data. This requirement poses a fundamental conflict with the principle of federated learning (FL), where the server typically may not have the representative dataset that workers do.
- **Clustering based:** Methods categorized under this approach involve clustering updates into two groups, with the smaller subset being identified as potentially malicious and consequently excluded from the model's learning process. Notably, techniques such as Auror [31] and multi-Krum (MKrum) [32] operate under the assumption that data across peers are independent and identically distributed (IID). This assumption, however, leads to increased rates of both false positives and negatives in scenarios where data are not IID [36]. Additionally, these methods necessitate prior knowledge regarding either the characteristics of the training data distribution [31] or an estimation of the anticipated number of attackers within the system [32].
- **Model behavior monitoring based:** Methods under this category operate under the assumption that malicious workers tend to exhibit similar behaviors, which means that their updates will be more similar to each other than to those of honest workers. Consequently, updates are subjected to penalties based on their degree of similarity. For example, FoolsGold (FGold) [30] and CONTRA [36] limit the contribution of potential attackers with similar updates by reducing their learning rates or preventing them from being selected. However, it is worth noting that these approaches can inadvertently penalize valuable updates that exhibit similarities, ultimately resulting in substantial reductions in model performance [45,46].
- **Update aggregation:** This approach employs resilient update aggregation techniques that are sensitive to outliers at the coordinate level. Such techniques encompass the use of statistical measures like the median [42], the trimmed mean (Tmean) [42], or the repeated median (RMedian) [47]. By adopting these methods, bad updates will have little to no influence on the global model after aggregation. It is worth noting, however, that while these methods yield commendable performance when dealing with updates originating from independent and identically distributed (IID) data, their effectiveness diminishes when handling updates from non-IID data sources. This is primarily due to their tendency to discard a significant portion of information

during the model aggregation process. Additionally, the estimation error associated with these techniques grows proportionally to the square root of the model's size [43]. Furthermore, the utilization of RMedian [47] entails substantial computational overhead due to the regression procedure it performs, while Tmean [42] demands explicit knowledge regarding the fraction of malicious workers within the system.

In contrast, our proposed cluster based detection technique stays robust under different data distributions and model sizes, and does not require prior knowledge about the number of attackers in the system.

3.2. Methodology: Proposed Cluster-Based Detection Strategy

Federated learning is designed to protect the privacy of data across different workers. And our proposed method ensures that it does not compromise this privacy. The following is a step-by-step breakdown of how this works:

Layer selection: Identifying the layer in the neural network that effectively captures the characteristics of each class is crucial. Typically, layers closer to the output are more class-specific. We find that the contradiction between the honest workers and compromised workers due to data poisoning attacks is reflected in the activation of the neurons of the second-last layer. Specifically, we find the activation of the neurons of the second-last layer, which is connected to the final output layer, is a better discriminative feature for attack detection as it can effectively capture the characteristics of each class.

Feature extraction: For each data point in a worker's local dataset, we extract the feature vector from the selected layer. These feature vectors represent the data in a high-dimensional space where similar items (from the same class) are expected to be closer together. As feature maps are high-dimensional, each client will perform a dimension reduction technique, e.g., Principal Component Analysis (PCA), on its activation value to convert it to a lower dimension. Then, each worker will share the converted lower dimensional feature maps for each local data point and its associated label with the server. Crucially, as this process involves sharing only the transformed (lower dimensional) activation maps from a single selected layer, it does not reveal any information about the private training data, and so, preserves the privacy of the data. This approach does not violate the privacy-preserving principles of federated learning protocols.

Class-wise cluster representation: Upon receiving the activation maps and class labels for every local data point from participating workers, the server employs a cluster-based representation for each worker. The clustering is performed separately for each class, and training samples from the same class label are also expected to be in the same feature space in cluster-based representation. This results in distinct clusters for each class within each worker's dataset.

Cluster comparison and attack detection: Finally, the server compares the class-wise cluster position among the workers to detect the workers affected by data-level poisoning. By looking for workers whose clusters for a particular class significantly deviate from the clusters of the same class of other workers, we can use statistical tests, in addition to visualization, to determine if the deviations are beyond the threshold. Workers with anomalous class-wise clusters are flagged for potential data poisoning attack. This detection process can be considered as a periodic check during the federated learning cycles. If a worker is flagged, it will be considered as a malicious worker affected by a data poisoning attack, and its contributions will be discarded and excluded from the federated training.

3.3. Results Analysis of Proposed Detection Approach

We conducted federated training on the MNIST handwritten digit dataset, where a number of workers participated in the training process to build the model. We simulated a federated training set where two workers were affected by data poisoning attacks. Among the two poisoned workers, one worker was attacked with label flipping and other one was attacked with dirty labeling. To launch the label-flipped data poisoning attack, we intentionally trained one worker (worker_3) on MNIST data, but with label-flipped samples (flipping the labels of digit 0 and digit 1). So, worker_3 manipulates its local data by swapping the labels of the training instances of class label 0 and class label 1 while keeping the training instances unchanged. And another worker (worker_4) is trained on the dirty labeled data where, images of public transport, e.g., bus, metro, airport, and battlefield vehicles, e.g., helicopter and tank, have been labeled as digit classes. So, worker_4 utilizes out-of-distribution samples (irrelevant samples), mislabels them (labels them as digit classes), and is trained on the manipulated data to launch the dirty label data poisoning attack.

Here, we employed a cluster-based representation for each worker and compared the class-wise cluster among the workers to detect the data-level poisoning. The assumption is that a worker trained on poisoned data produces clusters that significantly differ from the majority, indicating a potential data poisoning attack. For simplicity and easy visualization, we visualized only a few digit classes instead of all digit classes to visually inspect the clusters. Figure 6 demonstrates that worker_1 and worker_2 are honest workers and trained on their local MNIST digit data. And they are honest, which is evidenced by the nearly identical positions of class-wise clusters in the 3D feature space for the majority of workers. However, in the same Figure 6 (lower left), a notable difference is observed for worker_3. Here, the blue and orange clusters, which represent digit classes 0 and 1, have swapped positions in the feature space compared to the honest workers. This cluster swap is a result of a label-flipping attack, where the labels for digit classes 0 and 1 have been flipped, leading to the altered cluster positions for worker_3. It is important to note that the cluster positions for the other digit classes in worker_3 remain largely unchanged and are almost identical to those of the honest workers due to accurate labeling for these other digit classes.

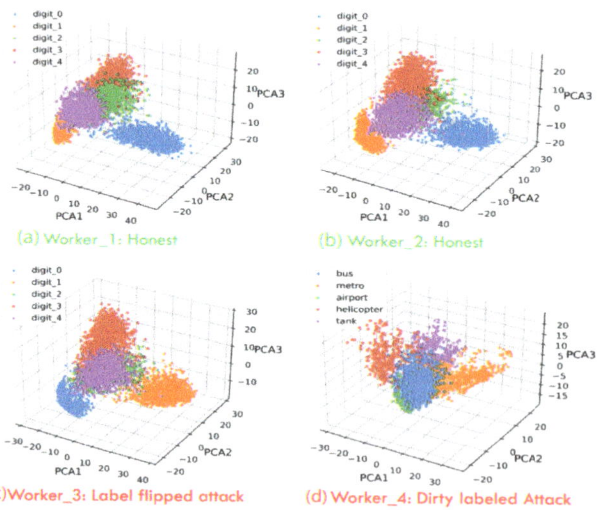

Figure 6. Clustering-based approach: (**a**) honest worker, (**b**) honest worker, (**c**) worker attacked with label-flipping of digit 0 and digit 1 classes, and (**d**) worker attacked with dirty labeling.

As depicted in Figure 6 (lower right), for worker_4, the class-wise cluster positions in the feature space for all classes are completely different from those of the honest workers. This discrepancy arises because worker_4 was trained on dirty labeled data, where images of buses, metros, airports, helicopters, and tanks were labeled as digit classes. Consequently, our cluster-based approach successfully identified both workers who were impacted by label-flipping and dirty labeling data poisoning attacks.

3.4. Effect of Attack on Model's Convergence

In our experiment, we simulated a federated learning (FL) environment with 25 local workers, among which 5 were intentionally compromised with data poisoning attacks. The presence of these malicious workers hindered the convergence of the global model. As shown in Figure 7a, the global model fails to converge even after 75 communication rounds when trained in the presence of such adversarial participants.

After detecting the malicious workers with our proposed detection method and discarding them from training, we evaluated the convergence behavior of the global model under two data distribution settings: independent and identically distributed (IID) and non-independent and identically distributed (non-IID). In the IID setting, each worker received a relatively balanced class distribution of training samples. In contrast, the non-IID setting was configured by assigning imbalanced class distributions to different workers. As in Figure 7, convergence in the IID and non-IID scenarios required only 25 and 40 rounds, respectively. So, by detecting the malicious workers and discarding them in model building, we found that the global model achieved convergence in significantly fewer training rounds. These findings highlight the detrimental impact of data poisoning on convergence and demonstrate that once malicious workers are effectively detected and discarded from training, convergence of the global model becomes stable.

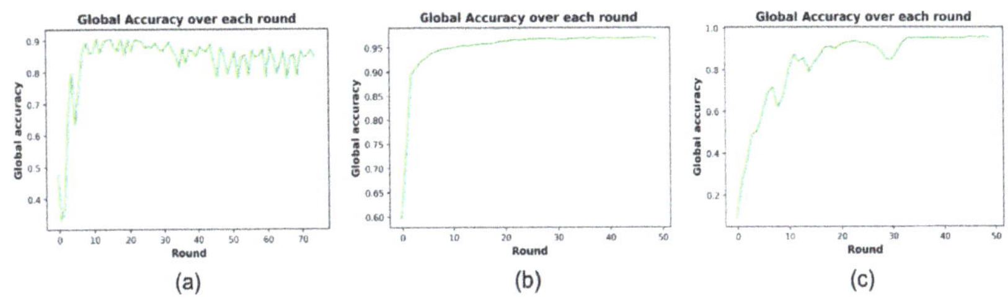

Figure 7. Effect on convergence in the presence of (**a**) malicious workers, (**b**) all honest workers in the IID setup, and (**c**) all honest workers in the non-IID setup.

4. Ablation Study

Thus far, we have evaluated our proposed prevention and detection approach on the image modality using the MNIST, Fashion-MNIST, and CIFAR-10 datasets. In this section, we demonstrate the effectiveness of our approach in the audio domain. Specifically, we conducted experiments using the AudioMNIST and UrbanSound8K audio datasets.

To assess robustness, we performed label-flipping attacks by altering a diverse percentage (ranging from 10% to 35%) of the training data, using several combinations of sources and target classes. The label-flipping configuration is denoted as a source class $\rightarrow$ target class pairing. For AudioMNIST, we considered the following pairings: 0: digit_0 $\rightarrow$ 2: digit_2, 0: digit_0 $\rightarrow$ 3: digit_3, 1: digit_1 $\rightarrow$ 5: digit_5, and 2: digit_2 $\rightarrow$ 4: digit_4. And for the UrbanSound8K dataset, we evaluated the pairings: car_horn $\rightarrow$ dog_bark, children_playing $\rightarrow$ drilling.

Our experimental results demonstrate that the proposed prevention mechanism effectively identifies and filters out label-flipped samples from local training. The approach achieved an average detection accuracy of 93% on the AudioMNIST and 90% on the UrbanSound8K datasets.

Furthermore, we evaluated the performance of our class-wise cluster representation-based detection approach for identifying compromised workers in the audio domain, using the UrbanSound8K dataset. In this setup, label flipping was applied to audio samples corresponding to the "Children_playing" and "Drilling" classes for Worker_2 (attacked worker). Consequently, in the cluster-based representation, the green and violet clusters—representing "Children_playing" and "Drilling"—were visibly swapped for Worker_2 in comparison with Worker_1 (honest worker), as shown in Figure 8. This behavior confirms the effectiveness of our detection strategy in the audio modality.

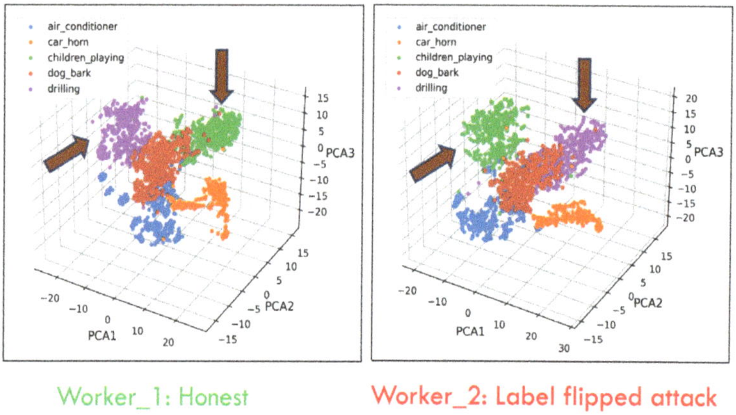

Figure 8. Class-wise cluster representation for workers. Honest worker (**left**) and attacked worker (**right**).

5. Discussions

Our framework assumes a trusted server and secure communication channels between clients and the server. The server is assumed to be a centralized coordinator with sufficient computational and storage resources to perform aggregation and clustering-based analyses. The clients represent generic edge devices—such as mobile phones, IoT nodes, or embedded systems—with a moderate local compute capacity sufficient for model training and feature extraction. The server is considered trustworthy, and communication between the server and clients is assumed to be authenticated and secure. The scope of this study is limited to resilience against data poisoning attacks and does not extend to privacy leakage from gradient inversion. Although we do not address gradient privacy in this work, our approach remains orthogonal to existing privacy-preserving mechanisms (e.g., differential privacy, secure aggregation) and can be integrated with such techniques without modifying the core detection pipeline.

Our current experiments were intentionally designed with 25 or fewer clients and moderate non-IID partitioning to provide a controlled yet meaningful environment for validating the core functionality of our proposed confident federated learning and cluster-based detection mechanisms. These design choices allowed for a clearer observation of system behavior under targeted data poisoning attacks. We fully agree that real-world FL deployments pose additional challenges, e.g., scalability to large numbers of clients.

Although our current study did not simulate large-scale or heterogeneous settings, we emphasize that our framework is conceptually agnostic to the number of clients and model topologies and does not rely on uniform architectures or strict synchronization assumptions. Our method operates at the data and activation levels, rather than requiring structural homogeneity. Moreover, our method is not inherently dependent on class cardinality, network depth, or the number of cross-validation folds, K. These factors may influence the stability or resolution of noise detection in practice, but the methodology itself—rooted in estimating the joint distribution of noisy and true labels via out-of-sample predictions—remains agnostic to such architectural or hyperparameter choices.

6. Conclusions

In this paper, we first investigated the feasibility and impact of data poisoning attacks in federated learning, demonstrating that as the number of malicious participants increases, the performance of the global model significantly deteriorates, particularly in terms of precision, recall, and overall accuracy. To counteract this, we evaluated the proposed method for detecting and excluding poisonous samples from local training to prevent label-flipped data poisoning attacks. Our strategy capitalizes on the local nature of FL, where workers retain access to their own data but not others'. By leveraging correctly labeled local data, our approach can identify mislabeled samples within a worker's dataset. However, when a local dataset is entirely or predominantly poisoned, this strategy becomes ineffective, underscoring the need for broader detection mechanisms to identify compromised participants.

We then proposed a robust detection mechanism that constructs class-wise cluster representations based on neuron activation maps from local models. These clusters are analyzed to identify and filter out malicious workers prior to model aggregation. Our experiments confirm the effectiveness of this method not only in detecting compromised workers but also in distinguishing between different types of attacks, such as label-flipping and dirty-labeling. Importantly, our approach remains resilient across varying data distributions and model complexities. Overall, our findings establish the robustness and adaptability of the proposed federated learning framework in mitigating data poisoning threats.

Author Contributions: Conceptualization, P.R.O. and A.G.; Methodology, P.R.O. and A.G.; Validation, P.R.O.; Resources, A.G.; Writing—original draft, P.R.O.; Writing—review and editing, P.R.O. and A.G.; Visualization, P.R.O.; Supervision, A.G.; Funding acquisition, A.G. All authors have read and agreed to the published version of the manuscript.

Funding: We acknowledge the support of the U.S. Army Grant W911NF21-20076.

Data Availability Statement: The data presented in this study are openly available in Github [Github] https://git-disl.github.io/GTDLBench/datasets/mnist_datasets#:~:text=MNIST%20in%20CSV,Datasets%20CIFAR%2D10, accessed on 20 July 2025.

Conflicts of Interest: The authors declare no conflict of interest.

References

1. Dean, J.; Corrado, G.; Monga, R.; Chen, K.; Devin, M.; Mao, M.; Ranzato, M.; Senior, A.; Tucker, P.; Yang, K.; et al. Large scale distributed deep networks. *Adv. Neural Inf. Process. Syst.* **2012**.
2. Duan, M.; Li, K.; Liao, X.; Li, K. A parallel multiclassification algorithm for big data using an extreme learning machine. *IEEE Trans. Neural Netw. Learn. Syst.* **2017**, *29*, 2337–2351. [CrossRef]
3. McMahan, B.; Moore, E.; Ramage, D.; Hampson, S.; y Arcas, B.A. Communication-efficient learning of deep networks from decentralized data. In Proceedings of the Artificial Intelligence and Statistics, PMLR, Fort Lauderdale, FL, USA, 20–22 April 2017; pp. 1273–1282.

4. Konečný, J.; McMahan, B.; Ramage, D. Federated optimization: Distributed optimization beyond the datacenter. *arXiv* **2015**, arXiv:1511.03575. [CrossRef]
5. Bonawitz, K.; Eichner, H.; Grieskamp, W.; Huba, D.; Ingerman, A.; Ivanov, V.; Kiddon, C.; Konečný, J.; Mazzocchi, S.; McMahan, B.; et al. Towards federated learning at scale: System design. *Proc. Mach. Learn. Syst.* **2019**, *1*, 374–388.
6. Ovi, P.R.; Dey, E.; Roy, N.; Gangopadhyay, A.; Erbacher, R.F. Towards developing a data security aware federated training framework in multi-modal contested environments. In Proceedings of the Artificial Intelligence and Machine Learning for Multi-Domain Operations Applications IV, Orlando, FL, USA, 3–7 April 2022; SPIE: Bellingham, WA, USA, 2022; Volume 12113, pp. 189–198.
7. Cho, H.; Mathur, A.; Kawsar, F. FLAME: Federated Learning Across Multi-device Environments. *arXiv* **2022**, arXiv:2202.08922. [CrossRef]
8. Tolpegin, V.; Truex, S.; Gursoy, M.E.; Liu, L. Data poisoning attacks against federated learning systems. In Proceedings of the European Symposium on Research in Computer Security, Guildford, UK, 14–18 September 2020; Springer: Berlin/Heidelberg, Germany, 2020; pp. 480–501.
9. Bhagoji, A.N.; Chakraborty, S.; Mittal, P.; Calo, S. Analyzing federated learning through an adversarial lens. In Proceedings of the International Conference on Machine Learning, PMLR, Long Beach, CA, USA, 9–15 June 2019; pp. 634–643.
10. Wu, Z.; Ling, Q.; Chen, T.; Giannakis, G.B. Federated variance-reduced stochastic gradient descent with robustness to byzantine attacks. *IEEE Trans. Signal Process.* **2020**, *68*, 4583–4596. [CrossRef]
11. Fang, M.; Cao, X.; Jia, J.; Gong, N. Local model poisoning attacks to {Byzantine-Robust} federated learning. In Proceedings of the 29th USENIX Security Symposium (USENIX Security 20), Boston, MA, USA, 12–14 August 2020; pp. 1605–1622.
12. Chen, X.; Liu, C.; Li, B.; Lu, K.; Song, D. Targeted backdoor attacks on deep learning systems using data poisoning. *arXiv* **2017**, arXiv:1712.05526. [CrossRef]
13. Lim, W.Y.B.; Luong, N.C.; Hoang, D.T.; Jiao, Y.; Liang, Y.C.; Yang, Q.; Niyato, D.; Miao, C. Federated learning in mobile edge networks: A comprehensive survey. *IEEE Commun. Surv. Tutor.* **2020**, *22*, 2031–2063. [CrossRef]
14. Xiao, H.; Xiao, H.; Eckert, C. Adversarial label flips attack on support vector machines. In *ECAI 2012*; IOS Press: Amsterdam, The Netherlands, 2012; pp. 870–875.
15. Northcutt, C.; Jiang, L.; Chuang, I. Confident learning: Estimating uncertainty in dataset labels. *J. Artif. Intell. Res.* **2021**, *70*, 1373–1411. [CrossRef]
16. Bagdasaryan, E.; Veit, A.; Hua, Y.; Estrin, D.; Shmatikov, V. How to backdoor federated learning. In Proceedings of the International Conference on Artificial Intelligence and Statistics, PMLR, Online, 26–28 August 2020; pp. 2938–2948.
17. Sun, Z.; Kairouz, P.; Suresh, A.T.; McMahan, H.B. Can you really backdoor federated learning? *arXiv* **2019**, arXiv:1911.07963. [CrossRef]
18. Melis, L.; Song, C.; De Cristofaro, E.; Shmatikov, V. Exploiting unintended feature leakage in collaborative learning. In Proceedings of the 2019 IEEE Symposium on Security and Privacy (SP), San Francisco, CA, USA, 19–23 May 2019; IEEE: Piscataway, NJ, USA, 2019; pp. 691–706.
19. Zhu, L.; Liu, Z.; Han, S. Deep leakage from gradients. *Adv. Neural Inf. Process. Syst.* 2019.
20. Ovi, P.R.; Dey, E.; Roy, N.; Gangopadhyay, A. Mixed Precision Quantization to Tackle Gradient Leakage Attacks in Federated Learning. *arXiv* **2022**, arXiv:2210.13457. [CrossRef]
21. Ovi, P.R.; Gangopadhyay, A. A comprehensive study of gradient inversion attacks in federated learning and baseline defense strategies. In Proceedings of the 2023 57th Annual Conference on Information Sciences and Systems (CISS), Baltimore, MD, USA, 22–24 March 2023; IEEE: Piscataway, NJ, USA, 2023; pp. 1–6.
22. Ovi, P.R.; Dey, E.; Roy, N.; Gangopadhyay, A. Mixed quantization enabled federated learning to tackle gradient inversion attacks. In Proceedings of the IEEE/CVF Conference on Computer Vision and Pattern Recognition, Vancouver, BC, Canada, 17–24 June 2023; pp. 5046–5054.
23. Ovi, P.R.; Gangopadhyay, A.; Erbacher, R.F.; Busart, C. Secure Federated Training: Detecting Compromised Nodes and Identifying the Type of Attacks. In Proceedings of the 2022 21st IEEE International Conference on Machine Learning and Applications (ICMLA), Nassau, Bahamas, 12–14 December 2022; pp. 1115–1120.
24. Sun, G.; Cong, Y.; Dong, J.; Wang, Q.; Lyu, L.; Liu, J. Data poisoning attacks on federated machine learning. *IEEE Internet Things J.* **2021**, *9*, 11365–11375. [CrossRef]
25. Ovi, P.R.; Gangopadhyay, A.; Erbacher, R.F.; Busart, C. Confident federated learning to tackle label flipped data poisoning attacks. In Proceedings of the Artificial Intelligence and Machine Learning for Multi-Domain Operations Applications V, Orlando, FL, USA, 1–4 May 2023; SPIE: Bellingham, WA, USA, 2023; Volume 12538, pp. 263–272.

26. Nasr, M.; Shokri, R.; Houmansadr, A. Comprehensive privacy analysis of deep learning: Passive and active white-box inference attacks against centralized and federated learning. In Proceedings of the 2019 IEEE Symposium on Security and Privacy (SP), San Francisco, CA, USA, 19–23 May 2019; pp. 739–753.
27. Gu, T.; Dolan-Gavitt, B.; Garg, S. Badnets: Identifying vulnerabilities in the machine learning model supply chain. *arXiv* **2017**, arXiv:1708.06733.
28. Baruch, G.; Baruch, M.; Goldberg, Y. A little is enough: Circumventing defenses for distributed learning. *Adv. Neural Inf. Process. Syst.* **2019**, *32*.
29. Biggio, B.; Nelson, B.; Laskov, P. Poisoning attacks against support vector machines. *arXiv* **2012**, arXiv:1206.6389.
30. Fung, C.; Yoon, C.J.; Beschastnikh, I. The limitations of federated learning in sybil settings. In Proceedings of the 23rd International Symposium on Research in Attacks, Intrusions and Defenses (RAID 2020), San Sebastian, Spain, 14–15 October 2020; pp. 301–316.
31. Shen, S.; Tople, S.; Saxena, P. Auror: Defending against poisoning attacks in collaborative deep learning systems. In Proceedings of the 32nd Annual Conference on Computer Security Applications, Los Angeles, CA, USA, 5–9 December 2016; pp. 508–519.
32. Blanchard, P.; El Mhamdi, E.M.; Guerraoui, R.; Stainer, J. Machine learning with adversaries: Byzantine tolerant gradient descent. *Adv. Neural Inf. Process. Syst.* **2017**.
33. Fung, C.; Yoon, C.J.; Beschastnikh, I. Mitigating sybils in federated learning poisoning. *arXiv* **2018**, arXiv:1808.04866.
34. Zhang, Z.; Cao, X.; Jia, J.; Gong, N.Z. FLDetector: Defending federated learning against model poisoning attacks via detecting malicious clients. In Proceedings of the 28th ACM SIGKDD Conference on Knowledge Discovery and Data Mining, Washington, DC, USA, 14–18 August 2022; pp. 2545–2555.
35. Liu, X.; Li, H.; Xu, G.; Chen, Z.; Huang, X.; Lu, R. Privacy-enhanced federated learning against poisoning adversaries. *IEEE Trans. Inf. Forensics Secur.* **2021**, *16*, 4574–4588. [CrossRef]
36. Awan, S.; Luo, B.; Li, F. Contra: Defending against poisoning attacks in federated learning. In Proceedings of the Computer Security–ESORICS 2021: 26th European Symposium on Research in Computer Security, Darmstadt, Germany, 4–8 October 2021; Proceedings, Part I 26; Springer: Berlin/Heidelberg, Germany, 2021; pp. 455–475.
37. Jebreel, N.M.; Domingo-Ferrer, J.; Sánchez, D.; Blanco-Justicia, A. Defending against the label-flipping attack in federated learning. *arXiv* **2022**, arXiv:2207.01982. [CrossRef]
38. Li, D.; Wong, W.E.; Wang, W.; Yao, Y.; Chau, M. Detection and mitigation of label-flipping attacks in federated learning systems with KPCA and K-means. In Proceedings of the 2021 8th International Conference on Dependable Systems and Their Applications (DSA), Yinchuan, China, 11–12 September 2021; pp. 551–559.
39. Ma, C.; Li, J.; Ding, M.; Wei, K.; Chen, W.; Poor, H.V. Federated learning with unreliable clients: Performance analysis and mechanism design. *IEEE Internet Things J.* **2021**, *8*, 17308–17319. [CrossRef]
40. Li, Z.; Sharma, V.; Mohanty, S.P. Preserving data privacy via federated learning: Challenges and solutions. *IEEE Consum. Electron. Mag.* **2020**, *9*, 8–16. [CrossRef]
41. Jagielski, M.; Oprea, A.; Biggio, B.; Liu, C.; Nita-Rotaru, C.; Li, B. Manipulating machine learning: Poisoning attacks and countermeasures for regression learning. In Proceedings of the 2018 IEEE symposium on security and privacy (SP), San Francisco, CA, USA, 21–23 May 2018; pp. 19–35.
42. Yin, D.; Chen, Y.; Kannan, R.; Bartlett, P. Byzantine-robust distributed learning: Towards optimal statistical rates. In Proceedings of the International Conference on Machine Learning, PMLR, Stockholm, Sweden, 10–15 July 2018; pp. 5650–5659.
43. Chang, H.; Shejwalkar, V.; Shokri, R.; Houmansadr, A. Cronus: Robust and heterogeneous collaborative learning with black-box knowledge transfer. *arXiv* **2019**, arXiv:1912.11279. [CrossRef]
44. Nelson, B.; Barreno, M.; Chi, F.J.; Joseph, A.D.; Rubinstein, B.I.; Saini, U.; Sutton, C.; Tygar, J.D.; Xia, K. Exploiting machine learning to subvert your spam filter. *LEET* **2008**, *8*, 16–17.
45. Li, S.; Ngai, E.; Ye, F.; Voigt, T. Auto-weighted robust federated learning with corrupted data sources. *ACM Trans. Intell. Syst. Technol. (TIST)* **2022**, *13*, 1–20. [CrossRef]
46. Nguyen, T.D.; Rieger, P.; De Viti, R.; Chen, H.; Brandenburg, B.B.; Yalame, H.; Möllering, H.; Fereidooni, H.; Marchal, S.; Miettinen, M.; et al. {FLAME}: Taming backdoors in federated learning. In Proceedings of the 31st USENIX Security Symposium (USENIX Security 22), Boston, MA, USA, 10–12 August 2022; pp. 1415–1432.
47. Siegel, A.F. Robust regression using repeated medians. *Biometrika* **1982**, *69*, 242–244. [CrossRef]

electronics

MDPI

Article

MAFUZZ: Adaptive Gradient-Guided Fuzz Testing for Satellite Internet Ground Terminals

Ang Cao, Yongli Zhao *, Xiaodan Yan *, Wei Wang, Jian Yang, Yuanjian Zhang and Ruiqi Liu

School of Electronic Engineering, Beijing University of Posts and Telecommunications, Beijing 100876, China; ca0522@bupt.edu.cn (A.C.); weiw@bupt.edu.cn (W.W.); jianyang@bupt.edu.cn (J.Y.); yuanjianzhang@bupt.edu.cn (Y.Z.); 202311624@bupt.cn (R.L.)

* Correspondence: yonglizhao@bupt.edu.cn (Y.Z.); xiaodanyan@bupt.edu.cn (X.Y.)

Abstract: With the proliferation of satellite internet systems, such as Starlink and OneWeb, ground terminals have become critical for ensuring end-user connectivity. However, the security of Satellite Internet Ground Terminals (SIGTs) remains underexplored. These Linux-based embedded systems are vulnerable to advanced attacks due to limited source code access and immature protection mechanisms. This paper presents MAFUZZ, an adaptive fuzzing framework guided by neural network gradients to uncover hidden vulnerabilities in SIGT binaries. MAFUZZ uses a lightweight machine learning model to identify input bytes that influence program behavior and applies gradient-based mutation accordingly. It also integrates an adaptive Havoc mechanism to enhance path diversity. We compare MAFUZZ with NEUZZ, a neural fuzzing tool that uses program smoothing to guide mutation through a static model. Our experiments on real-world Linux binaries show that MAFUZZ improves path coverage by an average of 17.4% over NEUZZ, demonstrating its effectiveness in vulnerability discovery and its practical value for securing satellite terminal software.

Keywords: satellite internet; user terminal; internet of things; linux embedded; fuzzy testing

1. Introduction

Satellite internet has garnered significant global research attention, particularly regarding its security. Leading the industry are SpaceX's Starlink, OneWeb, and Amazon's Kuiper [1]. Notably, Starlink's ground terminals have achieved widespread commercial deployment, with newer generations extending coverage to mobile platforms such as vehicles, ships, and aircraft.

While prior studies have focused extensively on inter-satellite laser links and satellite-to-ground microwave communications, the security of Satellite Internet Ground Terminals (SIGTs) remains underexplored. These terminals function as edge nodes within the satellite network, often built on Linux-based embedded platforms and exhibiting characteristics akin to Internet-of-Things (IoT) devices, such as constrained firmware, proprietary communication interfaces, and remote access capabilities. The existing literature in IoT security and firmware fuzzing has highlighted challenges such as closed-source binaries, incomplete verification, and inadequate input sanitization [2,3].

As illustrated in Figure 1, satellite internet communication architecture allows users to connect their personal computers or mobile devices wirelessly to SIGTs. These terminals upload user data to Low Earth Orbit (LEO) satellites, which then relay the data to ground gateways for internet access. Given their increasing ubiquity and external exposure, SIGTs are becoming attractive targets for attackers aiming to exploit vulnerabilities in embedded software, control protocols, and web-based management interfaces.

This paper aims to address this critical security gap by focusing on the automated vulnerability discovery of SIGT binary programs through adaptive gradient-guided fuzzing.

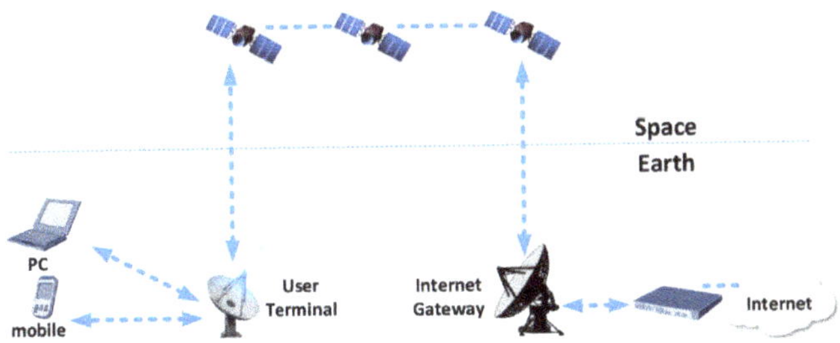

Figure 1. Satellite internet communication architecture.

SIGTs in satellite internet systems play a vital role in linking user devices to communication satellites [4]. These terminals receive commands from user applications or web interfaces and employ proprietary phased array technology to locate and connect to Low Earth Orbit (LEO) satellites within their range, facilitating the upload and download of user data. As emerging IoT [5] devices and commercial routers [6,7], SIGTs face security challenges similar to those of existing terrestrial IoT devices [3]. Most SIGTs utilize embedded Linux systems. For instance, Starlink's SIGTs share a similar internal structure with traditional Linux-embedded devices, utilizing binary programs on loopback and external ports for interactive functions. However, as early-stage IoT devices, many applications for these terminals remain immature, with their code security not thoroughly examined. Additionally, satellite internet providers typically offer interactive interfaces for user control and status monitoring of SIGTs. For example, Starlink provides applications and web management interfaces, which could be exploited by attackers for remote attacks, posing threats to user privacy and enabling malicious activities.

These practical concerns motivate the need for a proactive approach to binary-level vulnerability discovery in SIGTs.

Given this context, we have undertaken the following work on the security of SIGTs: We review past attack cases on Starlink's SIGTs, analyzing the methods and principles behind these attacks [2,8]. We conduct an in-depth analysis of the hardware and software architecture of Starlink's SIGTs [9]. This analysis aims to identify potential attack surfaces and construct a threat model. We address the challenges of acquiring binary program source code and the difficulties of reverse engineering and static analysis by proposing a fuzz testing method guided by neural network gradients. This method employs a neural network to approximate the relationship between seed inputs and program coverage, allowing it to compute input gradients and guide mutations toward paths that are more likely to trigger unexplored control-flow branches. We also designed an adaptive algorithm to automatically adjust the deterministic and havoc stages during the fuzz testing process. Our experimental results show that our method can achieve higher code coverage of the target binary programs in a shorter time [10,11].

2. Previous Attack Case Analysis

2.1. Fault Injection Attack

In the field of terminal security attack research, Lennert Wouters focused on exploring vulnerabilities in secure boot systems. He employed hardware attack techniques to design a custom circuit board called a modchip, which can temporarily disable decoupling capacitors used for power smoothing, inducing circuit faults. This allows for the circumvention of security protection mechanisms during the initialization process of the Linux bootloader. Once the security protection is bypassed, the modchip re-enables the decoupling capacitors, granting access to the underlying system of the Starlink's SIGTs. The core principle of this attack is to temporarily short-circuit the terminal's internal system, bypassing the security protection module during startup, thereby gaining access to the underlying system and allowing the execution of custom code on the Starlink system. Although this attack method is highly effective in achieving advanced malware injection, it is relatively difficult to implement because it requires complex physical hardware manipulation.

Notably, this type of physical-layer attack ultimately targets the software components of the system—particularly the bootloader, kernel, and initialization routines embedded in the firmware. These binaries are often closed-source and highly obfuscated, making static analysis challenging. Although such attacks are conducted at the hardware level, their ultimate objective is to compromise critical software binaries. This highlights the necessity of proactive vulnerability discovery mechanisms at the binary level. Our proposed framework, MAFUZZ, offers a dynamic and automated way to analyze these components. By applying adaptive gradient-guided fuzzing to the early boot stages, MAFUZZ enables the discovery of memory corruption, logic flaws, or unexpected state transitions that could be exploited during initialization. While MAFUZZ does not directly prevent physical intrusions, it strengthens firmware security by identifying software-layer vulnerabilities before they can be exploited by hardware-assisted attacks.

2.2. Remote Command Attack

In the realm of network security, researchers such as Joshua Smailes have conducted detailed analysis of the communication architecture employed by Starlink ground terminals [6,12]. Their investigations have revealed that both the front-end and back-end systems utilize Google Remote Procedure Call (gRPC) commands for interaction [13]. This approach facilitates high-performance and low-latency real-time communication. However, it also introduces vulnerabilities to potential tampering, allowing for the transmission of malicious commands. Furthermore, they noted the presence of the grpcurl command-line tool within the user's web management interface, enabling users to issue arbitrary gRPC requests and interact with gRPC servers.

Based on the analysis, Joshua Smailes utilized the Wireshark tool to capture and extract gRPC commands encapsulated within HTTP packets. By analyzing the format of these commands, they constructed initial seeds and performed fuzz testing using the grpcurl command-line interface, successfully triggering remote command reception crashes on the target ground terminal. This attack method exploits design flaws in the Starlink user web management interface, particularly in the command handler's input parsing logic.

Importantly, such command handlers are implemented as binary programs in the firmware and typically process external inputs without formal verification. These components are ideal candidates for fuzz testing to detect memory corruption, format string errors, and other parsing-related vulnerabilities. MAFUZZ provides an efficient solution for analyzing these closed-source gRPC handling binaries through gradient-guided seed mutation and adaptive exploration. By targeting this class of input-driven programs, MAFUZZ can help uncover critical flaws before they are exploited in remote command injection scenarios.

2.3. KA-SAT Attack

In the context of large-scale attacks on satellite networks, a significant cyberattack was launched by the Russian military intelligence agency (GRU) against ViaSat's KA-SAT satellite network just hours before Russia's invasion of Ukraine on 24 February 2022 [6]. This attack targeted critical communication equipment used by the Ukrainian Armed Forces—ViaSat SurfBeam 2 modems [14]. These modems were extensively utilized for tasks such as tactical communication, intelligence sharing, logistical support, and cyber defense. Their disruption severely degraded operational capabilities.

The attack unfolded in several phases: first, the attackers identified the KA-SAT network and its SurfBeam 2 modems [15], analyzed the configuration, and discovered a vulnerability in the VPN application setup. A Distributed Denial of Service (DDoS) attack followed, initially disrupting network availability. Then, leveraging the VPN vulnerability, the attackers gained unauthorized access to the management segment, from which they deployed the "AcidRain" malware [16] to remotely wipe device storage and disable modem functionality permanently.

While this attack does not originate from a fuzzing perspective, it highlights how firmware-level components—such as VPN clients, update agents, or configuration parsers—can serve as entry points for devastating exploits. These components are typically closed-source and embedded as binaries, making proactive vulnerability discovery difficult. MAFUZZ is designed to operate in exactly this context: as a binary-level fuzzing framework, it can dynamically explore and test such components to uncover input-handling flaws, unsafe state transitions, or logic errors. By applying MAFUZZ to SIGT firmware modules, it becomes possible to identify similar latent vulnerabilities before they are weaponized in attacks of this scale.

3. Threat Analysis and Model Construction

To effectively understand the attack surfaces of Satellite Internet Ground Terminals (SIGTs), it is essential to analyze the system from both physical and logical perspectives. Starlink SIGTs are composed of secure hardware modules, closed-source embedded firmware, and complex runtime communication interfaces. Each of these components may expose vulnerabilities that could be exploited for unauthorized access, command injection, or denial of service.

This section provides a comprehensive analysis of the Starlink ground terminal architecture from three dimensions—hardware, software, and runtime behavior—and constructs a corresponding threat model. This analysis directly supports the motivation for applying binary-level fuzzing, as many of the vulnerabilities identified reside in binary executables and cannot be detected through static inspection alone.

3.1. Starlink Terminal Hardware Structure Analysis

Similar to traditional Linux embedded devices, the internal hardware system of a STARLINK terminal is also built around a central System-on-Chip (SoC), which is responsible for storing all the files required for device operation and executing management programs. The specific core structure is illustrated in Figure 2.

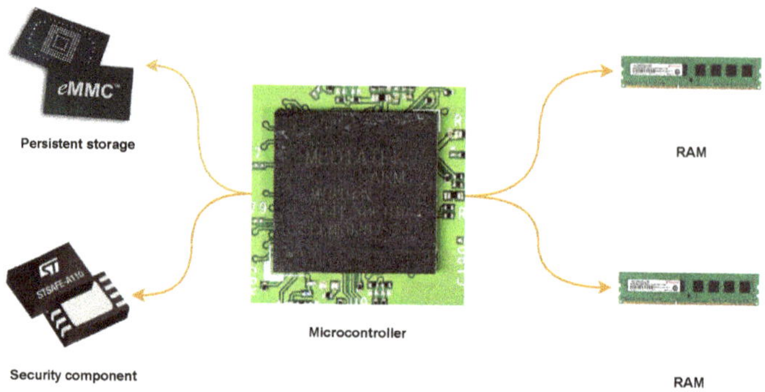

Figure 2. Starlink hardware core structure.

Below, we detail the various components of the core structure:

1. **Microcontroller:** A customized quad-core ARM Cortex-A53 processor, model STM GLLCCODGBF (STMicroelectronics, Geneva, Switzerland), responsible for executing program instructions from RAM or ROM.
2. **RAM:** Consists of two DDR3 chips (e.g., Micron Technology Inc., Boise, ID, USA), each with a capacity of 4 Gbit, providing necessary memory support for system operation.
3. **Persistent storage:** A 4 GB eMMC chip (e.g., Kingston Technology, Fountain Valley, CA, USA) is used to store all the files required for running the Linux system, which is also the primary target for attackers. Key files include the trusted firmware (TF-A), U-Boot bootloader, Linux kernel, and root filesystem.
4. **Security component:** STSAFE-A110 (STMicroelectronics, Geneva, Switzerland), which provides identity authentication and secure data management services for local or remote hosts.

For attackers, the primary step towards executing malicious code injection or other threatening activities is to gain elevated access privileges to the target system. Only with these privileges can attackers modify internal files and steal sensitive information. However, compared to typical IoT-embedded devices, Starlink ground terminals have implemented stricter security measures.

As shown in Figure 3, a Starlink ground terminal incorporates a TF-A secure chain verification module into its system boot process. The boot process is initiated by the ROM inside the microcontroller, and upon receiving instructions the eMMC first activates the TF-A security module. Guided by the TF-A secure trust chain, U-Boot, the system kernel, and, finally, the root filesystem are sequentially started.

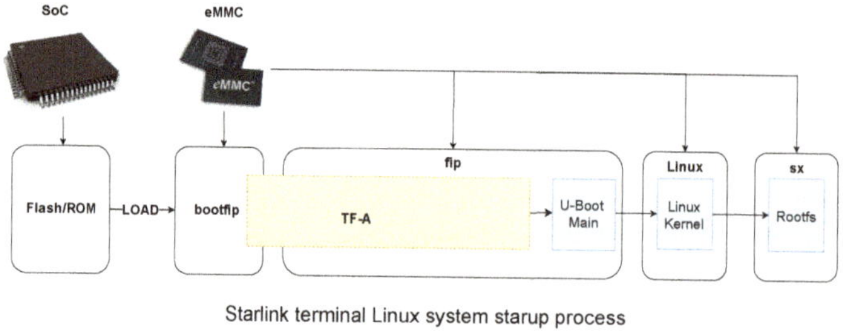

Figure 3. Starlink terminal Linux system startup process. Arrows indicate the boot sequence: TF-A and U-Boot load the Linux kernel and root filesystem from eMMC.

With the introduction of the trust chain, any modifications to the software in the memory are detected by the system. Therefore, if attackers want to achieve persistent modifications to the software, they must bypass the trust chain verification. An effective method is through fault injection, causing the initial signature check in the trust chain to fail, while simultaneously writing a patched firmware image that aims to skip subsequent verification steps. Once successfully written, attackers can enter the testing environment of the Starlink terminal through the USRT test interface.

Despite the existence of the TF-A secure chain and hardware-based verification, the system's resilience still relies significantly on the STM STSAFE-A110 secure element. This component handles identity authentication, cryptographic key protection, and boot integrity validation, leveraging tamper-resistant hardware and elliptic-curve signature mechanisms [17].

However, fault injection attacks—such as voltage glitches—can interrupt the boot process before STSAFE-A110 completes its validation. To counter such hybrid physical–software threats, the system must integrate hardware and firmware defense measures. For example, TF-A or U-Boot can implement runtime integrity checks and challenge–response verification using secrets stored in the secure element.

These cooperative mechanisms substantially enhance an SIGT's ability to detect and resist low-level intrusion attempts [18].

3.2. Starlink Terminal Runtime Structure Analysis

Starlink SIGTs, similar to common smart home IoT devices on the market, are equipped with corresponding mobile applications and web management interfaces. These external input interfaces undoubtedly provide potential avenues for attackers to remotely infiltrate the system. For traditional IoT devices, once an attacker obtains the terminal's internal binary programs and uses static or dynamic analysis to discover software vulnerabilities, they can exploit these vulnerabilities remotely on the target terminal to steal sensitive information or gain elevated administrative privileges.

However, the internal programs of SIGTs are highly complex. Even if the external interfaces used as attack entry points are identified and the internal binary programs are obtained through reverse engineering, executing remote exploits remains challenging without a thorough understanding of the terminal's runtime communication structure. This complexity arises because during the operation of the SIGT there are interactions with different access levels between the user terminal, the ground terminal's internal processes, and the cloud servers. This results in varying user access permissions and access levels for different internal binary programs, making it more difficult to exploit vulnerabilities in these programs. Therefore, a deep understanding of the internal communication architecture during the terminal's operation is crucial for carrying out remote network attacks.

As shown in Figure 4, the communication interaction architecture of a Starlink ground terminal mainly covers three levels: interaction between front-end applications and the internal processes of the terminal, interaction between remote servers and the internal processes of the terminal, and interaction among the internal processes of the terminal. Below is a detailed analysis of each interaction principle and its potential attack surfaces:

1. **Interaction between front-end applications and the internal processes of the terminal**: Within the terminal, there are back-end processes that interact with front-end applications. These applications remotely send commands via the gRPC protocol, including requests for terminal status, telemetry data, factory resets, software updates, and terminal orientation control. If attackers identify the format of gRPC requests and exploit vulnerabilities via dynamic analysis (e.g., fuzz testing), they may remotely

send malicious commands. Joshua Smailes et al. demonstrated this attack method on real terminals.

2. **Interaction between remote servers and the internal processes of the terminal**: Starlink's remote servers receive and respond to gRPC requests from terminal back-end processes. These servers interact with the terminal's control, update, and telemetry processes. If attackers discover vulnerabilities in this server–terminal interaction, they may leverage the server as a proxy to deliver malicious commands to internal processes.
3. **Interaction among the internal processes of the terminal**: These processes facilitate communication with front-end applications and satellites, mediated by the terminal control process. Internally, they exchange data via loopback ports using precompiled binary programs. Once communication interfaces are identified, attackers can focus on locating exploitable vulnerabilities in these binaries.

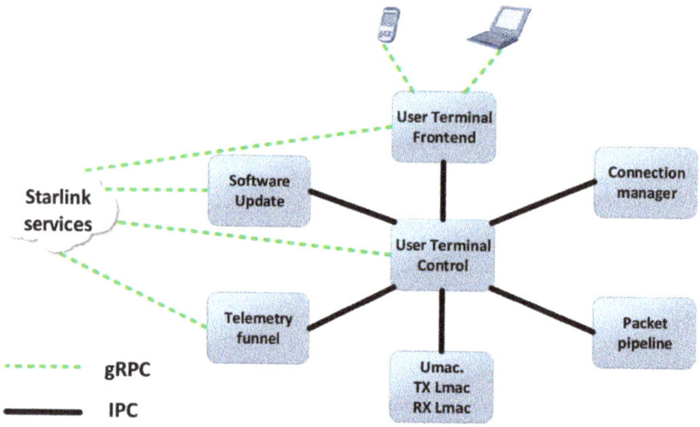

Figure 4. Starlink terminal communication architecture.

3.3. Threat Model Construction

Based on the preceding analysis of the Starlink ground terminal's hardware, software, and communication architecture, we constructed a three-layer threat model encompassing the physical layer, the network/software layer, and the protocol/communication layer, as illustrated in Figure 5. This model reflects varying attacker capabilities, access levels, and technical complexity across different layers of the system.

Physical layer: Attackers with physical access can extract firmware from the eMMC storage, inject modified images with patched trust chains (e.g., TF-A), and use modchip-based fault injection to bypass secure boot verification [18]. This type of attack offers deep system control but requires high precision, specialized equipment, and close physical proximity—making it powerful but difficult to scale.

Network/software layer: Without hardware access, remote adversaries can exploit vulnerabilities exposed by front-end-back-end interfaces (e.g., gRPC) or use fuzzing techniques to generate malformed inputs that target back-end binaries. These attacks are scalable and automatable but are constrained by the closed-source nature of firmware and limited semantic feedback during testing [19]. Recent studies have shown that such vulnerabilities are prevalent in commercial satellite modem firmware, where over a dozen exploitable flaws were identified across real-world devices [20], highlighting the practical relevance of embedded binary fuzzing.

Protocol/communication layer: During runtime, dynamic behaviors such as satellite handovers introduce unique risks. Improper state synchronization—such as inconsistent session contexts or re-used authentication tokens—may result in session desynchronization or replay attacks [21,22]. Furthermore, satellite–ground and inter-satellite links are typically encrypted using application-layer or MAC-layer protocols. While encryption enhances security, it obscures program behavior from fuzzing tools, reducing both input observability and mutation effectiveness [9].

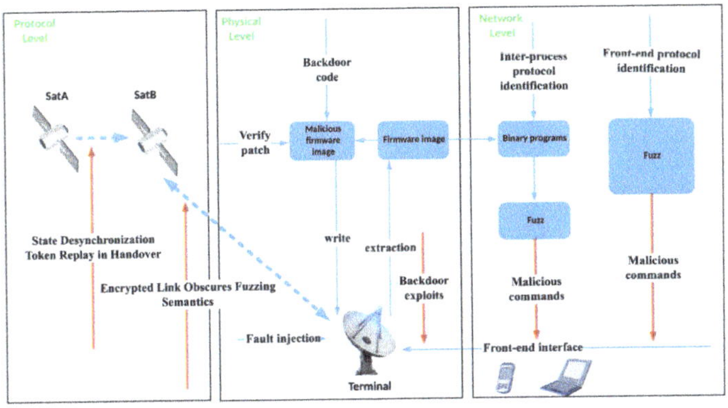

Figure 5. Three-layer threat model of a Starlink ground terminal: physical hardware attacks, software/network-based remote exploits, and protocol-level threats during satellite communication.

4. Fuzz

In this section, we will explore the principles of gradient-guided fuzz testing for efficiently discovering vulnerabilities in binary programs, and we will introduce our developed adaptive gradient-guided fuzz testing framework.

In summary, this threat model captures a spectrum of attack vectors: highly effective but hardware-dependent physical attacks, widely accessible but semantically opaque software attacks, and dynamic protocol-level threats that are both difficult to monitor and test. Collectively, these observations illustrate the unique challenges posed by SIGT systems—from physical tampering to protocol-level complexity. To address these issues, we introduce an adaptive fuzzing framework capable of dynamically navigating such deeply layered attack surfaces.

4.1. Gradient-Guided Fuzz Testing

Fuzz testing is a dynamic analysis vulnerability discovery technique that continuously sends mutated data to the target program to check if these inputs cause program errors or crashes [23]. Current mainstream binary fuzz testing tools, such as American fuzzy lop (AFL), adopt coverage-guided methods combined with the principles of evolutionary optimization algorithms, retaining only those inputs most likely to produce new code coverage to improve seed quality. However, evolutionary optimization algorithms tend to get stuck in local optima during the computation process [24], leading to a gradual decrease in efficiency in exploring new code paths. Gradient-guided optimization algorithms effectively address this issue [25].

The principle of achieving efficient fuzz testing using gradient guidance is illustrated in Figure 6. For the seed provided as input to the target program, the ith byte typically corresponds to a reference point of a conditional branch statement in the program. Therefore, if we can identify, through gradient guidance, the byte in each seed most likely to change the branch statement and mutate it accordingly, we may explore the sibling path of the original branch. For example, in Figure 6, mutating the value of seed[i] to be greater than x can transition the seed exploration path from l1 to l2. The gradient-guided algorithm can meet this requirement by first constructing a surrogate function to establish the relationship between seed bytes and their coverage paths then utilizing this function to calculate the gradient corresponding to each byte, thereby identifying the most promising mutation bytes. However, due to the complexity of real-world programs, constructing a function that can smoothly represent the causal relationship mentioned above is highly challenging.

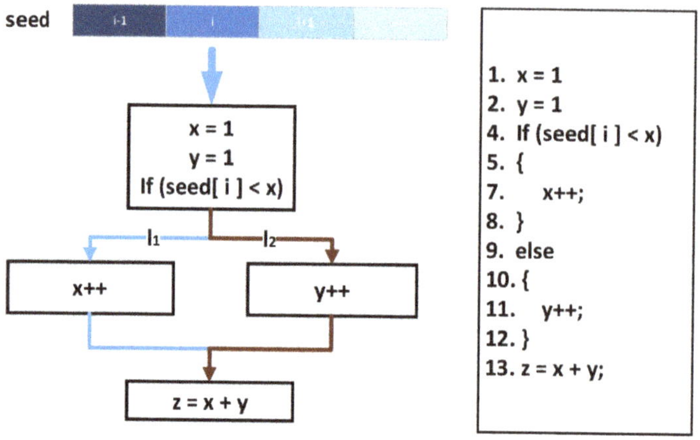

Figure 6. Program use case that explains gradient guidance.

4.2. Neural Program Smoothing Fuzz Testing

Given the limitations of current gradient-guided methods in fuzzing programs, She et al. proposed a fuzz testing tool called NEUZZ based on neural program smoothing [26,27]. NEUZZ is a pioneering framework that integrates deep learning into fuzzing by modeling how input bytes affect code coverage. It trains a neural network to learn the mapping from inputs to edge coverage and uses gradient backpropagation to identify mutation positions. This method utilizes a neural network model [28] to learn the functional relationship between input seed bytes and output coverage edges. It takes the byte sequences of each initial seed as input and outputs a vector representation of the corresponding coverage bitmap. Through the neural network [29,30], it captures the implicit correlations between seed byte sequences and program branches, and it then performs gradient backpropagation to identify the input bytes most likely to influence control flow transitions [31]. Subsequent mutations are guided by the magnitude of these gradients, enabling targeted exploration of previously unreached paths.

The specific process of NEUZZ is illustrated in Figure 7, and it can be divided into two stages: neural program smoothing and gradient-guided mutation. In the smoothing stage, NEUZZ constructs a mapping function between the seed byte positions and *edge bitmap*:

$$f : \{i, i+1, i+2, i+3, \dots\}^m \to \{l_1, l_2, l_3, l_4, \dots\}^n \quad (1)$$

All the initial seeds are first executed to collect the set of covered edges, defining the output bitmap's dimensionality n. Each input seed is recorded as a byte sequence of length m, representing the input dimensionality. For any given execution, if an edge is triggered then the corresponding bit in the output vector is set to 1; otherwise, to 0. For example, a seed activating edge_1 but not edge_2 yields an output like $\{1, 0, \text{edge}_3, \text{edge}_4, \dots\}$. The accumulated input–output pairs from all the seeds are then used to train the neural network. After training, gradient-based mutation is performed by computing the derivative of the output edge bitmap with respect to each input byte. These gradients serve as indicators of each byte's mutation potential.

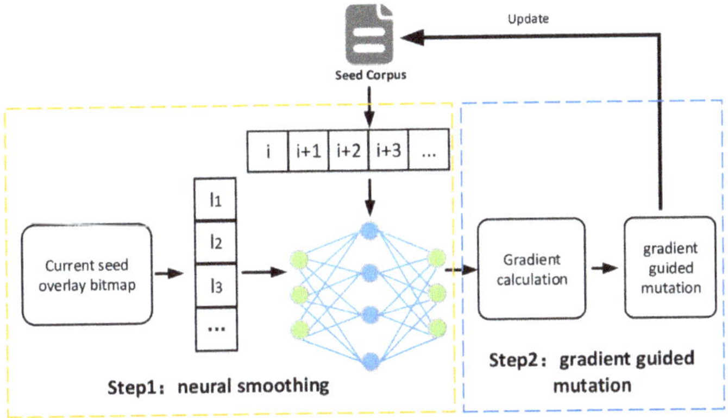

Figure 7. Neural program smoothing fuzzing.

To implement the smoothing step, NEUZZ uses a fully connected feedforward neural network with a single hidden layer, typically consisting of 4096 neurons with ReLU activation. The output layer uses a sigmoid function to predict the edge activation probabilities. This lightweight design ensures both modeling capacity and computational efficiency.

The NEUZZ authors report that the neural network structure plays a secondary role compared to input diversity: experiments using deeper networks or wider hidden layers achieved only marginal improvements in coverage while significantly increasing training cost and risk of overfitting. Conversely, removing the hidden layer degraded performance, due to limited nonlinear modeling capacity. These findings indicate that a one-hidden-layer architecture is sufficient to approximate the mapping from seed bytes to coverage edges, offering a good trade-off between accuracy, generalization, and overhead in fuzzing scenarios [26].

Experimental results demonstrate that NEUZZ achieves up to three times the edge coverage compared to traditional fuzzers like AFL over a 24 h run. It is particularly effective on large programs, where its learning-guided approach allows it to generalize internal branching logic and escape coverage plateaus. This advantage arises from the neural network's ability to generalize over the collective edge-activation patterns of all seed inputs [32,33]. The quality and diversity of the initial seed set directly impact the model's ability to capture complex branching behavior [34,35]. When the seed pool includes enough inputs to cover a broad range of sibling edge clusters, the neural model can guide mutations toward unexplored conditional branches more effectively. Conversely, a narrow seed distribution limits learning capacity and causes early saturation.

For Satellite Internet Ground Terminals (SIGTs), where binaries are large and obfuscated, NEUZZ's gradient-based exploration framework offers significant advantages. Its learned model can navigate the deep and complex control-flow structures typical of SIGT binaries, triggering deeper paths and discovering subtle logic vulnerabilities. These properties make NEUZZ—and its successors, like MAFUZZ—particularly well-suited for security analysis in embedded and closed-source systems.

Building on NEUZZ, MAFUZZ retains the surrogate modeling framework using a single-layer feedforward neural network trained to approximate the mapping from seed byte sequences to coverage edge vectors. The model is optimized via standard backpropagation, and the gradient of the predicted coverage vector with respect to the input bytes is used to locate high-impact mutation positions.

Unlike conventional software, SIGT firmware often contains highly discrete control logic, such as hardcoded state machines and nested branches, which may introduce gradient discontinuities. To maintain the effectiveness of gradient-guided mutation in such scenarios, MAFUZZ restricts mutation to high-confidence bytes (i.e., those with large gradient magnitudes), reduces reliance on weak or noisy gradients, and emphasizes seed corpus diversity during training. This ensures that the model can generalize over discontinuous coverage landscapes and still provide meaningful directional guidance for mutation.

4.3. Baseline Justification and Tool Comparison

To justify the selection of NEUZZ as the main baseline for our fuzzing framework, we conducted independent comparative experiments between AFL and NEUZZ. All the evaluations were performed on three representative Linux binaries—objdump, readelf, and harfbuzz—using identical testing conditions: a 12 h runtime per target and a common initial seed corpus. Table 1 presents the observed edge coverage results.

The data show that NEUZZ significantly outperformed AFL across all the benchmarks. In particular, NEUZZ achieved up to 9.0× higher coverage on objdump and 6.6× on readelf, highlighting the benefit of its neural program smoothing and gradient-guided mutation strategy. These findings support the validity of NEUZZ as a robust baseline for evaluating further enhancements in our proposed framework.

Table 1. Edge coverage comparison between AFL and NEUZZ under identical testing conditions.

Program	AFL	NEUZZ	NEUZZ Gain
objdump	426	3838	+9.0×
readelf	1420	9373	+6.6×
harfbuzz	7642	14,521	+1.9×

4.4. Adaptive Gradient-Guided Fuzzing

While NEUZZ demonstrates strong performance in gradient-guided fuzzing, its reliance on a static neural program smoothing process limits its ability to discover new execution paths once the initial sibling edge clusters are exhausted. In particular, when the initial seed pool lacks diversity, the neural network can only guide mutations within a constrained edge space, leading to early saturation and coverage stagnation.

To address this limitation, we propose a novel adaptive gradient-guided fuzzing framework—MAFUZZ—that introduces two key enhancements to the traditional NEUZZ architecture: (1) integration of a Havoc mutation mode, and (2) a dynamic controller to adjust the balance between gradient-guided and random mutation strategies during fuzzing.

Hybrid mutation design. MAFUZZ extends the NEUZZ mutation pipeline by incorporating AFL-style Havoc mutation operations, such as random bit flips, byte insertions, and deletions. These random mutations enable the exploration of previously unreachable sibling edge clusters, complementing the precision of gradient-guided mutation. When the neural model becomes saturated, Havoc provides a mechanism to escape local minima by generating novel seed variants.

Adaptive mode regulation. Instead of statically applying both mutation strategies, MAFUZZ dynamically adjusts their usage during fuzzing based on real-time coverage feedback. After each round of seed execution, the algorithm analyzes the proportion of explored edges in sibling clusters and accordingly adjusts the number of gradient-guided and Havoc mutations for the next round. When the average saturation ratio is low, the controller favors gradient mutation for efficiency; when the ratio is high, it emphasizes Havoc to increase diversity.

Mutation control algorithm. The mutation strategy control algorithm lies at the heart of MAFUZZ's adaptiveness. It evaluates the edge coverage status of the current seed pool and dynamically adjusts the balance between gradient-guided and Havoc mutation modes. The process consists of three stages, outlined as follows and corresponding to the structure of Algorithm 1:

Algorithm 1 Adaptive mutation pattern modulation

Input: *program, seeds*
Output: *guideNum, randNum*
1: **for** *seed*[*i*] $\in$ *seeds* **do**
2:    Edge[i] $\leftarrow$ SeedExecution(seeds[i])
3:    totalEdge[j] $\leftarrow$ totalEdge[j] + Edge[i]
4: **end for**
5: correspRelation $\leftarrow$ getEdgeRelation(program)
6: emptyArray $\leftarrow$ correspRelation
7: **for** *j* in totalEdge **do**
8:    **for** *edge* in correspRelation **do**
9:       **if** totalEdge[j] = edge **then**
10:          emptyArray[edge] $\leftarrow$ 1
11:       **end if**
12:    **end for**
13:    **for** $i \in emptyArray$ **do**
14:       ratio[i] $\leftarrow \frac{num}{\text{arrayLength}}$
15:       averageRatio $\leftarrow \frac{1}{n}\sum_{i=0}^{n} \text{ratio}[i]$
16:    **end for**
17: **end for**
18: **if** $averageRatio \in [0, \text{Threshold}]$ **then**
19:    guideNum $\leftarrow$ guideNum(1 + averageRatio)
20:    randNum $\leftarrow$ randNum(1 - averageRatio)
21: **end if**
22: **if** $averageRatio \in [\text{Threshold}, 1]$ **then**
23:    guideNum $\leftarrow$ guideNum(1 - averageRatio)
24:    randNum $\leftarrow$ randNum(1 + averageRatio)
25: **end if**
26: **return** *guideNum,randNum*

(1) Edge coverage aggregation (lines 1–4). Each seed in the seed pool is executed on the target binary, and the edges it triggers are recorded. These edges are aggregated into a global set, `totalEdge`, representing the complete set of coverage edges observed in the current round. This forms the empirical basis for evaluating exploration saturation.
(2) Sibling edge cluster analysis (lines 5–12). Using static analysis (e.g., disassembling with `objdump`), the control flow graph (CFG) of the program is extracted. From this, all sibling edge clusters—sets of control-flow-related edges—are constructed as `correspRelation`. A zero-initialized structure `emptyArray` is created to match this layout.

The algorithm then flags each edge in `totalEdge` within its respective cluster. For each sibling cluster, the ratio of visited edges is computed. Averaging across all the clusters yields the global `averageRatio`, which quantifies the current round's overall exploration depth.
(3) Adaptive mutation adjustment (lines 13–20). Based on the calculated `averageRatio` and a predefined `Threshold`, the algorithm adjusts the number of gradient-guided (`guideNum`) and Havoc-based (`randNum`) mutations:

- If `averageRatio` < `Threshold`, the seed pool is deemed underexplored. The algorithm increases `guideNum` and reduces `randNum` to exploit known edge clusters more efficiently.

- If `averageRatio` $\geq$ `Threshold`, it shifts emphasis to exploration by increasing `randNum` and decreasing `guideNum`.

This feedback loop allows MAFUZZ to dynamically balance exploitation and exploration as fuzzing progresses, effectively improving coverage across structurally diverse programs.

Figure 8 presents the architectural differences between NEUZZ and our proposed framework MAFUZZ. While retaining NEUZZ's neural smoothing and gradient-guided mutation modules, MAFUZZ introduces two key enhancements. First, a Havoc mutation module is incorporated to explore novel edge clusters that are unreachable via gradient-guided paths. Second, an adaptive controller dynamically regulates the ratio of guided versus random mutations based on the saturation level of explored edge clusters in the seed pool. This closed-loop architecture improves fuzzing efficiency by balancing precision and diversity in input mutations.

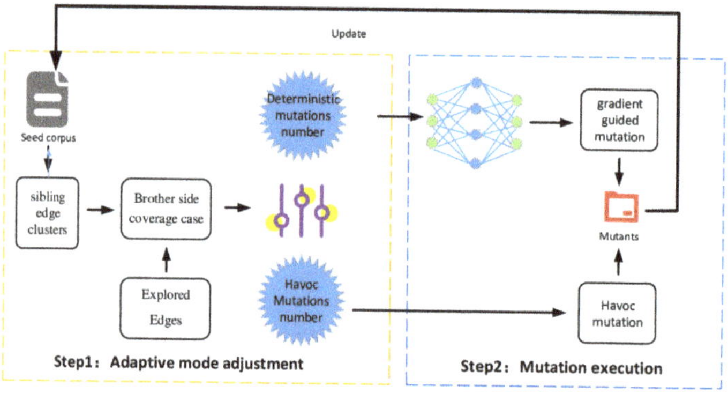

Figure 8. Structural comparison between the original NEUZZ architecture and the proposed MAFUZZ framework. The enhanced version introduces a Havoc mutation path and a dynamic mode controller to enable adaptive mutation strategy switching.

Framework overview. Figure 9 presents the overall workflow of MAFUZZ. Starting from an initial seed pool, inputs are processed by a neural smoothing model to estimate coverage gradients. An adaptive controller adjusts the ratio of gradient-guided and Havoc mutations based on coverage feedback (the two mutation types are applied sequentially, with gradient-guided mutation followed by Havoc). Mutated seeds are executed, and edge results are used to update the seed pool, forming a closed loop that continuously refines mutation strategies to improve path coverage.

Summary. In summary, MAFUZZ introduces a hybrid and adaptive mutation framework that combines the precision of gradient guidance with the exploratory strength of Havoc mutation. By dynamically regulating the two strategies according to the real-time saturation of edge clusters, MAFUZZ enhances the diversity and depth of seed mutation. This adaptive control significantly improves path coverage efficiency and robustness across different program complexities.

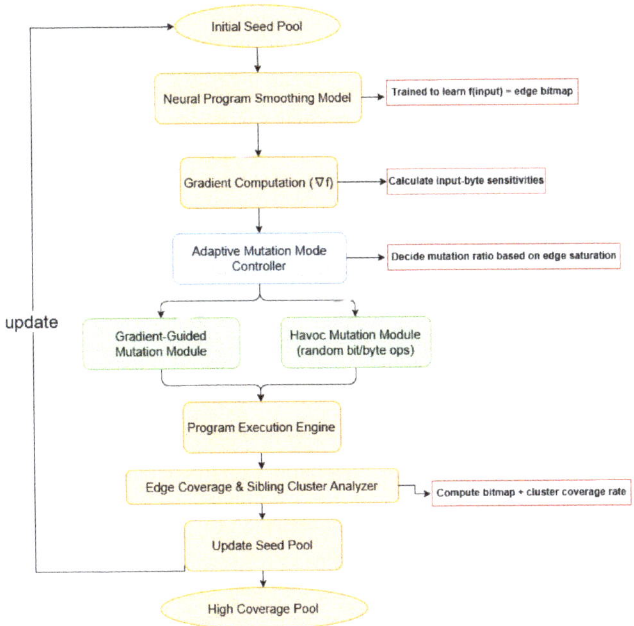

Figure 9. Workflow of the proposed adaptive fuzzing framework (MAFUZZ).

5. Experiment Validation

For this section, we conducted a two-part experimental study. The first part investigated the optimal threshold for adaptive mutation switching in our framework. The second part evaluated the fuzzing performance of MAFUZZ against NEUZZ under the selected threshold.

All our experiments were conducted on Ubuntu 18.04 (Canonical Ltd., London, UK) with an NVIDIA Tesla P4 GPU (NVIDIA Corporation, Santa Clara, CA, USA) for neural network acceleration. The targets included three widely used Linux binaries—`objdump`, `readelf`, and `harfbuzz`.

To ensure fair comparison, we first ran AFL on each target for 5 h to generate initial seed corpora. These seeds were re-used in both NEUZZ and MAFUZZ to eliminate variability and ensure identical initial conditions. The left table in Table 2 summarizes the number of seeds collected.

To avoid bias from model configuration, both tools used the same neural network architecture and training parameters. As shown in the right-hand column of Table 2, the network included one hidden layer with 4096 ReLU units, trained for 50 epochs using a learning rate of 0.01, binary cross-entropy loss, and early stopping.

Table 2. Initial seed counts (left) and shared neural network training configuration (right).

Seed Corpus		NN Training Parameters	
Program	**Seeds**	**Parameter**	**Value**
objdump	1586	Architecture	1 hidden layer (4096 ReLU)
readelf	1543	Learning rate	0.01
harfbuzz	1678	Epochs	50
		Loss function	Binary cross-entropy
		Optimizer	Adam
		Early stopping	Enabled

Each test configuration was repeated three times to ensure statistical reliability. During each run, we collected edge coverage at consistent intervals across 30 iterations. Figures 13–15 present the averaged edge coverage curves. From the results, we observe that NEUZZ showed rapid initial growth but plateaued early, likely due to its fixed model-based mutation strategy. In contrast, MAFUZZ continued to accumulate coverage at the later stages by dynamically switching to Havoc-based mutations when gradient-guided exploration reached saturation.

Table 5 summarizes the final average coverage for both tools, the absolute and relative improvements of MAFUZZ, and p-values from independent-samples t-tests. The results show consistent performance gains on all three programs, with average improvements ranging from +15.5% to +19.2%. All differences are statistically significant ($p < 0.001$), confirming that the observed gains were not due to chance.

Table 5. Comprehensive comparison of edge coverage between MAFUZZ and NEUZZ (12 h runtime, $n = 3$).

Program	NEUZZ ($\mu \pm \sigma$)	MAFUZZ ($\mu \pm \sigma$)	Gain (#)	Gain (%)	p-Value
`objdump`	3,838.0 ± 15.9	4,646.7 ± 24.0	+809	+15.5%	1.97×10^{-5}
`readelf`	9,373.0 ± 27.7	11,606.0 ± 60.0	+2,233	+19.2%	2.75×10^{-7}
`harfbuzz`	14,521.0 ± 42.1	17,086.0 ± 32.6	+2,565	+17.6%	4.88×10^{-6}

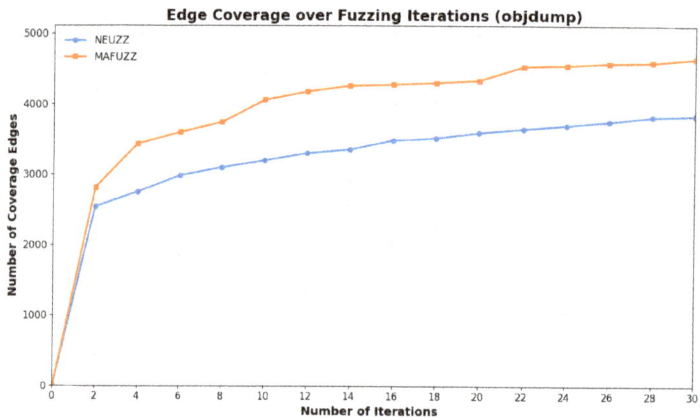

Figure 13. Mean edge coverage trajectory of NEUZZ vs. MAFUZZ on `readelf` (12 h, $n = 3$).

Discussion. As shown in Table 5 and Figure 16, MAFUZZ consistently delivered higher final edge coverage than NEUZZ across all the benchmarks. These results validate the design rationale of MAFUZZ: adaptive threshold-driven control enables effective switching between exploration and exploitation. When the seed space becomes saturated under gradient guidance, the system automatically increases the proportion of Havoc mutations, allowing the discovery of new sibling edge clusters that would otherwise be missed. This flexibility leads to deeper path exploration and better overall fuzzing effectiveness. The low standard deviations and statistically significant p-values ($p < 0.001$) confirm the stability and reliability of these improvements.

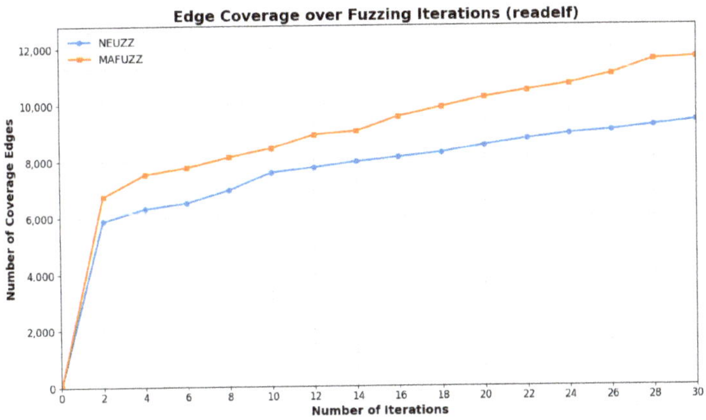

Figure 14. Mean edge coverage trajectory of NEUZZ vs. MAFUZZ on `objdump` (12 h, $n = 3$).

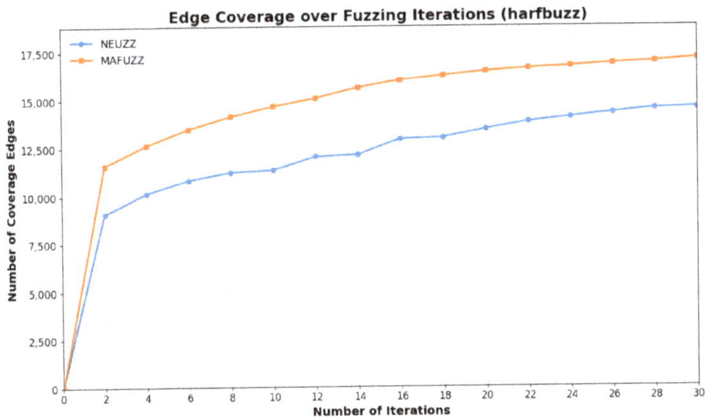

Figure 15. Mean edge coverage trajectory of NEUZZ vs. MAFUZZ on `harfbuzz` (12 h, $n = 3$).

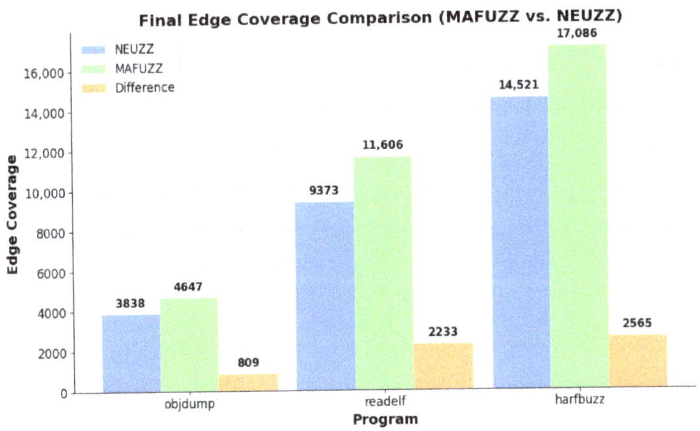

Figure 16. Final average edge coverage on all benchmarks (MAFUZZ vs. NEUZZ, $n = 3$).

5.3. Firmware Vulnerabilities and Mitigation Strategies in Satellite Terminals

MAFUZZ revealed several common binary flaws in satellite ground terminals:

- **Memory overflows**: from unchecked buffers or integer operations.
- **Invalid state transitions**: due to missing control logic.
- **Unhandled errors**: in malformed input processing.
- **Unsafe command parsing**: without format or field validation.

These issues affect back-end firmware modules directly and may lead to crashes, logic faults, or silent failures. Table 6 summarizes lightweight mitigation strategies tailored for embedded terminal systems.

Table 6. Typical vulnerabilities and corresponding mitigation strategies.

Vulnerability in Satellite Terminal Firmware	Recommended Mitigation
Memory overflows	Enable stack canaries, ASLR; apply static analysis to prevent unsafe memory use.
Invalid state transitions	Use finite state machines (FSMs); validate state logic and log violations.
Unhandled input errors	Standardize error codes; add fallback paths and fault recovery handlers.
Unsafe command parsing	Define structured formats (e.g., TLV); validate type, length, and value constraints.

6. Conclusions

In this paper, we conducted a comprehensive security analysis of Satellite Internet Ground Terminals (SIGTs), including real-world attack case studies, hardware/software architecture examination, and threat model construction. To address the identified vulnerabilities—especially those residing in closed-source binary firmware—we propose MAFUZZ, an adaptive gradient-guided fuzzing framework tailored to the characteristics of SIGT environments.

MAFUZZ integrates neural gradient mutation with a Havoc-style mutation strategy and adaptively balances the two, based on edge coverage feedback. This design enables it to effectively escape local plateaus and discover previously unreachable paths in complex embedded binaries.

Our experiments on three representative Linux binaries demonstrate that MAFUZZ consistently outperforms the state-of-the-art NEUZZ fuzzer. Specifically, MAFUZZ achieves an average path coverage improvement of +17.4%, with gains of +15.5% on objdump, +19.2% on readelf, and +17.6% on harfbuzz, as shown in Table 5. These results are statistically significant and validate the effectiveness of the adaptive mutation strategy, particularly in resource-constrained and semantically opaque environments such as SIGT firmware.

In future work, we plan to extend our framework to real-world satellite terminal firmware. This includes analyzing the runtime interaction data between the SIGT and its front-end interfaces and implementing targeted binary fuzzing based on observed protocol flows. We expect this work to further improve automated vulnerability discovery in satellite communication systems and contribute to the overall security of emerging space–ground infrastructure.

Author Contributions: Conceptualization, A.C.; Methodology, A.C., Y.Z. (Yongli Zhao) and Y.Z. (Yuanjian Zhang); Validation, J.Y.; Investigation, R.L.; Writing—original draft, A.C.; Writing—review & editing, X.Y. and W.W. All authors have read and agreed to the published version of the manuscript.

Funding: This work was supported in part by the National Natural Science Foundation of China under Grant No. 62425105, 62350001, 62021005, and 62206019.

Data Availability Statement: Data are contained within the article.

Conflicts of Interest: The authors declare no conflict of interest.

References

1. Jennings, R. The challenge to develop the perfect flat panel satellite communications terminal: The perfect SATCOM terminal. *IEEE Microw. Mag.* **2023**, *24*, 22–29. [CrossRef]
2. Eceiza, M.; Flores, J.L.; Iturbe, M. Fuzzing the Internet of Things: A review on the techniques and challenges for efficient vul-nerability discovery in embedded systems. *IEEE Internet Things J.* **2021**, *8*, 10390–10411. [CrossRef]
3. Neshenko, N.; Bou-Harb, E.; Crichigno, J.; Kaddoum, G.; Ghani, N. Demystifying IoT security: An exhaustive survey on IoT vulnerabilities and a first empirical look on internet-scale IoT exploitations. *IEEE Commun. Surv. Tutor.* **2019**, *21*, 2702–2733. [CrossRef]
4. Grayver, E.; Nelson, R.; McDonald, E.; Sorensen, E.; Romano, S. Position and navigation using Starlink. In Proceedings of the 2024 IEEE Aerospace Conference, Big Sky, MT, USA, 2–9 March 2024; pp. 1–12.
5. Asplund, M.; Nadjm-Tehrani, S. *Secure IT Systems: 25th Nordic Conference, NordSec 2020, Virtual Event, November 23–24. 2020, Proceedings*; Springer International Publishing: Berlin/Heidelberg, Germany, 2021; Volume 12556, pp. 75–174.
6. Jeitner, P.; Shulman, H.; Teichmann, L.; Waidner, M. XDRI attacks—and how to enhance resilience of residential routers. In Proceedings of the 31st USENIX Security Symposium (USENIX Security 22), Boston, MA, USA, 10–12 August 2022; pp. 4473–4490.
7. Ceylan, O.; Caglar, A.; Tugrel, H.B.; Cakar, H.O.; Kislal, A.O.; Kula, K.; Yagci, H.B. Small satellites rock a software-defined radio modem and ground station design for Cube satellite communication. *IEEE Microw. Mag.* **2016**, *17*, 26–33. [CrossRef]
8. Ahmad, I.; Suomalainen, J.; Porambage, P.; Gurtov, A.; Huusko, J.; Hoyhtya, M. Security of satellite-terrestrial communications: Challenges and potential solutions. *IEEE Access* **2022**, *10*, 96038–96052. [CrossRef]
9. Yu, L.; Hao, J.; Ma, J.; Sun, Y.; Zhao, Y.; Luo, B. A comprehensive analysis of security vulnerabilities and attacks in satellite modems. In Proceedings of the 2024 ACM SIGSAC Conference on Computer and Communications Security, Salt Lake City, UT, USA, 14–18 October 2024; pp. 3287–3301.
10. Anand, P.; Singh, Y.; Selwal, A.; Alazab, M.; Tanwar, S.; Kumar, N. IoT vulnerability assessment for sustainable computing: Threats, current solutions, and open challenges. *IEEE Access* **2020**, *8*, 168825–168853. [CrossRef]
11. Xiao, L.; Wan, X.; Lu, X.; Zhang, Y.; Wu, D. IoT security techniques based on machine learning: How do IoT devices use AI to enhance security? *IEEE Signal Process. Mag.* **2018**, *35*, 41–49. [CrossRef]
12. Smailes, J.; Salkield, E.; Köhler, S.; Birnbach, S.; Martinovic, I. Dishing out DoS: How to disable and secure the Starlink user terminal. *arXiv* **2023**, arXiv:2303.00582. [CrossRef]
13. Niemietz, M.; Schwenk, J. Owning your home network: Router security revisited. *arXiv* **2015**, arXiv:1506.04112. [CrossRef]
14. Poirier, C.; Soesanto, S. Hacking the cosmos: Cyber operations against the space sector: A case study from the war in Ukraine. *ETH Zur. Rep.* **2024**, *48*, 1–48.
15. Boschetti, N.G.; Gordon, N.G.; Falco, G. Space Cybersecurity Lessons Learned from the Viasat Cyberattack. In Proceedings of the ASCEND 2022, American Institute of Aeronautics and Astronautics (AIAA), Las Vegas, NV, USA, 24–26 October 2022; p. 4380. [CrossRef]
16. Guerrero-Saade, J.A.; Van Amerongen, M. AcidRain: A Modem Wiper Rains Down on Europe. *Sentinel Labs*, 31 March 2022. Available online: https://www.sentinelone.com/labs/acidrain-a-modem-wiper-rains-down-on-europe/ (accessed on 6 June 2025).
17. STMicroelectronics. STSAFE-A110: Authentication Secure Element for Embedded Systems. ST Datasheet. 2023. Available online: https://www.st.com/en/secure-mcus/stsafe-a110.html (accessed on 6 June 2025).
18. Wouters, L.; Trickel, S.; Kennedy, D.; Ragsdale, B. Glitched on Earth by Humans: A Black Box Security Evaluation of the SpaceX Starlink User Terminal. In Proceedings of the Black Hat USA, Las Vegas, NV, USA, 6–11 August 2022. Available online: https://i.blackhat.com/USA-22/Wednesday/US-22-Wouters-Glitched-On-Earth.pdf (accessed on 6 June 2025).
19. Willbold, J.; Schloegel, M.; Göhler, F.; Scharnowski, T.; Bars, N.; Wörner, S.; Schiller, N.; Holz, T. Scaling software security analysis to satellites: Automated fuzz testing and its unique challenges. In Proceedings of the 2024 IEEE Aerospace Conference, Big Sky, MT, USA, 2–9 March 2024; pp. 1–12.

20. Miller, C.; Valasek, C. Fuzz by numbers: Fuzzing and taint analysis for protocol reverse engineering. In Proceedings of the Black Hat USA, Las Vegas, NV, USA, 2–7 August 2008.
21. Xie, T.; Zhu, Y.; Yang, J.; Wu, L. Dynamic handover security in LEO satellite networks. *IEEE Commun. Mag.* **2023**, *61*, 52–58.
22. Qu, Z.; Zhu, G.; Zhang, J.; Wang, Y. LEO satellite constellations for 5G and beyond: How will they integrate with terrestrial networks? *IEEE Netw.* **2021**, *35*, 130-137.
23. Klees, G.; Ruef, A.; Cooper, B.; Wei, S.; Hicks, M. Evaluating fuzz testing. In Proceedings of the 2018 ACM SIGSAC Conference on Computer and Communications Security, Toronto, ON, Canada, 15–19 October 2018; pp. 2123–2138.
24. Boehme, M.; Cadar, C.; Roychoudhury, A. Fuzzing: Challenges and reflections. *Commun. ACM* **2021**, *64*, 46–53. [CrossRef]
25. Gopalakrishnan, G.; Qadeer, S. *Computer Aided Verification: 23rd International Conference, CAV 2011, Snowbird, UT, USA, July 14–20. 2011. Proceedings*; Lecture Notes in Computer Science; Springer: Berlin/Heidelberg, Germany, 2011; Volume 6806.
26. She, D.; Pei, K.; Epstein, D.; Yang, J.; Ray, B.; Jana, S. NEUZZ: Efficient fuzzing with neural program smoothing. In Proceedings of the IEEE Symposium on Security and Privacy (SP), San Francisco, CA, USA, 19–23 May 2019; pp. 803–817.
27. Wang, Y.; Wu, Z.; Wei, Q.; Wang, Q. Neufuzz: Efficient fuzzing with deep neural network. *IEEE Access* **2019**, *7*, 36340–36352. [CrossRef]
28. Nichols, N.; Raugas, M.; Jasper, R.; Hilliard, N. Faster fuzzing: Reinitialization with deep neural models. *arXiv* **2017**, arXiv:1711.02807. [CrossRef]
29. Godefroid, P.; Peleg, H.; Singh, R. Learn&Fuzz: Machine learning for input fuzzing. In Proceedings of the 2017 32nd IEEE/ACM International Conference on Automated Software Engineering (ASE), Urbana, IL, USA, 30 October–3 November 2017; pp. 50–59.
30. Li, S.; Xie, X.; Lin, Y.; Li, Y.; Feng, R.; Li, X.; Ge, W.; Dong, J.S. Deep Learning for Coverage-Guided Fuzzing: How Far Are We? *IEEE Trans. Dependable Secur. Comput.* **2022**. [CrossRef]
31. Zong, P.; Lv, T.; Wang, D.; Deng, Z.; Liang, R.; Chen, K. FuzzGuard: Filtering out unreachable inputs in directed grey-box fuzzing through deep learning. In Proceedings of the 29th USENIX Security Symposium (USENIX Security 20), Boston, MA, USA, 12–14 August 2020; pp. 2255–2269.
32. Bai, T.; Huang, S.; Huang, Y.; Wang, X.; Xia, C.; Qu, Y.; Yang, Z. CriticalFuzz: A critical neuron coverage-guided fuzz testing framework for deep neural networks. *Inf. Softw. Technol.* **2024**, *172*, 107476. [CrossRef]
33. Deng, Y.; Xia, C.S.; Peng, H.; Yang, C.; Zhang, L. Large language models are zero-shot fuzzers: Fuzzing deep-learning libraries via large language models. In Proceedings of the 32nd ACM SIGSOFT International Symposium on Software Testing and Analysis, Seattle, WA, USA, 17–21 July 2023; pp. 423–435.
34. Odena, A.; Olsson, C.; Andersen, D.; Goodfellow, I. Tensorfuzz: Debugging neural networks with coverage-guided fuzzing. In Proceedings of the International Conference on Machine Learning, Long Beach, CA, USA, 9–15 June 2019; pp. 4901–4911.
35. Xie, X.; Ma, L.; Juefei-Xu, F.; Xue, M.; Chen, H.; Liu, Y.; Zhao, J.; Li, B.; Yin, J.; See, S. Deephunter: A coverage-guided fuzz testing framework for deep neural networks. In Proceedings of the 28th ACM SIGSOFT International Symposium on Software Testing and Analysis, Beijing, China, 15–19 July 2019; pp. 146–157.

electronics

MDPI

Article

Mitigating DDoS Attacks in LEO Satellite Networks Through Bottleneck Minimize Routing

Fangzhou Meng, Xiaodan Yan *, Yuanjian Zhang, Jian Yang, Ang Cao, Ruiqi Liu and Yongli Zhao *

School of Electronic Engineering, Beijing University of Posts and Telecommunications, Beijing 100876, China; fzmeng@bupt.edu.cn (F.M.); yuanjianzhang@bupt.edu.cn (Y.Z.); jianyang@bupt.edu.cn (J.Y.); ca0522@bupt.edu.cn (A.C.); 2023110624@bupt.cn (R.L.)

* Correspondence: xiaodanyan@bupt.edu.cn (X.Y.); yonglizhao@bupt.edu.cn (Y.Z.)

Abstract: In this paper, we focus on defending against distributed denial-of-service (DDoS) attacks in a low-earth-orbit (LEO) satellite network (LSN). To enhance the security of LSN, we propose the K-Bottleneck Minimize routing method. The algorithm ensures path diversity while avoiding vulnerable bottleneck paths, which significantly increases the cost for attackers. Additionally, the attacker's detectability is reduced. The results show that the algorithm avoids the bottleneck paths that are vulnerable to attacks, improves the attacker's cost by about 13.1% and 16.6% on average and median, and improves the detectability of attackers by 48.5% and 45.4% on average and median. The algorithm generates multiple non-overlapping inter-satellite paths, preventing the exploitation of bottleneck paths and ensuring better robustness and attack resistance.

Keywords: LEO satellite network; routing algorithm; bottleneck; DDoS

1. Introduction

1.1. System Context and Challenge

Satellite communication systems have undergone a fundamental paradigm shift in their operational and governance models. Although the satellite-communications sector was long dominated by government agencies and international consortia (e.g., NASA and ESA), it has recently experienced an unprecedented surge in commercial participation. Private entities such as SpaceX's Starlink, Telesat, and OneWeb are now spearheading the deployment of LSNs through mega-constellations, aiming to deliver global broadband coverage [1].

From a service perspective, satellite Internet bridges critical gaps where terrestrial infrastructure is impractical [2], such as maritime, aviation, and rural regions [3]. According to statistics published by the International Telecommunication Union (ITU) as of 2022, approximately 2.7 billion individuals worldwide remain unconnected to the Internet, highlighting a persistent global digital divide. This disparity is further underscored by the uneven distribution of connectivity: while 82% of urban populations had adopted Internet access, this figure represents approximately 1.8 times the adoption rate observed in rural areas [4]. However, challenges remain in spectrum coordination, orbital debris mitigation, and energy efficiency for satellite power systems. These factors will shape the next evolution of LEO networks.

As shown in Figure 1, the LSN consists of an inter-satellite link (ISL) consisting of a large number of satellites, and a ground-satellite link (GSL) for ground coverage. Modern LSNs leverage ISLs to achieve two critical advantages: ultralow latency through

https://doi.org/10.3390/electronics14122376

optimized orbital routing, and enhanced throughput via spatial multiplexing. Beyond technical merits, their global footprint addresses critical connectivity gaps in terrestrial infrastructure, enabling emergency response [5], remote scientific expeditions, and disaster recovery operations.

Figure 1. LEO satellite network.

The commercial viability of this model is evidenced by SpaceX's milestone of 4 million subscribers as of September 2024 [6], accompanied by rapid constellation expansion. As of 8 April 2025, orbital registries document 11,414 operational satellites in Earth's orbit, with SpaceX's Starlink constellation dominating the landscape. Quantitative analysis from [7] reveals that 7161 Starlink satellites are currently active—constituting 62.7% of all active orbital assets. This unprecedented concentration underscores Starlink's dominance in global satellite infrastructure, far exceeding the cumulative deployments of all other operators combined. In accordance with the FCC report [8], we adopted the Starlink S1 shell topology, which has 72 orbital planes, each with 22 satellites, a height of 550 km, and an orbital inclination of 53°, each with 4 ISLs.

Previous research on satellite networks has predominantly focused on performance optimization, including communication capacity enhancement [9,10], latency reduction through ISL routing [11], and novel constellation designs [12]. However, the rapid commercialization of LSNs has introduced new security challenges that remain insufficiently addressed. In contrast to traditional satellite networks operated by governmental agencies, commercial mega-constellations often prioritize scalability and cost-efficiency, which often results in cybersecurity being treated as a secondary concern. For instance, the dense mesh topology of ISLs, while enabling low-latency routing, creates a larger attack surface for adversaries to exploit [13]. Recent studies highlight risks such as spoofing attacks on GSLs [14], and eavesdropping threats on satellite signals [6]. These systemic vulnerabilities pose critical risks to mission-critical operations, extending beyond launch platform integrity to encompass ground and space-based communications infrastructure, telemetry networks, spacecraft tracking mechanisms, and mission-critical command subsystems [15]. Regulatory frameworks governing cybersecurity in the space domain remain severely underdeveloped, particularly among commercial satellite operators. This lack of regulatory oversight becomes particularly concerning given the critical role that LSNs are expected to play in both civilian and defense communications. According to [16], the incidence of satellite system attacks increased fivefold during the period from 2009 to 2018 compared to the preceding decade (2000–2008), reflecting a significant escalation in the frequency and intensity of threat activity.

The public disclosure of satellite deployment details (e.g., FCC technical specifications) [17] enables attackers to reconstruct network topologies with high precision. The prevailing reliance on shortest-path routing in LSNs creates predictable traffic patterns, as evidenced by routing analyses in operational constellations [18]. Such patterns have proven attractive to adversaries and have been directly exploited in real world incidents. In November 2022, Starlink suffered a DDoS attack on the layer, which caused some users' satellite services to be disrupted for a period of time [19]. In March 2025, a hacking group claimed responsibility for a cyberattack on 116 Iranian ships that resulted in a full-scale blow to the tanker's satellite communications system [20].

On the Internet, routing bottlenecks are structural weaknesses. In terrestrial Internet infrastructure, route-cost minimization heuristics led to traffic convergence on a small set of high-centrality links, inadvertently creating structural chokepoints. Similarly, in LSNs, such traffic concentration arises due to topology-aware routing optimizations that prioritize minimal hop counts or latency, often at the expense of robustness. The ICARUS [21] framework has experimentally validated that such bottlenecks can be exploited in LSNs through coordinated botnet traffic, though specific performance impacts require further empirical measurement. Attackers can use network probing tools to discover the transmission path from the source node to the destination node [22]. As depicted in Figure 2, adversaries can strategically target three critical attack surfaces in LSNs: uplink and downlink jamming through distributed botnets and ISL flooding using coordinated payloads. The differently colored arrows in the diagram represent traffic from different directions that converges at the bottleneck link.

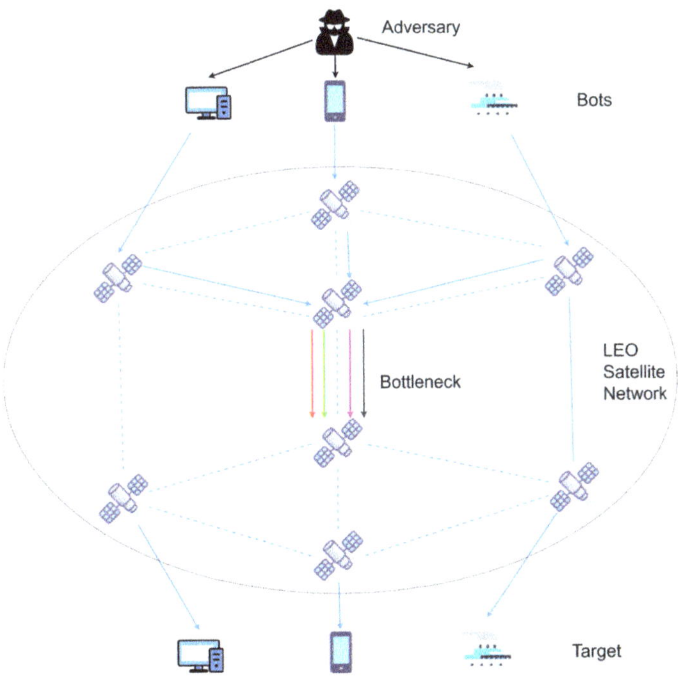

Figure 2. An example of adversary attacking LSN.

This paper presents a routing algorithm, in which we conducted statistical modeling of the bottleneck paths in LSN. We propose the K-Bottleneck Minimize routing algorithm, which aims to minimize the bottleneck weight during path generation. This algorithm increases the cost for the attacker to launch DDoS attacks and enhances the detectability of the attacker, providing greater security for LSN.

1.2. Motivation

Since bottleneck paths exist in the network, once attackers identify and continuously probe these bottleneck links, they can repeatedly locate them with low-rate probing traffic, and then launch concentrated floods at critical moments, seriously damaging network availability; once an attacker identifies and continuously probes these bottleneck links, they can repeatedly locate them with low-rate probing traffic and then unleash a concentrated flood at critical moments, severely impairing network availability.

Current multipath routing implementations predominantly rely on random or load balancing to enhance path unpredictability [23], yet fundamentally fail to mitigate bottleneck exploitation risks. Even emerging intelligent solutions, such as deep learning-based anomaly detection [15] or blockchain-secured routing [24], show limited practicality in resource-constrained LSN environments due to their high computational overhead. At the control layer, several studies have focused on fractional-order multi-agent systems [25], incorporating adaptive mechanisms to counteract time-varying attack gains induced by deception attacks [26]. This comprehensive survey [27] shows that intrusion detection system (IDS) methods have been introduced in spatial networks, but their computational overhead may introduce non-trivial detection delays under bursty or high-volume traffic and may also cause detection performance degradation under high-volume traffic.

Prior work [28] has shown that under malicious intervention Border Gateway Protocol (BGP) prefix hijacking can concentrate originally dispersed routes onto a single bottleneck link. Further amplifying the bottleneck effect [29] demonstrated, in their LSN study, that by leveraging publicly available TLE orbital data and simple throughput probes, attackers can accurately identify and continuously overwhelm the current busiest ground–satellite link, achieving up to a 3.4× reduction in global user traffic. This implies that unless defenses incorporate an assessment of high-risk bottlenecks and avoid them, attackers can repeatedly probe and reuse the same hotspot links, continuously evading mitigation.

Despite these demonstrated risks, no existing LSN DDoS mitigation framework systematically incorporates bottleneck risk profiling into routing weight optimization models. This oversight perpetuates the exposure of high-frequency attack surfaces, underscoring the urgent need for risk routing paradigms.

1.3. Contribution

This paper proposes a routing algorithm and statistically models the bottleneck path in LSN. We propose the K-Bottleneck Minimize routing algorithm, which aims to minimize the bottleneck weight during path generation. This algorithm increases the cost for the attacker to launch DDoS attacks and enhances the detectability of the attacker, providing greater security for LSN.

2. Background and Related Work

2.1. LEO Satellite Network

LSN integrates two fundamental components: a space segment comprising numerous LEO satellites interconnected via ISLs, and a ground segment consisting of user terminals and gateway stations [30]. Satellite Internet represents a revolutionary approach to global connectivity by leveraging constellations of LEO satellites. Unlike traditional geostationary (GEO) satellites operating at 36,000 km altitude, modern LEO constellations orbit below 2000 km, significantly reducing signal latency to 10–30 ms [31], while their 53° inclination angles ensure concentrated coverage over economically critical mid-latitude regions. This architectural shift enables near-fiber-optic performance for real-time applications like video conferencing and online gaming.

The technological advancement of modern satellite constellations is primarily driven by two disruptive innovations: cost-effective mass production of miniaturized satellites and pioneering reusable launch architectures. Empirical data illustrates this progression: early-generation satellites documented in [32] weighed approximately 260 kg, whereas contemporary Starlink V2 variants exhibit a threefold mass increase to 800 kg, reflecting enhanced payload capacity. Concurrently, SpaceX's Falcon 9 booster has achieved unprecedented reusability milestones, with [33] reporting its 17th successful mission deploying 28 satellites—a testament to operational maturity in reusable rocket technology. Scaling ambitions further materialize through payload optimization; current Falcon 9 configurations accommodate up to 60 satellites per launch [34], while the developmental next-generation Starship megarocket prototype promises exponential capacity expansion, projected to deliver over 400 Starlink satellites per mission upon operational deployment.

This paradigm shifts from traditional bent-pipe relay systems to a three-stage data delivery model: terrestrial users first uplink data to overhead satellites via phased-array antennas. The data is then routed through multiple ISL hops across orbital planes using laser communication terminals (LCTs). Finally, destination satellites downlink the processed data to ground stations [35]. The first-generation Starlink architecture, in its initial deployment configuration, leverages X/Ku-band and Ka-band for user and ground station links to enable bidirectional low-latency communications [36]. This enables 4 Gbps user link throughput alongside 20 Gbps full-duplex ISL capacities [21], forming a high-efficiency space-terrestrial integrated network.

2.2. Denial of Service Attack

Denial of service (DoS) attacks disrupt target systems by exhausting computational resources through malicious traffic overload. The evolution to DDoS attacks enables attackers to coordinate geographically dispersed botnets—compromised devices spanning thousands of networks—to amplify attack magnitude exponentially. A seminal 1999 DDoS incident against the University of Minnesota incapacitated critical servers for 48 h, demonstrating early Internet vulnerabilities.

Modern variants like Coremelt's link-flooding attack (LFA) exploit legitimate-appearing traffic between botnet nodes to congest critical network links rather than end-hosts, evading conventional intrusion detection systems [37]. Crossfire extends this paradigm by decoupling control-plane stability from data-plane attacks, enabling persistent regional service degradation through strategic target selection [38].

In satellite network contexts, the ICARUS framework adapts these principles to LSN environments. Attackers leverage compromised ground terminals across multiple regions to generate coordinated "normal" traffic patterns, strategically selecting source-destination pairs to saturate uplinks, downlinks, or inter-satellite connections.

As reported in [39], attackers are increasingly adopting hybrid DDoS strategies that combine carpet-bombing techniques with TCP reflection and amplification attacks, leading to highly disruptive traffic patterns across distributed ground terminals and satellite links, such as satellite ISPs or terminal services. These approaches indirectly launch amplified attacks against specific downstream targets.

Lu et al. proposed DoSat [17], a DDoS attack model targeting LEO satellite networks by combining link flooding with temporal lensing. By leveraging the time-varying topology of satellite constellations, DoSat concentrates attack traffic to overwhelm target links.

Simulations show that it reduces attack cost by approximately 20% compared to prior methods such as ICARUS, while maintaining stealth.

2.3. Satellite Security

The routing paradigms of terrestrial networks and LSNs exhibits fundamental differences. Terrestrial infrastructures benefit from stable node distributions and quasi-static topologies, whereas LSN routing must address dynamic orbital reconfigurations and stringent resource constraints. This volatility renders conventional security mechanisms inapplicable, necessitating domain-specific secure routing frameworks for space environments. In this context, several researchers have proposed innovative solutions to address these unique challenges.

Some studies enhance the unpredictability of path selection by incorporating random or predefined weighting mechanisms into routing. Ref. [40] developed Secure Enhanced Multipath Routing (SEMR), leveraging randomized breadth-first search (BFS) to generate unpredictable paths. Ref. [41] introduced Load-Balanced Multipath Routing (LBMR), employing Least Common Multiple (LCM)-based weight allocation for temporal-aware traffic splitting. Ref. [42] proposed an enhanced ant-colony pheromone model combined with an optional forwarding mechanism. When a node becomes inundated by traffic, both its heuristic value and pheromone concentration are dynamically reduced, promptly steering traffic toward healthy links to defend against DDoS attacks.

In a ground-relay–assisted Starlink topology, Ref. [43] introduced a hop-count–prioritized shortest-path scheme that splits a session's traffic across two path segments and instantaneously activates a backup route as soon as a failure is detected on the primary link. Ref. [44] proposed advanced k-RAND, a random routing algorithm. This algorithm integrates Bayesian optimization to dynamically blend classic routing strategies. The experimental results demonstrate a 2.05% increase in attacker costs compared to static algorithms, validating its adaptive defense capabilities.

To ensure the trusted identities of satellite nodes and the security of their messages, blockchain technology has recently been incorporated into routing and multicast design. In [45], blockchain was integrated aboard satellites by designating each satellite node as a network participant; smart contracts and a distributed ledger were then employed to execute encrypted in-orbit data transmissions. Ref. [46] proposed a blockchain-based trustworthy multicast routing framework that leverages decentralized node authentication and combines an ant-colony algorithm with a scenario-aware hybrid switching strategy to isolate malicious nodes, construct a trusted multicast tree, and implement DDoS defense.

Some researchers have also explored machine learning- or deep learning-assisted DDoS defense. Huang et al. [47] introduced a Graph Neural Network-based MultiPath Traffic Engineering (GNN-MPTE), which centrally computes multiple disjoint paths at the ground controller to circumvent attacked links and automatically distribute traffic onto healthy paths. Ref. [48] proposed a deep learning-based trust-routing framework that combines Dempster–Shafer (D–S) evidence theory with variational autoencoder (VAE) based anomaly detection, integrating the generated security factors into an ant-colony algorithm to dynamically avoid malicious nodes.

There are several other security enhancement schemes that also offer valuable strategies for mitigating DDoS attacks. Ref. [49] proposed a distributed node–trust evaluation and secure-routing framework that collects inter-node interaction data to compute both direct and indirect trust, then fuses these via a D-S framework to derive an overall trust score—significantly improving the packet-delivery ratio and reducing packet-loss rate. Ref. [50] introduced an ICN network architecture that integrates a centralized software-defined networking (SDN) control plane with an information-centric networking (ICN) data plane. By leveraging the controller's global view to dynamically install flow rules and employing content naming with in-network caching of popular content, the framework can rapidly redirect or cache malicious requests under DDoS attacks, thereby distributing load and alleviating stress on core links.

The main characteristics and drawbacks of these representative DDoS mitigation techniques are compared in Table 1.

Table 1. State-of-the-art DDoS defense techniques in LSN.

Paper	Key Idea	Limitation
[40]	Randomized BFS to build multiple disjoint paths and disperse DDoS traffic	The randomized path is often not the shortest and may go around distant satellites
[41]	Least Common Multiple-based dynamic billing to balance load	Cannot reflect real-time or historical risk
[42]	Enhanced ant-colony: pheromone on congested nodes decays, steering traffic away	DDoS attacks may cause routing to suboptimal or wrong paths by distorting heuristic
[43]	Segment Routing with pre-installed snapshots for latency-aware detours	Reliant on terrestrial relays and not suited for sparse or long-haul networks
[44]	Bayesian optimization to mix shortest-path and randomized routing dynamically	Routing strategies change frequently, and forwarding tables frequently fluctuate
[45]	Integrated Blockchain in satellite node, verify the legitimacy of data sources	Smart contracts and a distributed ledger bring delays of more than seconds
[46]	Combining Blockchain and ant-colony, building multicast trees to isolate attackers.	High blockchain latency and communication overhead limit real-time defense
[47]	GNN-driven, latency and stability-aware traffic splitting/dropping of attack flows	Training and updating rely on historical snapshots, difficult to respond to changing attacks
[48]	Combining D-S preprocessing and VAE anomaly detection to generate security factors guiding routing	Only fluctuations in trust vectors and does not track sudden traffic spikes, thus failing to distinguish legitimate bursts from DDoS floods
[49]	Distributed D–S trust fusion in OSPF to automatically isolate suspicious nodes	Collection and fusion of interactive data is heavy; convergence speed is slow in large network
[50]	SDN flow rules and ICN edge caching to redirect malicious requests and offload core routers	Requires SDN and ICN deployment, with controller scalability and cache challenges

Prior schemes improve path unpredictability but introduce excessive path stretch and ignore the inherent risk of each route. Deep learning and blockchain approaches, however, incur high deployment overhead and cannot block stealthy DDoS attacks on board satellites in real time. Our work delivers a practical routing strategy for satellite networks that steers traffic away from high-risk bottleneck links while ensuring that path lengths remain bounded.

3. Model

3.1. Attacker Model

Although routing strategies are not publicly disclosed by satellite operators and vary across service providers, attackers can obtain routing information in two ways: one is to infer using public satellite topology data, and the other is to actively detect through ground terminals. LSN often maintains network stability at the second level. For example, Starlink changes the network every 15 s [51], so an attacker's maximum window to exploit any static snapshot is only 15 s. During this interval, bots continue to use a fixed set of pre-planned paths and traffic-distribution plans to launch its flows. Our simulation is also based on the static network in this case. To evaluate the attack, we adopt the adversary's perspective and focus on two critical metrics: Cost and MaxUp.

Cost quantifies the resource investment required to achieve attack objectives. For stealth-oriented attacks, they must distribute traffic across a large botnet to avoid detection, which increases coordination difficulty and operational overhead, thereby raising the overall attack cost. The cost of the attack is measured in Gbps. In actual attack and defense studies of satellite networks [52], the attack traffic generation capacity of a single bot is about tens of Mbps. To paralyze an ISL with a capacity of 20 Gbps, for example, a bot sends 40 Mbps, the attacker needs to coordinate at least 500 zombie devices to form an attack cluster.

For MaxUp, there is usually an anomaly detection mechanism based on link utilization in LSN. When the instantaneous bandwidth utilization of any ground-satellite uplink increases too much compared to its historical average level, an alarm can be triggered, and defenses such as traffic cleaning or node isolation can be initiated. In order to avoid such monitoring, attackers must disperse the total attack traffic to multiple uplinks to avoid excessive bandwidth surges on a single link. The maximum absolute bandwidth increment of this uplink attack traffic is defined as MaxUp to characterize the detectability of the attack. MaxUp is normalized to the bandwidth of an uplink. In the worst case, the attacker needs to fully saturate the satellite's uplink, and the MaxUp at this time is 1.

3.1.1. Link and Path Discovery

The attacker creates a network diagram based on the existing satellite link and the distribution of controlled nodes. For each controlled node, uplinks and downlinks are added to its neighboring satellites. Then, for any two ordered combinations of controlled nodes, the Dijkstra algorithm is used to determine their shortest transmission path.

3.1.2. Path Filtering

Let P be the set of all paths in the network. The attacker will target one or more links and find all bots combinations that pass through these links via the shortest path. The attacker only selects and retains those paths that pass through the target in the attack direction.

3.1.3. Calculation of Feasible Attack Flows

The attack traffic to be allocated on each attack direction path j is a non-negative variable x_j. The objective is to minimize the sum of x_j.

$$min\sum_{j=1}^{\mathrm{m}} x_j \tag{1}$$

For the total links L in the network, the attacker seeks a traffic distribution on these links and satisfies the following two constraints:

1. For all target links $T \in L$, the traffic needs slightly higher than the capacity C_T to ensure congestion:

$$\sum_{j\in P_T} x_j > C_T \tag{2}$$

2. For all non-target links $U \in L$, the traffic needs slightly higher than the capacity C_U, to ensure that traffic does not become congested:

$$\sum_{j\in P_U} x_j < C_U \tag{3}$$

By satisfying these two sets of constraints, the target link can be squeezed with the minimum bandwidth without causing congestion on other links.

After the solution x_j is obtanined, let D be the maximum absolute bandwidth increase in the uplink, MaxUp, as follows:

$$D = \max_{L\in E_{uplink}} \sum_{j\in P_T} x_j \tag{4}$$

3.1.4. Iterative Solution

If the initial budget D cannot meet feasibility requirements, the opponent will continue to reduce D and repeatedly solve the above feasibility problem until the minimum value D_{min} is found, which can still cause congestion on the target link.

3.2. Defendence Model

We compute frequently recurring bottleneck paths under routing policies within the ICARUS framework. This generates a critical edge set that identifies high-risk links along with their attack frequency. Edges with higher frequencies handle greater traffic volumes, making them the most vulnerable components of the LSN and highly susceptible to targeted attacks.

Under the K-Bottleneck Minimize strategy, each candidate path evaluates the overall vulnerability by accumulating the risk weights of the links it passes through and prioritizes paths with the smallest weights to avoid high-risk links. In this way, the most vulnerable high-capacity links in the network will be effectively bypassed. If attackers want to achieve the same destructive effect, they must use more bots or use higher bandwidth to attack multiple candidate links at the same time.

As illustrated in Figure 3a, adversaries first perform active probing from compromised terminals to map routing paths and then utilize this information to orchestrate DDoS attacks. As illustrated in Figure 3b, our routing mechanism strategically avoids these critical links. While attackers previously required minimal traffic to congest highly utilized bottleneck links, the diversion strategy forces them to generate significantly larger attack volumes, leveraging the high-capacity nature of ISLs to achieve comparable disruption.

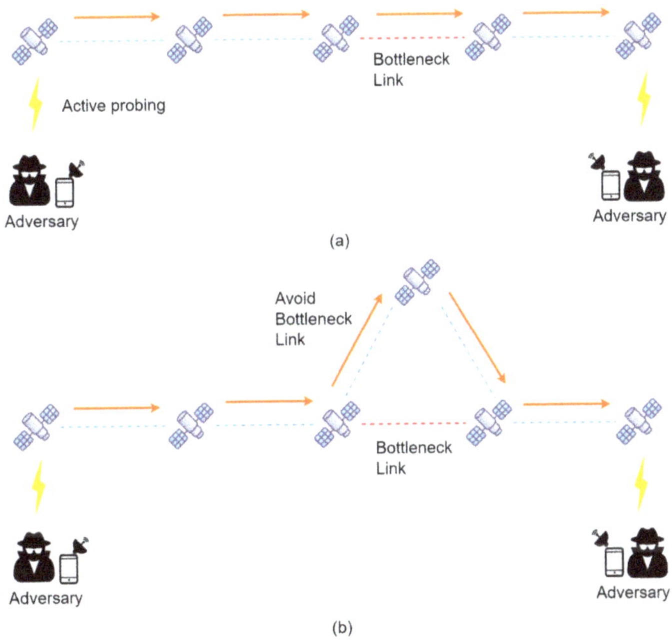

Figure 3. Mitigation DDoS attack through Bottleneck Minimize routing scheme. (**a**) Attacker probes to obtain LSN information; (**b**) Routing avoids the bottleneck link via alternate paths.

To characterize the distribution patterns of these metrics, we employ cumulative distribution function (CDF) plots. The CDF is a fundamental statistical function that characterizes the probability that a random variable X takes a value less than or equal to a specified threshold x, thereby capturing the overall distributional characteristics of the dataset. The formal definition of the CDF is given in Equation (5):

$$F_X(x) = P(X \leq x) \tag{5}$$

where X represents the random variable under analysis, and $F_X(x)$ quantifies the cumulative probability across the distribution. This approach enables evaluation of attack by mapping the likelihood of adversarial success under varying resource constraints.

4. Algorithm

The goal is to optimize multi-path selection while minimizing the bottleneck weight of paths, with the frequency of bottleneck path occurrences used as a weight. We adopted a custom approach that covetously iterates over the culling of edges.

We cluster the frequency distribution of statistically identified bottleneck edges within the network to establish systematical evaluation. Each bottleneck edge is assigned a vulnerability level through a nonlinear classification methodology that employs exponential scaling to amplify inter-category distinctions. This approach heightens sensitivity to high-risk scenarios during decision-making processes while quantitatively reflecting the cumulative risk impact of bottleneck edges on network-wide stability.

The goal is to extract up to k edge-disjoint paths from source s_d to destination t_d that minimize bottleneck weight, subject to latency and iteration constraints. Under no circumstances should the latency of any chosen path exceed that of an equivalent terrestrial fiber-optic link. As shown in Algorithm 1, we propose a K-Bottleneck Minimize algorithm to avoid the bottleneck risk path in LSN. The algorithm proceeds as follows:

Shortest-Path Search: Run a weighted Dijkstra on the current graph G (V, E). Find the shortest path from source satellite s_d to target satellite t_d. If no path exists, terminate.

Length Check and Edge Pruning: Measure the end-to-end path length of the candidate path. If it exceeds the fiber-equivalent bound, identify the single link with the greatest propagation delay, and mark it as unavailable.

Accept and Disjoint Enforcement: Once a path meets the length constraint, record it in the solution set, then remove its ISLs while permitting node reuse to ensure edge disjoint in subsequent iterations. Then, continue to calculate until paths are found or the attempt limit is reached.

Our network uses the Starlink S1 constellation, which means it has 1584 satellites, each with four ISLs, which means a total of 6336 ISLs. The number of k paths can be customized as needed. In our experiment, we fix the number of paths to 5. Following prior work [53], we first compute the fiber length by multiplying the great-circle distance between endpoints by a path-stretch factor of 1.53. We then estimate the one-way latency by dividing this length by the speed of light in fiber, which is approximately two-thirds of its vacuum value. We limit the maximum number of attempts to k + 3, and the majority of candidate paths are either pruned or accepted on the first search invocation, making secondary computation infrequent. By imposing a retry cap, the algorithm ensures sufficient flexibility to handle the pathological cases while bounding any excessive overhead from redundant re-search operations.

Algorithm 1. K-Bottleneck Minimize

Input: $G\ (V, E)$; source satellite s_d, target satellite t_d, fiber length *fiber_len*
Output: routing in $G\ (V, E)$

```
While count < k and attempt < max_attampts do
    Attempt ← Attempt + 1
    path ← Shortest Simple Path ( s_d, t_d, weight = 'Bottleneck_Weight')
    If path is None
        Break While
    End If
    If Length (path) > fiber_len
        max_edge ← edge with max length in path
        Set G [max_edge] not available
        Continue While
    End If
    Count ← count + 1
    ISL_edges ← Extract_ISL_Edges (path)
    If not ISL_edges
        Break While
    End If
    For edges in ISL_edges
        Remove edges in G (V, E)
    End For
    Return path_list
End While
```

5. Simulation and Result

5.1. Simulation Setup

The experiments were conducted under Ubuntu 20.04 LTS, and the hardware configuration included an Intel Core i5-13600K processor (14 cores, 20 threads, 3.5 GHz) and 32 GB DDR4 memory. This experiment is based on the open-source ICARUS model, using Python 3.7.16 and NetworkX 2.5.1. We use the S1 shell of the Starlink constellation for our LSN analysis. Table 2 shows our LSN setup parameters and values. In order to keep pace with the original model [21], we used the standardized bandwidth mentioned in the paper. The ISL bandwidth is 20 Gbps and the GSL bandwidth is 4 Gbps.

Table 2. LSN setup.

Parameters	Values
Satellite	1584
Orbits	72
Satellites per orbit	22
Elevation	550 km
Inclination	53°
Satellite-to-satellite Bandwidth	20 Gbps
Satellite-to-ground Bandwidth	4 Gbps

We first construct the LSN constellations by building the ISL topology from the given parameters, generating uniform grid points on the Earth's surface, and loading weighted, normalized GDP data. Ground–satellite coverage is computed at the minimum elevation angle, after which risk weights are assigned to all links. Then, source–destination pairs are randomly sampled according to grid weights. For each candidate path, bandwidth allocation is attempted: if every link on the path has sufficient residual capacity, the allocation is applied; otherwise, the path is discarded. We use an empty network without any benign traffic background in the network because it will be more of a resource burden for the attacker. Then, we execute our routing algorithm on these prepared topologies and finally execute the attack mechanism.

5.2. Result

As illustrated in Figure 4, the CDF of attacker costs demonstrates that our K-Bottleneck Minimize routing algorithm substantially increases adversarial resource requirements compared to K-SP and K-DG satellite routing schemes. The gradual ascent of the curve in low-cost regions suggests limited initial impact on path selection strategies, while its flattened progression in high-cost intervals reveals progressive cost escalation during sustained attacks, achieving our design objective. This cost inflation stems from attackers being compelled to select low-utilization paths rather than exploiting bottleneck links with concentrated traffic flows, thereby increasing total required attack traffic volume.

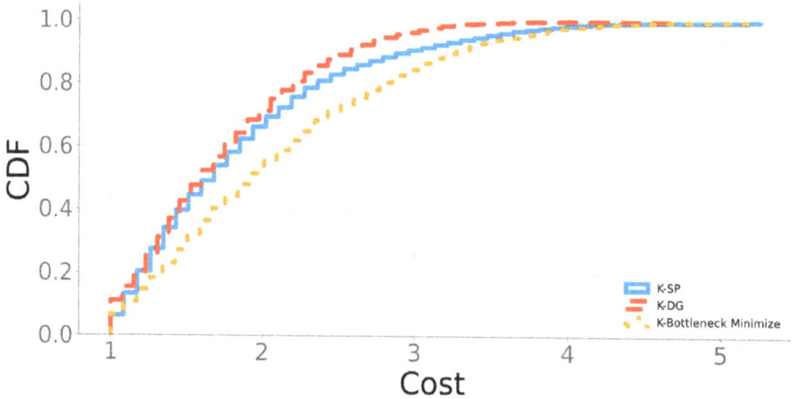

Figure 4. CDF of adversary's cost launching attack on LSN.

Figure 5 presents mean and median attack costs across compared algorithms. In Figure 5a, our proposed method achieves the highest average cost among all strategies, demonstrating improvements of 13.1% over K-SP and 21.6% over K-DG. In Figure 5b, it also attains the highest median cost, showing gains of 16.6% and 20.3% compared to K-SP and K-DG, respectively. These statistically significant increments validate the algorithm's effectiveness in elevating attack barriers, particularly crucial for large-scale LSN deployments. The elevated cost requirements indicate that potential attackers would need to coordinate botnets of a considerably larger scale to successfully penetrate such defenses. This inherent advantage not only enhances the security of LSN infrastructures but also creates substantial economic and operational barriers for would-be attackers, as the resource requirements for mounting effective attacks become prohibitively high.

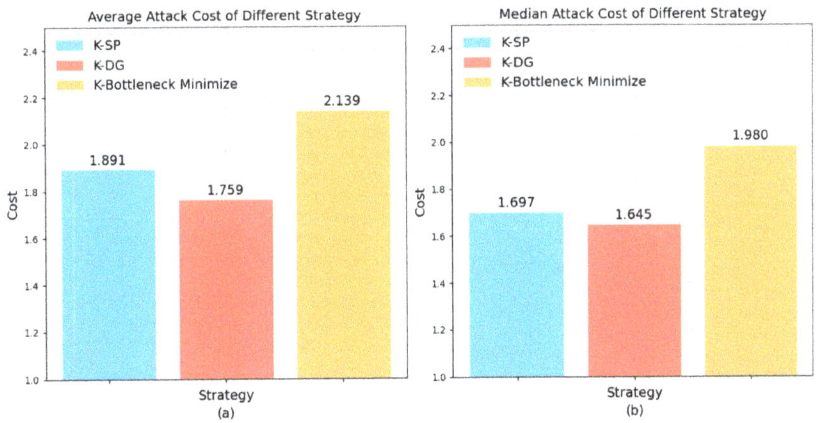

Figure 5. Attack cost of different strategy. (**a**) Average attack cost for each strategy; (**b**) Median attack cost for each strategy.

The detectability analysis in Figure 6 reveals that K-Bottleneck Minimize exhibits the highest MaxUp values among compared schemes, indicating greater susceptibility to satellite operator detection. This trend correlates with the cost CDF pattern, as achieving equivalent congestion effects under K-Bottleneck Minimize necessitates larger traffic volumes, thereby amplifying observable anomalies for network monitoring systems.

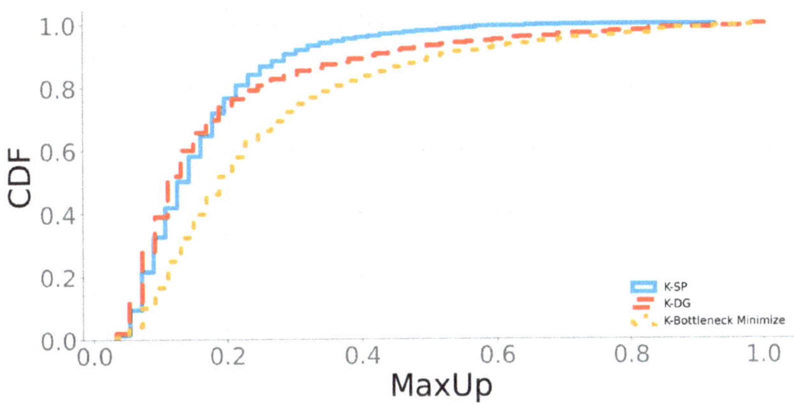

Figure 6. CDF of adversary MaxUp launching attack on LSN.

The experimental evaluation reveals the remarkable effectiveness of the K-Bottleneck Minimize strategy in defending against DDoS attacks. Figure 7 illustrates the average and median attack MaxUp values across the algorithms under comparison. As shown in Figure 7a, K-Bottleneck Minimize achieves an average MaxUp value of 0.251, which is 48.5% higher than the 0.169 average recorded by K-SP. This performance advantage extends to comparisons with K-DG, exceeding the K-DG average of 0.192 by 30.7%. In Figure 7b, when examining the median values, K-Bottleneck Minimize maintains its superiority with a 0.205 value, representing a 45.4% improvement over K-SP 0.141 median. The comparison shows an even more striking difference, where outperforms K-DG 0.131 median by 56.5%.

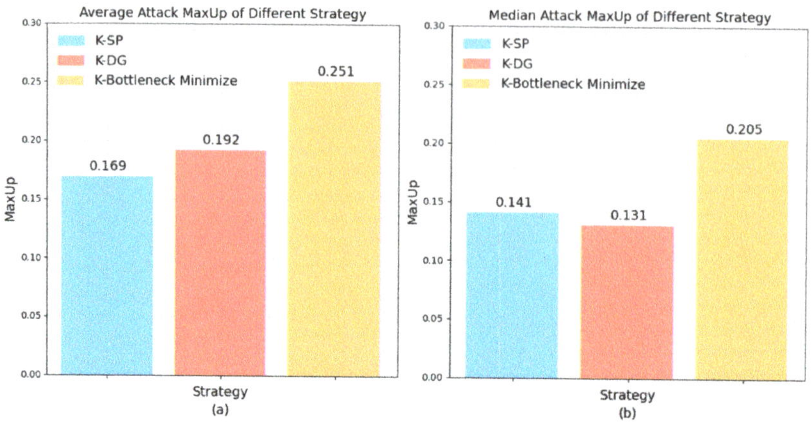

Figure 7. Attack MaxUp of different strategy. (**a**) Average attack MaxUp for each strategy; (**b**) Median attack MaxUp for each strategy.

These substantial improvements in MaxUp metrics directly translate to enhanced network security. The elevated thresholds force attackers to generate traffic surges of significantly greater magnitude, increasing the likelihood of anomalous patterns being detected. As a result, the deployment of K-Bottleneck Minimize not only imposes prohibitive resource demands on adversaries but also enables network administrators to more readily identify sudden traffic anomalies. This facilitates earlier detection of potential attacks and allows for more effective and timely threat mitigation.

5.3. Complexity Analysis

In terms of time complexity, K-SP's is finding the shortest k paths between sources by using the Yen's algorithm. In the worst case, however, every newly discovered path of length up to V may require enumerating all of its spur nodes, which incurs a base cost of $O(kV(E + VlogV))$. But once it is found that the actual length of a candidate path exceeds *fiber_len*, further spur enumeration of the path is stopped immediately. Let the average number of spur nodes for each path in the actual graph is N. Since $N \ll V$, the number of shortest path searches required during actual runtime is much less than the theoretical worst case. Then, it needs to repeat by k times to find paths. Hence, the end-to-end time complexity for K-SP routing is as follows:

$$O(kN(E + VlogV)) \tag{6}$$

The K-DG strategy iteratively invokes a single-source Dijkstra search to extract one shortest path per iteration and uses a *fiber_len* cutoff to prune in advance, costing $O(E + VlogV)$ each time. Once a path is accepted, its constituent ISLs, uplinks, or downlinks are pruned from the graph. If at any point the path contains no ISL segments, the algorithm terminates early. This iterative process continues until k paths have been found or no further paths exist, yielding the following total routing complexity:

$$O(k(E + VlogV)) \tag{7}$$

The core of the K-Bottleneck Minimize algorithm is its repeated invocation of single-source Dijkstra search under weighted risk metrics. A single Dijkstra run on a graph with V vertices and E edges require $O(E + VlogV)$ time when implemented with a binary-heap priority queue. Since we extract up to k edge-disjoint paths and allow a bounded number of retries, we perform $O(k)$ for such Dijkstra computations. As with the previous two strategies, we enforce the *fiber_len* bound. However, rather than simply discarding any path whose total length exceeds bound, we iteratively identify and remove its longest edge and re-run Dijkstra to obtain the next candidate. In each iteration, we also traverse the selected path of N edges in $O(N)$ time to check the cumulative length and to disable any individual edge that would push the path over the bound. Consequently, the overall time complexity of the routing procedure is as follows:

$$O(k(E + VlogV + N)) \quad (8)$$

The computation time cost of the three algorithms is shown in Figure 8.

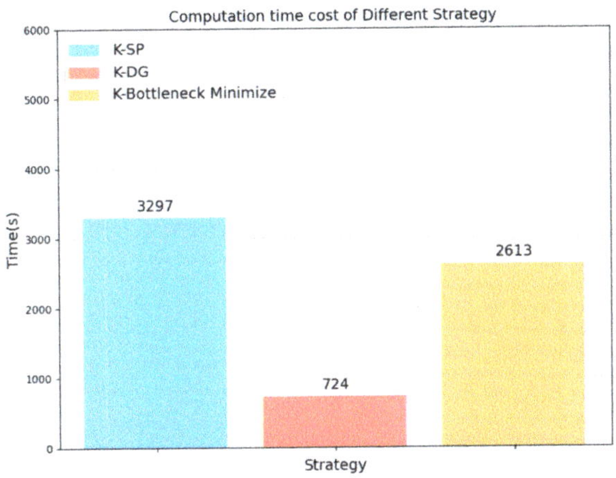

Figure 8. Computation time cost of different strategy.

We measure the computational cost of different algorithms by actual computation time. Under our experimental conditions, routing computation across the entire Starlink S1 constellation required 3297 s for K-SP, 724 s for K-DG, and 2613 s for K-Bottleneck Minimize. The markedly longer runtime of K-SP arises from its additional overhead: each new path generation invokes a spur-node search, and for every source–destination pair, K-SP exhaustively generates paths until it either finds all k routes or exhausts all feasible options, which leads to the highest total computation cost.

By contrast, both K-DG and K-Bottleneck Minimize terminate upon discovering the first ground–satellite–ground direct route. In K-DG, each time a path is successfully selected and appended to the result set, only one complete Dijkstra search is required; subsequent edge-pruning operations do not trigger further shortest-path computations, accounting for its reduced total runtime. K-Bottleneck Minimize likewise performs one Dijkstra search, but whenever a candidate path exceeds the length limit and its longest edge must be discarded, each retry entails another full shortest-path run. Its attempt-limit mechanism effectively curtails repeated computation when feasible paths are scarce, and if k valid paths cannot be assembled after multiple attempts, the algorithm terminates early—resulting in a total runtime above that of K-DG.

5.4. Limitation

In comparison to the K-SP strategy, our K-Bottleneck Minimize algorithm achieves a marked reduction in overall computational effort; however, it still incurs greater overhead than the K-DG approach. This limitation stems from the requirement that, whenever a candidate path violates the prescribed fiber-length bound, the algorithm must excise its single longest, high-risk edge and then re-invoke a full shortest-path computation under the risk metric. Although the maximum path length $O(N)$ is strictly bounded, each prune-and-recompute cycle carries a penalty. When such cycles are performed repeatedly, their aggregate contribution to total runtime becomes non-negligible.

6. Conclusions

This paper addresses DDoS attacks in LSN by introducing a K-Bottleneck Minimize routing algorithm. First, we leverage the ICARUS framework to measure each link's bottleneck occurrence frequency and map it into a nonlinear risk weight. Under the constraint that the end-to-end latency does not exceed the equivalent fiber-optic delay threshold, Dijkstra iteration weighted by bottleneck weights is used to generate up to k edge-disjoint paths by pruning ISL to avoid high-risk links.

Simulation on the Starlink S1 topology demonstrates that, relative to the classical K-SP approach, K-Bottleneck Minimize raises the average attacker cost by 13.1% and the median cost by 16.6%; against the K-DG algorithm, the corresponding gains are 21.6% and 20.3%. In terms of MaxUp, our method delivers a 48.5% increase in mean detection probability and a 45.4% uplift in the median compared to K-SP. Against K-DG, our method increases the mean MaxUp by 30.7% and the median by 56.5%. This proves that our algorithm can effectively improve the cost and detectability of attackers. This greatly increases the probability of attackers being detected.

The total computation times for K-SP, K-DG, and our K-Bottleneck Minimize algorithms are 3297 s, 724 s, and 2613 s, respectively. While K-DG remains the fastest, completing in roughly 4.5 times faster than K-SP. Our K-Bottleneck Minimize approach still achieves a reduction in routing-calculation time compared to K-SP and incurs an overhead relative to K-DG. Compared with the most common K-SP algorithm, our routing calculation time is still reduced, which shows that our algorithm still has room for application in large-scale satellite scenarios.

Our future work will focus on reducing time overhead by streamlining path pruning and using multi-objective optimization to balance latency and bandwidth and integrate continuous monitoring with load-aware controls. These refinements aim to deliver more efficient adaptive routing and further bolster DDoS resilience in LEO satellite systems.

Author Contributions: Conceptualization, F.M. and Y.Z. (Yuanjian Zhang); methodology, F.M. and Y.Z. (Yuanjian Zhang); software, F.M.; formal analysis, J.Y.; investigation, A.C. and R.L.; writing—original draft preparation, F.M.; writing—review and editing, F.M. and X.Y.; supervision, X.Y.; funding acquisition, X.Y. and Y.Z. (Yongli Zhao). All authors have read and agreed to the published version of the manuscript.

Funding: This work was supported in part by the National Natural Science Foundation of China under Grant 62206019.

Data Availability Statement: Data are contained within the article.

Conflicts of Interest: The authors declare no conflicts of interest.

References

1. Lai, Z.; Wang, Y.; Li, H.; Wu, Q.; Zhang, Q.; Hou, Y.; Liu, J.; Li, Y. Your Mega-Constellations Can Be Slim: A Cost-Effective Approach for Constructing Survivable and Performant LEO Satellite Networks. In Proceedings of the IEEE INFOCOM 2024-IEEE Conference on Computer Communications, Vancouver, BC, Canada, 20–23 May 2024; pp. 521–530.
2. Sun, Y.; Peng, M.; Zhang, S.; Lin, G.; Zhang, P. Integrated satellite-terrestrial networks: Architectures, key techniques, and experimental progress. *IEEE Netw.* **2022**, *36*, 191–198. [CrossRef]

3. Kodheli, O.; Lagunas, E.; Maturo, N.; Sharma, S.K.; Shankar, B.; Montoya, J.F.M.; Duncan, J.C.M.; Spano, D.; Chatzinotas, S.; Kisseleff, S. Satellite communications in the new space era: A survey and future challenges. *IEEE Commun. Surv. Tutor.* **2020**, *23*, 70–109. [CrossRef]
4. Luo, X.; Chen, H.-H.; Guo, Q. LEO/VLEO satellite communications in 6G and beyond networks–technologies, applications, and challenges. *IEEE Netw.* **2024**, *38*, 273–285. [CrossRef]
5. Cui, Y.; Xi, Z.; Zhang, X. A Game Between Cyber Attack and Defense Under the Topology of Satellite Networks. In Proceedings of the International Conference on Guidance, Navigation and Control, Changsha, China, 9–11 August 2024; pp. 5113–5125.
6. Starlink's Soaring Subscriber Milestone in 2024: A Closer Look at the Satellite Internet Service's Growth. Available online: https://newspaceeconomy.ca/2024/09/26/starlinks-soaring-subscriber-milestone-in-2024-a-closer-look-at-the-satellite-internet-services-growth/ (accessed on 30 April 2025).
7. McDowell, J. Jonathan's Space Pages. Available online: https://planet4589.org/space/stats/active.html (accessed on 8 April 2025).
8. FCC. *SpaceX Non-Geostationary Satellite System, Modification on Satellite Space Station Filing*; FCC: Washington, DC, USA, 2019.
9. Kim, H.; Lee, H.; Heo, J.; Bang, J.; Hong, D. Ephemeris-based Sum Capacity Enhancement in Multi-Satellite Communication Systems. *IEEE Trans. Veh. Technol.* **2025**, 1–14. [CrossRef]
10. Liu, K.; Wang, L.; Chen, M. Robust multifunctional single-tone training sequence for free-space optical communication in strong turbulence. *Opt. Express* **2025**, *33*, 21660–21677. [CrossRef]
11. Do, P.H.; Le, T.D.; Berezkin, A.; Kirichek, R. Optimizing Resource Allocation for Multi-beam Satellites Using Genetic Algorithm Variations. In Proceedings of the International Conference on Distributed Computer and Communication Networks, Moscow, Russia, 23–27 September 2024; pp. 16–29.
12. Yang, Y.; Wu, X.; Li, J.; Zang, J.; Lu, J.; Zgeib, R. Configuration Design Method of Mega Constellation for Low Earth Orbit Observation. *Space Sci. Technol.* **2024**, *4*, 0175. [CrossRef]
13. Wang, R.; Kishk, M.A.; Alouini, M.-S. Stochastic geometry-based low latency routing in massive LEO satellite networks. *IEEE Trans. Aerosp. Electron. Syst.* **2022**, *58*, 3881–3894. [CrossRef]
14. Kumar, R.; Arnon, S. Improving physical layer security of ground stations against geo satellite spoofing attacks. In Proceedings of the International Symposium on Cyber Security, Cryptology, and Machine Learning, Be'er Sheva, Israel, 19–20 December 2024; pp. 458–470.
15. Salim, S.; Moustafa, N.; Reisslein, M. Cybersecurity of satellite communications systems: A comprehensive survey of the space, ground, and links segments. *IEEE Commun. Surv. Tutor.* **2024**, *27*, 372–425. [CrossRef]
16. Manulis, M.; Bridges, C.P.; Harrison, R.; Sekar, V.; Davis, A. Cyber security in new space: Analysis of threats, key enabling technologies and challenges. *Int. J. Inf. Secur.* **2021**, *20*, 287–311. [CrossRef]
17. Lu, T.; Ding, X.; Shang, J.; Zhao, P.; Zhang, H. DoSat: A DDoS Attack on the Vulnerable Time-Varying Topology of LEO Satellite Networks. In Proceedings of the International Conference on Applied Cryptography and Network Security, Munich, Germany, 23–26 June 2025; pp. 265–282.
18. Guo, W.; Xu, J.; Pei, Y.; Yin, L.; Jiang, C.; Ge, N. A distributed collaborative entrance Defense framework against DDoS attacks on satellite internet. *IEEE Internet Things J.* **2022**, *9*, 15497–15510. [CrossRef]
19. Wang, Y.; Li, H.; Lai, Z.; Li, J. StarMaze: Ring-based Attack in Satellite Internet Constellations. In Proceedings of the 2024 IEEE/ACM 32nd International Symposium on Quality of Service (IWQoS), Guangzhou, China, 19–21 June 2024; pp. 1–10.
20. Ribeiro, A. Cydome Analyzes Lab Dookhtegan Cyber Attack on Iranian Oil Tankers, Provides Mitigation Action. Available online: https://industrialcyber.co/transport/cydome-analyzes-lab-dookhtegan-cyber-attack-on-iranian-oil-tankers-provides-mitigation-action/ (accessed on 19 March 2025).
21. Giuliari, G.; Ciussani, T.; Perrig, A.; Singla, A. {ICARUS}: Attacking low earth orbit satellite networks. In Proceedings of the 2021 USENIX Annual Technical Conference (USENIX ATC 21), Santa Clara, CA, USA, 14–16 July 2021; pp. 317–331.
22. Kim, J.; Nam, J.; Lee, S.; Yegneswaran, V.; Porras, P.; Shin, S. BottleNet: Hiding network bottlenecks using SDN-based topology deception. *IEEE Trans. Inf. Forensics Secur.* **2021**, *16*, 3138–3153. [CrossRef]
23. Yan, Y.; Han, G.; Xu, H. A survey on secure routing protocols for satellite network. *J. Netw. Comput. Appl.* **2019**, *145*, 102415. [CrossRef]
24. Ibrahim, H.; Shouman, M.A.; El-Fishawy, N.A.; Ahmed, A. Literature review of blockchain technology in space industry: Challenges and applications. In Proceedings of the 2021 International Conference on Electronic Engineering (ICEEM), Menouf, Egypt, 3–4 July 2021; pp. 1–8.
25. Sharafian, A.; Ali, A.; Ullah, I.; Khalifa, T.R.; Bai, X.; Qiu, L. Fuzzy adaptive control for consensus tracking in multiagent systems with incommensurate fractional-order dynamics: Application to power systems. *Inf. Sci.* **2025**, *689*, 121455. [CrossRef]
26. Sharafian, A.; Naeem, H.Y.; Ullah, I.; Ali, A.; Qiu, L.; Bai, X. Resilience to deception attacks in consensus tracking control of incommensurate fractional-order power systems via adaptive RBF neural network. *Expert Syst. Appl.* **2025**, *283*, 127763. [CrossRef]
27. Zhuo, M.; Liu, L.; Zhou, S.; Tian, Z. Survey on security issues of routing and anomaly detection for space information networks. *Sci. Rep.* **2021**, *11*, 22261. [CrossRef]

28. Yang, Y.; Yin, X.; Shi, X.; Wang, Z.; He, J.; Fu, T.Z.; Winslett, M. Inter-domain routing bottlenecks and their aggravation. *Comput. Netw.* **2019**, *162*, 106839. [CrossRef]
29. Deng, Y.; Wu, Q.; Lai, Z.; Gu, C.; Li, H.; Li, Y.; Liu, J. Time-varying Bottleneck Links in LEO Satellite Networks: Identification, Exploits, and Countermeasures. In Proceedings of the Network and Distributed System Security Symposium, San Diego, CA, USA, 16–17 February 1995.
30. Zhang, Y.; Wu, Q.; Lai, Z.; Li, H. Enabling low-latency-capable satellite-ground topology for emerging LEO satellite networks. In Proceedings of the IEEE INFOCOM 2022-IEEE Conference on Computer Communications, Virtual, 2–5 May 2022; pp. 1329–1338.
31. Guo, B.; Zhang, Z.; Atapattu, S.; Pan, M.; Yan, Y.; Xiong, Z.; Li, H. Enabling Real-time Computing and Transmission Services in Large-Scale LEO Satellite Networks. *IEEE Trans. Veh. Technol.* **2025**. [CrossRef]
32. Pultarova, T. Starlink Satellites: Facts, Tracking and Impact on Astronomy. Available online: https://www.space.com/spacex-starlink-satellites.html (accessed on 30 April 2025).
33. Pearlman, R.Z. SpaceX Launches 28 Starlink Satellites to Orbit on 1st Half of Spaceflight Doubleheader (Video, Photos). Available online: https://www.space.com/space-exploration/launches-spacecraft/spacex-launches-28-starlink-satellites-to-orbit-on-1st-half-of-spaceflight-doubleheader-photos (accessed on 30 April 2025).
34. How Many Satellites Does Musk's Starlink Have in Orbit? An Expert Analysis. Available online: https://www.historytools.org/companies/how-many-satellites-does-musks-starlink-have-in-orbit?utm_source (accessed on 30 April 2025).
35. Chen, Q.; Giambene, G.; Yang, L.; Fan, C.; Chen, X. Analysis of inter-satellite link paths for LEO mega-constellation networks. *IEEE Trans. Veh. Technol.* **2021**, *70*, 2743–2755. [CrossRef]
36. Gomez-del-Hoyo, P.; Samczynski, P. Starlink-based passive radar for Earth's surface imaging: First experimental results. *IEEE J. Sel. Top. Appl. Earth Obs. Remote Sens.* **2024**, *17*, 13949–13965. [CrossRef]
37. Studer, A.; Perrig, A. The coremelt attack. In Proceedings of the European Symposium on Research in Computer Security, Bydgoszcz, Poland, 16–20 September 2024; pp. 37–52.
38. Kang, M.S.; Lee, S.B.; Gligor, V.D. The crossfire attack. In Proceedings of the 2013 IEEE symposium on security and privacy, San Francisco, CA, USA, 19–22 May 2013; pp. 127–141.
39. Hildebrand, C. Satellite Companies, ISPs Feeling the Heat from Hackers. Available online: https://www.netscout.com/blog/satellite-companies-isps-feeling-heat-hackers (accessed on 30 April 2025).
40. Sarkar, S.; Datta, R. A secure and energy-efficient stochastic multipath routing for self-organized mobile ad hoc networks. *Ad Hoc Netw.* **2016**, *37*, 209–227. [CrossRef]
41. Bhattacharya, A.; Sinha, K. An efficient protocol for load-balanced multipath routing in mobile ad hoc networks. *Ad Hoc Netw.* **2017**, *63*, 104–114. [CrossRef]
42. Nie, W.; Chen, Y.; Wang, Y.; Wang, P.; Li, M.; Ning, L. Routing networking technology based on improved ant colony algorithm in space-air-ground integrated network. *EURASIP J. Adv. Signal Process.* **2024**, *2024*, 34. [CrossRef]
43. Zhang, S.; Li, X.; Yeung, K.L. Segment routing for traffic engineering and effective recovery in low-earth orbit satellite constellations. *Digit. Commun. Netw.* **2024**, *10*, 706–715. [CrossRef]
44. Fratty, R.; Saar, Y.; Kumar, R.; Arnon, S. Random routing algorithm for enhancing the cybersecurity of LEO satellite networks. *Electronics* **2023**, *12*, 518. [CrossRef]
45. de La Beaujardiere, J.; Mital, R.; Mital, R. Blockchain application within a multi-sensor satellite architecture. In Proceedings of the IGARSS 2019-2019 IEEE International Geoscience and Remote Sensing Symposium, Yokohama, Japan, 28 July–2 August 2019; pp. 5293–5296.
46. Song, J.; Ju, Y.; Wang, Y.; Zou, Y.; Deng, C.; Yuan, X.; Chen, C. Blockchain Identity Authentication-Aided Trustworthy Multicast Routing Strategy for LEO Satellite Networks. In Proceedings of the 2023 IEEE International Conferences on Internet of Things (iThings) and IEEE Green Computing & Communications (GreenCom) and IEEE Cyber, Physical & Social Computing (CPSCom) and IEEE Smart Data (SmartData) and IEEE Congress on Cybermatics (Cybermatics), Danzhou, China, 17–21 December 2023; pp. 256–261.
47. Huang, Y.; Yang, D.; Feng, B.; Tian, A.; Dong, P.; Yu, S.; Zhang, H. A GNN-enabled multipath routing algorithm for spatial-temporal varying LEO satellite networks. *IEEE Trans. Veh. Technol.* **2023**, *73*, 5454–5468. [CrossRef]
48. Liu, Z.; Rong, J.; Jiang, Y.; Zhang, L. Satellite network security routing technology based on deep learning and trust management. *Sensors* **2023**, *23*, 8474. [CrossRef]
49. Li, H.; Shi, D.; Wang, W.; Liao, D.; Gadekallu, T.R.; Yu, K. Secure routing for LEO satellite network survivability. *Comput. Netw.* **2022**, *211*, 109011. [CrossRef]
50. Liu, Z.; Zhu, J.; Zhang, J.; Liu, Q. Routing algorithm design of satellite network architecture based on SDN and ICN. *Int. J. Satell. Commun. Netw.* **2020**, *38*, 1–15. [CrossRef]
51. Tanveer, H.B.; Puchol, M.; Singh, R.; Bianchi, A.; Nithyanand, R. Making sense of constellations: Methodologies for understanding starlink's scheduling algorithms. In Proceedings of the Companion of the 19th International Conference on Emerging Networking EXperiments and Technologies, Paris, France, 5–8 December 2023; pp. 37–43.

52. Brodkin, J. SpaceX Starlink Speeds Revealed as Beta Users Get Downloads of 11 to 60 Mbps. Available online: https://arstechnica.com/information-technology/2020/08/spacex-starlink-beta-tests-show-speeds-up-to-60mbps-latency-as-low-as-31ms/ (accessed on 25 May 2025).
53. Singla, A.; Chandrasekaran, B.; Godfrey, P.B.; Maggs, B. The internet at the speed of light. In Proceedings of the 13th ACM Workshop on Hot Topics in Networks, Los Angeles, CA, USA, 27–28 October 2014; pp. 1–7.

electronics

MDPI

Article

A Practical Human-Centric Risk Management (HRM) Methodology

Kitty Kioskli [1,*], Eleni Seralidou [1] and Nineta Polemi [1,2]

[1] trustilio B.V., Vijzelstraat 68, 1017 HL Amsterdam, The Netherlands; eleni.seralidou@trustilio.com (E.S.); nineta.polemi@trustilio.com (N.P.)
[2] Department of Informatics, University of Piraeus, 185 34 Piraeus, Greece
* Correspondence: kitty.kioskli@trustilio.com

Abstract: Various standards (e.g., ISO 27000x, ISO 31000:2018) and methodologies (e.g., NIST SP 800-53, NIST SP 800-37, NIST SP 800-161, ETSI TS 102 165-1, NISTIR 8286) are available for risk assessment. However, these standards often overlook the human element. Studies have shown that adversary profiles (AP), which detail the maturity of attackers, significantly affect vulnerability assessments and risk calculations. Similarly, the maturity of the users interacting with the Information and Communication Technologies (ICT) system in adopting security practices impacts risk calculations. In this paper, we identify and estimate the maturity of user profiles (UP) and propose an enhanced risk assessment methodology, HRM (based on ISO 27001), that incorporates the human element into the risk evaluation. Social measures, such as awareness programs, training, and behavioral interventions, alongside technical controls, are included in the Human-Centric Risk Management (HRM) risk treatment phase. These measures enhance user security hygiene and resilience, reducing risks and ensuring comprehensive security strategies in SMEs.

Keywords: human-centric risk management; adversary profiles; user maturity; socio-technical risk assessment; cyber psychology

1. Introduction

Human threats pose significant risks to Information and Communication Technologies (ICT) system security but are often overlooked in traditional risk management. These threats include malicious or unintentional actions like unauthorized access, intellectual property theft, system sabotage, and user errors. They exploit human vulnerabilities such as lack of awareness, inadequate security culture, poor cyber hygiene, and low cyber maturity among users. Factors like a lack of training, stress, cognitive issues, and multitasking further exacerbate these risks. Attackers often use social engineering techniques to manipulate users into compromising security through methods like phishing and disinformation.

ISO 27001 mandates regular risk assessments to identify and mitigate potential threats and vulnerabilities, including those related to human factors. Effective risk management should consider security culture, employee behavior, and psychological profiles. Tailored risk treatment measures should include both technical controls and social interventions such as awareness programs, training, and co-creation workshops. Small Medium Enterprises (SMEs) should begin by identifying employee vulnerabilities and implementing targeted social controls to reduce these risks.

The Human-Centric Risk Management (HRM) methodology proposed in this paper integrates socio-psychological techniques with existing technical risk management tools to address human threats. HRM uses open-source risk management tools (e.g., ENISA,

 https://doi.org/10.3390/electronics14030486

OWASP, MISP, Cyberwatching) and co-creation workshops to identify and estimate human-related vulnerabilities and effectively manage these risks.

The rest of the paper is organized as follows:

1.1. Human-Centric Risk Management (HRM) Objectives and Main Principles

The Human-Centric Risk Management (HRM) methodology integrates human factor considerations into the ISO 27001 framework [1], enabling SMEs to manage their security risks more effectively by incorporating profiles of their ICT users (e.g., administrators, defenders, operators, employees, third parties). HRM proactively identifies and addresses human threats, implementing best practices for security management to strengthen SMEs' overall security posture and protect valuable assets from evolving cyber threats.

Numerous standards (e.g., ISO 27000x [2], ISO 31000:2018 [3]) and methodologies (e.g., NIST SP 800-53, NIST SP 800-37 [4]) exist for risk assessment, evaluating cybersecurity risks for each threat as the product of vulnerabilities (weaknesses) of the assets, impact (consequences), and the frequency and probability of the threats occurring:

$$\text{Risk} = \text{Threat (T)} \times \text{Vulnerability (V)} \times \text{Impact (I)} \tag{1}$$

Alternatively, the literature sometimes defines risk as [5,6]:

$$\text{Likelihood (L)} = \text{Threat (T)} \times \text{Vulnerability (V)} \tag{2}$$

$$\text{Risk} = \text{Likelihood (L)} \times \text{Impact (I)} \tag{3}$$

However, these standard evaluations often overlook the threats related to adversaries or ICT users. Several studies [7–9] have shown that adversaries' profiles (AP) (i.e., traits that impact the maturity of the adversary to conduct a successful attack) affect the estimation of vulnerabilities and, consequently, the calculation of risks. Specifically, Study [7] analyzed the role of attackers' technical skills and resources in determining the likelihood of exploitation. Study [8] focused on the psychological and behavioral traits of adversaries, highlighting how motivations and persistence influence attack outcomes. Study [9] examined sector-specific adversary capabilities, showing how threat actors' knowledge of organizational systems impacts the success rate of cyberattacks. Similarly, ICT user profiles (UP) (i.e., traits that impact their maturity to adopt secure behavior) influence risk estimation and treatment plans, necessitating both technical and social measures (e.g., awareness raising, training, behavior change interventions, co-creation workshops).

Existing standards and methodologies focus on technical controls to treat risks, often ignoring the necessary social mitigation measures that help ICT users strengthen their personal security hygiene and resilience to cyber-attacks. These social measures reduce human vulnerabilities and the occurrence of human threats, ultimately decreasing risks and ensuring appropriate technical and human-related controls are implemented within the specific operational environment of the SME.

HRM delves deeper into the human element of users who defend and interact with the SME's ICT to identify human threats and vulnerabilities, proposing targeted technical and social controls that can be easily adopted by employees. HRM methodology proposes that the traditional risk models can be enhanced by considering the strength of the Adversary Profile (AP) and the minimum strength of ICT User Profiles (UPs):

$$\text{Risk} = \text{T} \times \text{V} \times \text{I} \times \text{AP} \times 1/\text{UP} \tag{4}$$

or alternatively:

$$\text{Risk} = \text{L} \times \text{I} \times \text{AP} \times 1/\text{UP} \tag{5}$$

HRM's compliance with ISO 27001, with its emphasis on human factors, ensures a holistic approach to risk management that effectively reduces human vulnerabilities and strengthens cybersecurity resilience within SMEs.

1.2. HRM Tools for Estimating Technical Risks

Any available open-source risk assessment (RA) and Risk Management (RM) tool can be used to assess technical cyber risks as for example the ENISA, OWASP, MISP, and Cyberwatching tools:

The ENISA Risk Management (RM) Toolbox [10] is a toolbox that includes methodologies for risk assessment, treatment options, incident response procedures, and guidelines for developing cybersecurity policies. It interprets risk scenarios using its own terminology, asset classifications, and threat taxonomies, standardizing results to a common risk matrix for comparable outcomes. The ENISA toolbox offers guidance, templates, and best practices for risk assessment, treatment, and communication in cybersecurity risk management.

The OWASP Risk Assessment Calculator [11,12] is a tool that helps organizations conduct risk assessments focused on web application security, identifying and prioritizing risks based on impact, likelihood, and exposure. Key features include risk identification, analysis, prioritization, documentation, and customization. The OWASP Risk Assessment Calculator enhances web application security and helps mitigate cybersecurity risks proactively.

The MISP Project [13] is an open-source Threat Intelligence and Sharing Platform that facilitates the exchange of threat intelligence and Indicators of Compromise (IoCs) related to malware, attacks, and other threats within a trusted community. It uses a distributed model to share technical and non-technical information in closed, semi-private, or open communities. This enhances the detection of targeted attacks, improves accuracy, and reduces false positives. According to MISP documentation, it is used to store, share, and collaborate on cybersecurity indicators and malware analysis, as well as to detect and prevent attacks, frauds, or threats against ICT infrastructures, organizations, or individuals. MISP is designed for information sharing rather than risk management.

The Cyberwatching Cyber Risk Temperature Tool [14] consists of a questionnaire divided into two main sections: the first asks the respondent to provide a personal evaluation of their company's IT security, while the second includes technical questions. The questions cover various topics to analyze the company in different areas, such as:

- Specific knowledge of the company's cybersecurity;
- The methodologies employed within the company;
- The distribution of administrative fees on systems;
- The information segmentation policy;
- Authentication policies for accessing corporate systems;
- Previous assessments conducted.

Based on their scores, SMEs will be categorized into different profiles according to their vulnerability level.

1.3. HRM Socio-Psychological Instruments for Estimating Social Risks

Socio-psychological instruments play a crucial role in managing human threats within the context of risk management by assessing and mitigating the impact of human factors on cybersecurity and organizational safety. These instruments evaluate psychological and social behaviors that influence security practices. For instance, the Security Behavior Intentions scale measures attitudes toward security behaviors like password management and software updates, which are essential for maintaining robust cybersecurity practices [15].

Moreover, addressing psychosocial risks in the workplace is integral to a comprehensive risk management approach. Psychosocial risks, such as excessive workloads, lack of role clarity, and inadequate managerial support can lead to stress, anxiety, and depression, negatively impacting employees' mental health and increasing their vulnerability to cyber threats. Structured interventions, including training programs and awareness campaigns, are necessary to enhance employees' mental health and mitigate these vulnerabilities.

By incorporating socio-psychological factors into the risk management framework, organizations can better understand and address the human elements that contribute to security risks. This holistic approach improves the overall security posture and resilience against cyber threats, as it considers both technical and human aspects of cybersecurity [16].

HRM uses the Behavior Model (B=MAT) developed by Fogg [17] to identify the type of cue needed to encourage the appropriate action, depending on an individual's motivation and ability to perform the act. According to Fogg, the likelihood of a behavior (B) occurring is a product of Motivation (M), Ability (A), and the appropriate Trigger (T), and hence this is referred to as the B=MAT model.

Models such as the Five Factor Theory (FFT) and behavioral theories like Fogg's B=MAT model provide frameworks for understanding motivations and actions. These models can be used to analyze the security behaviors of users.

In HRM, we use extended psychological profiles as defined in [18] to analyze not only motivations, abilities, and triggers (Fogg's model) but also personality traits and social characteristics.

Cyber profiling is the instrument used to identify human threats and vulnerabilities of ICT users as a proactive measure to select targeted social controls that will reduce employees' vulnerabilities to human threats. HRM methodology uses a multidimensional cyber psychological profile for users to evaluate the factors that determine secure behaviors.

Co-creation workshops are also used to develop a comprehensive and effective risk treatment plan. These workshops are participatory events where ICT users collaborate. The adoption of security measures is streamlined through these workshops, designed to directly engage users in the development process, thereby enhancing the likelihood of triggering secure behavior. The fundamental goal of HRM co-creation workshops is to leverage the collective intelligence and diverse psychological profiles of ICT users, a strategy shown to foster broader engagement in cybersecurity practices [19].

Key features of HRM co-creation workshops include:

- **Diversity of Participants**: These workshops prioritize the inclusion of a diverse range of ICT users, such as organizational insiders (e.g., CISOs, risk managers, incident handlers, defenders, administrators, and general employees), suppliers or supply chain partners, and third parties (e.g., suppliers, auditors, external penetration testers). This diversity is crucial for capturing a wide array of perspectives and experiences, which enriches the security discourse [20];
- **Collaboration**: Participants are encouraged to collaborate in a structured setting, facilitated by experienced leaders. This approach mirrors effective teamwork strategies that are essential for problem-solving and innovation in cybersecurity [21];
- **Interactive Activities**: Employing methods such as brainstorming sessions, design thinking exercises, and prototyping fosters a creative and engaging environment. These activities are foundational to generating practical and innovative solutions [22];
- **Risk Treatment Generation and Refinement**: The workshops focus on co-developing a comprehensive set of social and technical measures that ICT users embrace and comprehend, which are refined through collaboration into viable security controls. This process aligns with best practices in risk management [23].

Co-creation workshops with various stakeholders enhance innovation and ensure relevant outcomes. Bringing together company management, ICT users, supply chain partners, industrial collaborators, policymakers, and researchers, these workshops develop effective risk mitigation plans and policies. Ramaswamy and Ozcan [24] highlight the strategic advantage of co-creation in fostering innovation and competitive advantage. By incorporating diverse perspectives, these workshops produce user-centric solutions, leading to higher adoption rates and greater stakeholder satisfaction. HRM supports the idea that security policies are better embraced when all ICT users and stakeholders participate in their creation.

HRM has developed an extended profile based on traits that identify ICT users' secure behavior and adversaries' profiles as have been developed by the authors [18] and outlined in this paper.

2. Comprehensive User and Adversary Profiling for Enhanced Cybersecurity Readiness

2.1. ICT User Profile (UP)

The proposed traits (Table 1) in the ICT user profile (UP) that define their maturity in adopting security practices include personality traits, social characteristics, technical skills, and capabilities relevant to their business roles within the SME. For instance, security professionals (e.g., CISOs, Risk Managers, auditors) are expected to possess skills defined in the European Cybersecurity Skills Framework (ECSF) [25], while general employees should have skills related to personal cyber hygiene [4,26].

Table 1. HRM-multi dimensional profile of ICT user with secure behavior example (source: created by the authors).

HRM ICT Users' Profiles (HRM-UP)	
Personality Traits	
Vigilance	Consistently remains alert and attentive to potential security threats, and is proactive in identifying and addressing suspicious activities.
Responsibility, Curiosity	Takes full ownership of their role, with an innate curiosity that drives them to deepen their understanding of cybersecurity threats and vulnerabilities.
Adaptable-Openness to experiences	Displays flexibility and openness to new security technologies, strategies, and approaches that enhance their security posture. Possesses a blend of intellect and creativity, demonstrates originality, and shows a keen scientific interest alongside a spirit of adventurousness.
Resilient	Has the capacity to cope with stress, setbacks, and failures, demonstrating resilience by quickly bouncing back and steadfastly maintaining a strong focus on achieving security objectives.
Social Traits	
Social exposure	Adapts to conventional social norms with ease, excelling in forging strong bonds with each co-worker. Collaborates effectively with colleagues, security teams, and external partners to tackle security challenges, sharing information and insights for collective benefit.
Conventional relationships	Effortlessly establishes professional virtual relationships, fostering collaborations and creating synergies.
Ethical	Individuals with integrity prioritize honesty, transparency, and respect, steadfastly adhering to ethical principles and professional codes of conduct.

Personal cyber hygiene practices encompass using strong passwords, regularly updating software, using reputable antivirus software, avoiding public Wi-Fi for sensitive transactions, recognizing and avoiding phishing attempts, regularly backing up data, reviewing and adjusting privacy settings, ensuring secure file sharing, and maintaining physical security.

Additional traits proposed in Table 1 include motivations that encourage secure user behavior, as well as triggers (opportunities/measures) that SMEs can adopt.

The assessment of secure behavior levels among ICT users is facilitated through the use of anonymized questionnaires, a method supported by research indicating its effectiveness in gathering sensitive data [27].

To select appropriate social measures for improving security behavior, co-creation workshops are employed.

2.2. Adversary Profile (AP)

Similarly, the estimated attackers' profile proposed by Kioskli and Polemi [28] (see Table 2) offers a comprehensive, multi-dimensional, and measurable profile of attackers based on psychological, behavioral, societal, and technical abilities, as well as personality traits, using the Five Factor Model (FFM) and Fogg's Behavioral Model.

Table 2. Estimated Attackers' Profiles (HRM-AP) [28].

Personality Traits	Description and Examples
Extraversion	Gregariousness (e.g., social engagement in attackers' groups); assertiveness/outspokenness (e.g., leadership skills); activity/energy level (e.g., enjoys a busy life); positive emotions/mood (e.g., happiness)
Conscientiousness	Orderliness/Neatness (e.g., well-organized) Striving/Perseverance (e.g., aims to achieve excellence) Self-Discipline (e.g., persistent engagement to goals) Dutifulness/Carefulness (e.g., strong sense of duty), Self-Efficacy (e.g., confidence to achieve goals)
Openness to experiences	Intellect/Creativity Imaginative (e.g., intellectual style) Scientifically Interested/Originality (e.g., evidence-based) Adventurousness (e.g., experiences of different things)
Social—Behavioral Traits	**Description and Examples**
Selected social exposure	Difficult to adapt to conventional social norms (e.g., events) Easy to build virtual anonymous, professional relationships (e.g., using anonymous identity has contacts with other attackers in the Deep Web) Easy to build strong e-bonds in hacking communities (e.g., these communities are closed to the public)
Not conventional relationships	Difficult to build physical relationships or contacts Easy to build professional (with other attackers) virtual, anonymous relationships under their moral code (us versus them approach)
Not talkative	Difficult to initiate small casual talk or social talk Difficult to express him/herself
Manipulative	Easy manipulating people via electronic means (e.g., phishing)

2.3. Measuring Profiles

The HRM profile calculations (UP and AP) adopt the scales in [29], where indicative measures are proposed (see Table 3):

Table 3. HRM-Quantification of UP/AP (Source: created by the authors).

Levels	Description	Semi-Quantitative Values		UP/AP Score of Profile	Indicative Social Measures Needed
Very High (VH)-5	Sophisticated	96–100	10	>96% of each of the traits in each category	social and technical threat intelligence updates, ethical training, advance cybersecurity exercises

Table 3. *Cont.*

Levels	Description	Semi-Quantitative Values		UP/AP Score of Profile	Indicative Social Measures Needed
High (H)-4	Experienced	80–95	8	>80%	ethical training, cybersecurity exercises, social and technical threat intelligence updates, ethical training
Medium (M)-3	Moderate	21–79	5	>21%	secure behavior intervention, training in operational cybersecurity, cybersecurity exercises
Basic (B)-2	Basic	5–20	2	>5%	awareness, secure behavior interventions, training in operational cybersecurity exercises
Low (I)-1	Insufficient	1–4	0	<5%	awareness, secure behavior interventions, training in basic concepts, basic cyber exercises

3. Phases of the HRM Methodology and Implementation

The HRM methodology comprises the following three main phases according to standards (Figure 1):

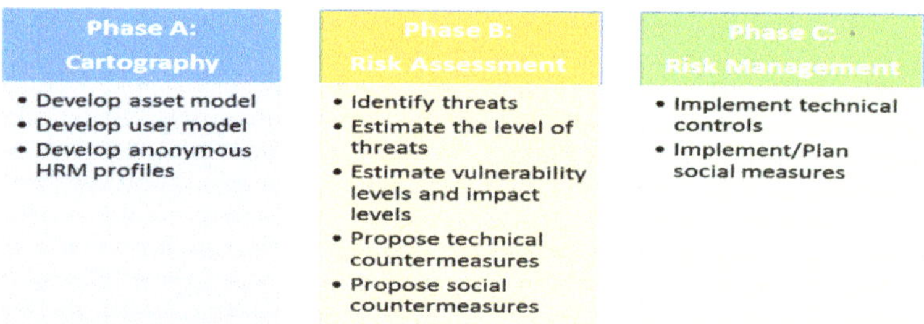

Figure 1. HRM phases (source: created by the authors).

3.1. Phase A: Cartography (Set Boundaries)

A1: Develop asset inventory

An inventory of all assets under assessment should be developed and maintained, recording details such as in Table 4:

Table 4. Asset inventory example (source: created by the authors).

	General Information	Technical Specifications	Location and Owner	Network Configuration (for Servers)	Implementation of Controls—History of Updates
1	Asset ID: Unique identifier for each piece of equipment.	Processor: Type and speed of the processor.	Location: Physical location of the asset.	IP Address: Network IP address.	Controls implemented
2	Asset Type: Differentiates between PCs and servers.	RAM: Amount of memory in GB.	Owner of Asset (Assigned to): Name of the employee responsible for the asset.	Role: Function or role of the server (e.g., file server, web server).	Update history of controls

Table 4. *Cont.*

	General Information	Technical Specifications	Location and Owner	Network Configuration (for Servers)	Implementation of Controls—History of Updates
3	Brand/Model: Specific model of the hardware.	Storage: Size and type of storage (e.g., SSD, HDD).	Owner/User(s) of asset: interacting entity.	-	Testing date of controls
4	Serial Number: Manufacturer's serial number. Date of purchase	Operating System: Installed operating system and version.	-	-	-

A2: Model the interaction of the assets

Provide diagrams that identify the interrelations of the assets under assessment using a Business Model Processing (BMP) tool using specific symbolism e.g., solid lines with arrows indicate the direction of data flow between devices (e.g., from workstations to servers, servers to storage). Dotted lines might indicate wireless connections or less direct interactions (e.g., mobile devices connecting via Wi-Fi). An example of an asset model is (Figure 2):

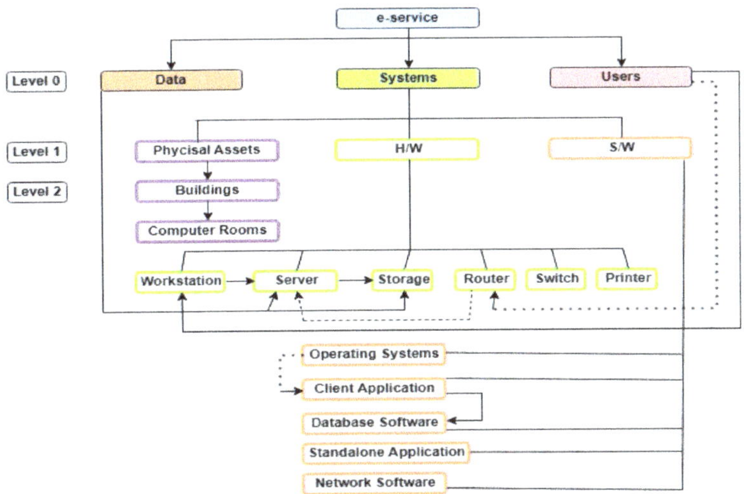

Figure 2. Asset model (source: created by the authors).

There are various open-source BPM tools that can be used e.g., bpmn.io "https://bpmn.io/ (accessed on 15 December 2024)", Modelio "https://www.modelio.org/index.htm (accessed on 15 December 2024)", Camunda Modeler "https://camunda.com/ (accessed on 15 December 2024)", Bizagi Modeler "https://bizagi.com/en (accessed on 15 December 2024)", Bonita BPM "https://www.bonitasoft.com/ (accessed on 15 December 2024)", Activiti "https://www.activiti.org/ (accessed on 15 December 2024)", jBPM "https://www.jbpm.org/ (accessed on 15 December 2024)", and ADONIS: Community Edition "https://www.adonis-community.com/en/ (accessed on 15 December 2024)".

A3: Develop user model

Identify all ICT users (found in phase A1 above for all assets under assessment) that own or use the asset(s) of the ICT system which is in the perimeter of this assessment. Develop a user inventory including information, e.g., as shown in the next table (Table 5):

Table 5. User inventory (source: created by the authors).

	User ID: 001	User ID: 002	...
General Information	Name: Full name of the employee/Role/Location/Contact	...	-
System and Credential System Access	Privileges, List of systems the user has access to (e.g., CRM, ERP, Email),	...	-
Supervisor and Interrelations	Direct supervisor or manager interactions with other users (model interaction)	...	-

Furthermore, there exists a user model describing the interaction among users, e.g., in Figure 3:

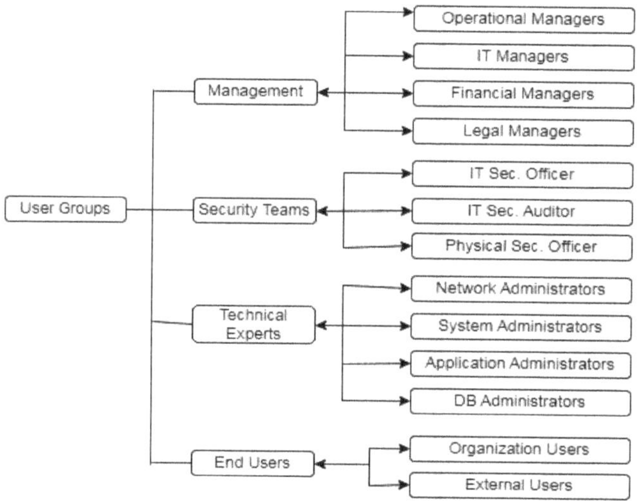

Figure 3. User model (source: created by the authors).

A4: Develop and estimate anonymous HRM-UP and potential HRM-AP

In this phase, we first develop an enhanced user inventory following the next steps:

(a) For all ICT users, compile anonymous profiles using Table 1;
(b) Measure the UP profiles using the scales in Table 3 during the co-creation workshops;
(c) Develop the HRM-User inventory by adding to the user inventory in Table 6, the UP scores, and social measures implemented and pending.

Then, we identify and measure the profiles of the potential adversaries by following the next steps:

(a) Compile the profiles of potential adversaries using Table 2:
To compile adversary profiles, we analyze past history, including previous attacks and sector-specific threat intelligence. Using Table 2, adversaries are classified based on their personality traits (e.g., extraversion, conscientiousness, openness to experiences) and social-behavioral traits (e.g., manipulative behavior, selected social exposure). For example, an adversary active in hacking communities and demonstrating leadership in forums would score highly in Extraversion, while one persistently employing new attack techniques would score highly in Openness to Experiences. Traits such as Manipulative Behavior are evaluated based on their ability to conduct phishing or

social engineering attacks. This classification is supported by historical data and incident analysis;

(b) Measure the Adversaries Profiles (AP) using the scales in Table 3. Adversary traits from Table 2 are scored on a semi-quantitative scale (1–5) based on historical data, threat intelligence, and crowd-sourced insights. These individual trait scores are aggregated into a composite AP score, which is then categorized using Table 3 thresholds (e.g., Very High = 96–100%, High = 80–95%). Adversaries with higher AP scores represent greater sophistication and require advanced social and technical measures, such as ethical training and cybersecurity exercises, while lower scores suggest basic awareness and secure behavior interventions are sufficient. This approach ensures targeted and proportional risk treatment.

Table 6. HRM-user inventory (source: created by the authors).

	User ID: 001	User ID: 002	...
General Information	Name: Full name of the employee/Role/Location/Contact	...	-
System and Credential System Access	Privileges, List of systems the user has access to (e.g., CRM, ERP, email)	...	-
Supervisor and Interrelations	Direct supervisor or manager interactions with other users (model interaction)	...	-
UP score	See Table 3 above	...	-
Social Measures Implemented/Required	See Table 3 above	...	...

3.2. Phase B: Risk Assessment

Risk assessments should identify, quantify, and prioritize information security risks against defined criteria for risk acceptance and objectives relevant to the organization.

The results should guide and determine the appropriate management action and priorities for managing information security risks and for implementing controls selected to protect against these risks.

Assessing risks and selecting controls may need to be performed repeatedly across different parts of the organization and information systems and to respond to changes.

The process should systematically estimate the magnitude of risks (risk analysis) and compare risks against risk criteria to determine their significance (risk evaluation).

The information security risk assessment should have a clearly defined scope and complement risk assessments in other aspects of the business, where appropriate. The steps we follow are:

B1—Identify the threats (physical/cyber/human);

B2—Estimate the level of threats;

B3—Estimate vulnerability levels and impact levels;

B4—Estimate the risk level;

B5—Propose technical countermeasures;

B6—Propose further social measures.

To propose appropriate social measures, co-creation workshops are employed. In these workshops, ICT users collaborate to generate and refine ideas for social and technical security measures, ensuring these are pragmatic and readily adoptable [30].

3.3. Phase C: Risk Management (Treatment)

Having identified and evaluated the risk level in the risk assessment phase, as it was described in the previous paragraphs, the next step involves the identification of the actions that must take place in order to manage the detected threats and propose specific treatment plans, according to the Interoperable EU Risk Management Framework [10]. More specifically, the risk treatment process is mapped with the ISO 27005 [31] and its objective is the selection of the treatment options that are suitable for the risks that have been identified. Some potential treatment options may include risk mitigation, avoidance, and sharing etc.

For the implementation of technical and social measures, we use co-creation workshops where the SME governance members share business intelligence and cost-benefit analysis expertise to select those selected measures for implementation and testing. The proposed technical and social measures (from Phase B—B5) can be implemented immediately, can be postponed, or ignored. A risk treatment plan needs to be compiled and Tables 4 and 5 need to be updated.

4. Applying HRM Methodology for Risk Management in Healthcare SMEs: A Comprehensive Use Case

An SME healthcare enterprise (HSME), operating across two separate facilities, offers e-health services to its personnel and patients. These services encompass, amongst others, e-diagnosis, e-prescriptions, and the handling of patients' sensitive data.

Through this use case, all phases of the above HRM methodology will be demonstrated step by step.

4.1. Phase A (Cartography)

Steps A1–A2:

The interconnected facilities enable users with varying access levels to retrieve private patient data from a shared, encrypted database. Each facility operates with a server and personal computers networked together, facilitating communication with the database. Given this setup, the enterprise must implement comprehensive security measures to safeguard its ICT systems effectively.

In the current use case, a doctor connects to a specific PC with his/her own personal account in order to check patients' data. During this process, it comes to his/her attention that many sensitive data are missing. The doctor's personal account has a specific data access policy that allows for accessing, entering, and altering the data only for his/her patients from any computer in the HSME's facilities.

Following the HRM methodology in the first phase (Cartography), firstly an asset inventory must be developed, where the identification of all assets under assessment must be included. In the current use case, as it is depicted in Figure 4, all physical, telecom, IT, data, services, and users' assets are recorded. Hence, the facilities' buildings, the telecommunication and network equipment, the database, the software, hardware and data, the communication services for the data exchange, and the users, like doctors and patients, are identified and documented.

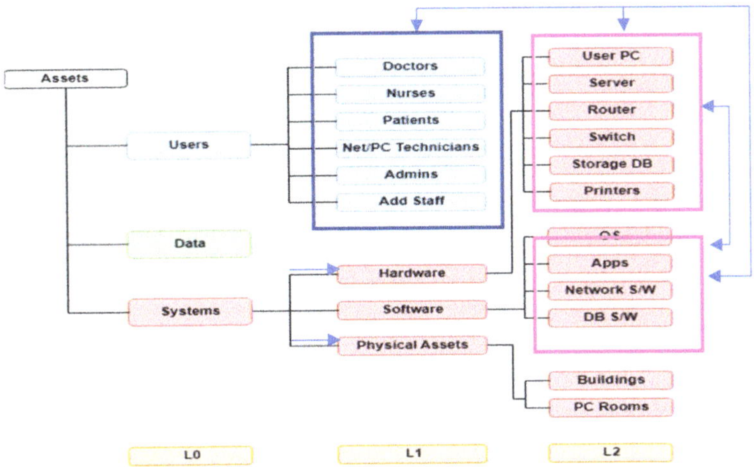

Figure 4. HSMEs users'/assets model (source: created by the authors).

Hardware devices, software applications, personnel, physical location, utilities, and organizational infrastructure fall into this category. In the current use case, primary assets include accessing patient data for treatment and personal patient information accessed by doctors. Supporting assets encompass PCs, servers, and networks in the hardware category; doctors, system administrators, and personnel with access as normal or privileged users in the personnel category; suppliers of specific systems; physical rooms or offices housing hardware equipment in the location and utilities category; and the existing cloud, network, and hosting services in the organizational infrastructure category. The information can be summarized in the next asset inventory (Table 7):

Table 7. Asset inventory (source: created by the authors).

General Information	Technical Specifications	Location and Owner	Network Configuration (for Servers)	Implementation of Controls—History of Updates
Asset ID: Unique identifier for each asset.	Software suite for patient records, network infrastructure etc.	Location: physical location of the asset.	Wired and wireless setup	Controls implemented
Asset Type: Software or Hardware	Software suite for patients records /Server hardware for data storage	Owner of Asset (assigned to): name of the employee responsible of the asset.	Role: function or role of the software or hardware	Update history of controls
Brand/Model: Specific model of the software or hardware.	Electronic Medical Records (EMR) system, database management platform etc.	Owner/user(s) of asset: doctor, nurse, admin etc	-	Testing date of controls
Serial Number: Manufacturer's serial number. Date of purchase	Software versions, hardware specifications	-	-	-

All the above-mentioned assets provide valuable information from a technical perspective. Additionally, the description of all assets' interdependencies and the development of the user model of the ICT system under assessment in the healthcare entity must be conducted.

Focusing on the user functions of one facility of the HSME, the users that are involved are doctors, patients, nurses, system admins, system technicians, and additional staff. All the users have access to the HSME's personal computers with accounts that have different user access rights, depending on their specialty. For example, each doctor has access to his/her patient data only, and nurses have access to specific medication depending on their department placement. The system admin has access to the server and personal computers for all user accounts and data stored in the database. The system technicians have additional access to all systems' infrastructures including PCs and network devices etc. (Figure 4).

In the current HRM methodology phase, the next step includes anonymous user profile development and secure level behaviors estimation, taking into account the included information in Table 1, in order to produce the social mitigation measures to enhance users' secure behavior.

Step A3:

The users that interact in our scenario are: two doctors, two patients, one nurse, one admin, one technician, and one member of additional staff. The co-creation workshops have been conducted and the scores of the profiles have been estimated as summarized in the next Table (Table 8):

Table 8. HRM-user inventory (source: created by the authors).

	User ID: 001-Doctor1	**User ID: 002-Nurse**	...
General Information	Name: Full name of the employee/Role/Location/Contact	...	
System and Credential System Access	Privileges, list of systems the user has access to (e.g., CRM, ERP, email),		
Supervisor and Interrelations	Direct supervisor or manager interactions with other users (model interaction)		-
UP score	Basic (B)-2		
Social Measures Implemented/Required	According to Table 3 the measures needed are: awareness, secure behavior interventions, training in operational cybersecurity exercises		

4.2. *Phase B: Risk Assessment*

Moving to the next phase of the HRM methodology, Risk Assessment strategies are implemented. The ENISA RM Toolbox is utilized to execute Phase B strategies. According to the toolbox, the initial steps involve defining attack/risk scenarios and identifying assets from a technical perspective, which were covered in the previous phase. The following paragraphs outline the subsequent technical representation steps.

Additionally, it is important to note that the ENISA RM Toolbox includes four libraries: Terms mappings, Assets mappings, Threats mappings, and Risk-Impact levels mappings.

In the first library, based on the current-use case scenario, we identify the frameworks and methodologies terminology. Utilizing the toolbox glossary and terminology sample library, we search for definitions of terms and incidents to fully understand the system's situation based on ISO/IEC 27005:2018 [32] and the ENISA IT Security Risk Management Methodology v1.2. For example, the definition of "Threat" according to ISO/IEC 27005:2018 is "potential cause of an unwanted incident, which can result in harm to a system or organization", matching 100% with ISO/IEC 27000:2018's definition [33].

In the second library, we identify the assets of the current scenario. Specifically, primary assets in HSMEs include all core business processes, functions, services provided to external parties and information/data supporting business processes or activities of the organization, as outlined in ISO/IEC 27005:2018. These assets are sensitive and include processes essential for the organization's mission. Information and data are also classified as primary assets, encompassing vital information necessary for the organization's mission or business, as defined by national privacy laws. Similar principles are applied in the IT Security Risk Management Methodology v1.2.

Steps B1 and B2—Identify the threats (physical/cyber/human):

Following asset identification, the next step involves threats-mapping using the third library of the ENISA RM Toolbox. This library allows for the identification of various threat types according to the IT Security Risk Management Methodology v1.2 and ISO/IEC 27005:2018. It provides additional details such as threat types, security dimensions, involved assets, and examples.

For the current use case, Table 9 lists the identified threats. These threats can occur unintentionally or intentionally through accidental or deliberate actions, impacting assets such as hardware devices or software and applications, affecting confidentiality, integrity, and/or availability.

Table 9. Threats identification (source: created by the authors).

Threat	Category	Security Dimension	Action	Assets	Explanation
Hardware or Software failure	Industrial	Availability	Deliberate or Accidental	H/W devices and equipment—S/W and applications	Failures in the equipment (e.g., user PC, server, router etc.) and/or programs (e.g., apps, OS etc.)
User errors	Errors and unintentional failures	Confidentiality, Integrity, Availability	Accidental	H/W devices and equipment—S/W and applications—organizational infrastructure	Mistakes by persons when using the services, data, etc. For example, making a mistake in saving data, or in a PC's usage.
Threat of system/security administrator errors	Errors and unintentional failures	Confidentiality, Integrity, Availability	Accidental	H/W devices and equipment—S/W and applications—organizational infrastructure	Mistakes by persons with responsibilities for installation and operation of the systems/system's security. For example, the PC technician can unintentionally cause the system failure of a user PC or server.
Destruction of information	Errors and unintentional failures	Availability	Accidental	All the categories of supporting assets	The accidental loss of the information due to a user's (doctor or nurse) mistake.

Table 9. *Cont.*

Threat	Category	Security Dimension	Action	Assets	Explanation
S/W vulnera-bilities	Errors and unintentional failures	Confidentiality, Integrity, Availability	Accidental	S/W and applications	Defects in the code that cause a defective operation without intention on the part of the user but with consequences to the data confidentiality, integrity, availability or to its capacity to operate. This can be detected in apps or OS, for example.
Abuse of access privileges	Willful attacks	Confidentiality, Integrity, Availability	Deliberate	S/W and applications—Locations and Utilities—organizational infrastructure	When users abuse their privilege level to carry out tasks that are not their responsibility, there are problems. For example, a user might use a doctor's account and delete patients' data.
Misuse	Willful attacks	Confidentiality, Integrity, Availability	Deliberate	S/W and applications—Locations and Utilities—organizational infrastructure	The use of system resources for unplanned purposes, typically of personal interest. For example, a user connects an app or to a PC inside the HSME's facility.

The identified threats in this case include hardware or software failures, user errors, and unauthorized access, covering a range of severity levels (Table 9).

Steps B3–B4:

Based on the identified assets and risks, the risk assessment process can now begin for the current-use case scenario. Primary assets at risk include accessing and managing patient health records, prescriptions, dosages, and scheduled health checks, along with compromising the security of personal patient and doctor data.

Supporting assets affected include HSME hardware, software, personnel, system suppliers, and infrastructure. Potential issues include hardware or software malfunctions leading to data loss, unintentional breaches of data confidentiality, integrity, or availability by HSME personnel, and risks associated with system suppliers not meeting HSME requirements. The placement of systems in HSME facilities may also invite unauthorized access.

The OWASP risk-rating methodology uses the standard model (Risk = Likelihood × Impact). During risk identification, information on threats, types of attacks, vulnerability levels, and potential impacts is gathered to assess risks.

In this use case, the risk of patient data loss is identified. The first step involves estimating the "Likelihood" level. For example, in the case of unauthorized access threats, where attackers gain unauthorized system access, determining threat agent and vulnerability factors is crucial.

For adversary factors (threat agents), the goal is to estimate the likelihood of a successful attack based on skill level, motive, opportunity, and size, rated on a scale from 0 to 9. In the worst-case scenario, potential threats include anonymous internet users with network and programming skills and high motivation for significant rewards, requiring access or resources, as outlined in Table 10. More specifically, the values for Skill Level, Motive, Opportunity, and Size are assigned using the OWASP risk-rating methodology. Skill Level is determined by IT security professionals based on the technical expertise needed for an attack. Motive reflects the high motivation for attackers, assessed by security analysts considering the value of patient data. Opportunity is based on the accessibility of vulnerabilities, evaluated by system administrators. Size represents the potential impact of the attack, assigned by risk management teams and senior leadership through collaborative assessment.

Table 10. Threat agent factors (source: created by the authors).

Threat	Skill Level	Motive	Opportunity	Size
Unauthorized access	6	9	4	9

For a more realistic assessment, we use the HRM-AP score (refer to Tables 2 and 3), which considers additional traits of the adversary (threat actor).

Regarding vulnerability factors, the aim is to estimate the likelihood of a specific vulnerability in terms of ease of discovery, exploitability, awareness, and intrusion detection, rated on a scale from 0 to 9. Table 11 illustrates a scenario where the vulnerability of unauthorized access is easily discoverable and exploitable using automated tools. Threat agents are aware of this vulnerability, making exploitation feasible through logging and reviewing. More specifically, the values for Ease of Discovery, Ease of Exploit, Awareness, and Intrusion Detection are assigned using the HRM-AP score. Ease of Discovery reflects how easily the vulnerability can be found by attackers, rated by security analysts based on available tools and techniques. Ease of Exploit indicates the difficulty for attackers to exploit the vulnerability, evaluated by system administrators considering known exploits and automation tools. Awareness represents how well attackers are aware of the vulnerability, assessed by IT security teams based on public information and threat intelligence. Intrusion Detection reflects how likely the vulnerability is to be detected by existing security measures, rated by network security specialists based on detection capabilities.

Table 11. Vulnerability factors (source: created by the authors).

Threat	Ease of Discovery	Ease of Exploit	Awareness	Intrusion Detection
Unauthorized access	7	9	6	3

Likelihood also depends on the secure behavior of all ICT users interacting with the asset. According to HRM, accuracy improves by considering this factor. The next step is to estimate the Impact, which includes Technical and Business Impact factors.

Regarding Technical Impact, considerations include confidentiality, integrity, availability, and accountability to gauge the magnitude of impact. Table 12 illustrates scenarios such as extensive critical data disclosure, serious data corruption, and primary services interruption caused by completely anonymous individuals. More specifically, the values for Loss of Confidentiality, Loss of Integrity, Loss of Availability, and Loss of Accountability are assigned using the HRM methodology. Loss of Confidentiality reflects the potential exposure of sensitive data, evaluated by data protection specialists based on the type of information at risk. Loss of Integrity indicates the severity of potential data corruption, assessed by system administrators based on the criticality of the affected systems. Loss of Availability represents the impact of a service interruption, rated by network engineers considering the potential disruption to operations. Loss of Accountability reflects the difficulty in tracing malicious actions, rated by security experts based on the likelihood of exploiting the system without detection.

Table 12. Technical impact factors (source: created by the authors).

Threat	Loss of Confidentiality	Loss of Integrity	Loss of Availability	Loss of Accountability
Unauthorized access	7	7	7	9

For the Business Impact factors, considerations include financial damage, reputation damage, non-compliance, and privacy violations. Table 13 presents scenarios such as a minor effect on business profit, loss of goodwill in reputation, and a high-profile violation involving thousands of people's data. More specifically, the values for Financial Damage, Reputation Damage, Non-Compliance, and Privacy Violation are assigned using the HRM methodology. Financial Damage reflects the potential monetary loss, assessed by financial analysts based on the business impact of the breach. Reputation Damage indicates the harm to the organization's public image, evaluated by public relations specialists considering the scope of affected stakeholders. Non-Compliance reflects the legal and regulatory implications, rated by compliance officers based on industry standards and legal requirements. Privacy Violation represents the degree of harm to individuals' privacy, evaluated by privacy officers considering the sensitivity of the exposed data.

Table 13. Business impact factors (source: created by the authors).

Threat	Financial Damage	Reputation Damage	Non-Compliance	Privacy Violation
Unauthorized access	3	5	7	7

Using the OWASP Risk Rating Calculator [11] it is possible to determine the severity of the risk by calculating it. For the case described in the above paragraphs, the results of the calculation produces a high overall risk severity for the unauthorized access threat scenario.

In the above calculations, ICT user profiles have not been fully considered (only partially for the AP score). In HRM methodology, we would multiply the OWASP score with the 1/min {UP score} of all users interacting with the asset.

To estimate the HRM score for the unauthorized-access-to-sensitive-patient-data scenario, we use the following formula from the HRM methodology:

$$\text{Risk} = T \times V \times I \times AP \times 1/UP$$

In this case:

- **T** is the Threat (unauthorized access to patient data);
- **V** is the Vulnerability (potential for unauthorized access due to weak access control);
- **I** is the Impact (severity of unauthorized data access);
- **AP** is the Adversary Profile (e.g., motivated, skilled attackers with resources);
- **UP** is the ICT User Profile (doctors' compliance with security protocols).

For this scenario:

The AP score considers the adversary's skills (7), motive (8), opportunity (6), and size (7).

The UP score is derived based on doctors' compliance and secure behavior, assumed to be 8 for this case.

By multiplying these values, we can calculate the HRM score, which reveals the overall high-risk level for unauthorized access. This score highlights the need for stringent access controls and comprehensive security measures.

Steps B5 and B6:

HSMEs must mitigate risks by implementing:

- **Technical Controls**: Advanced access control, data encryption, network and endpoint security;
- **Administrative Controls**: Policy development, access management, employee training, and security audits;
- **Physical Controls**: Access control systems, surveillance, alarms, and restricted-access storage;
- **Social Controls**: Enhance software and IT skills based on personality traits, social factors, and technical skills identified earlier.

Effective threat management includes educating employees about cyber threats, training in modern technologies, regular cybersecurity workshops, phishing simulations, incident response programs, data protection seminars, and promoting strong passwords and multi-factor authentication.

By combining these controls, HSMEs can effectively mitigate unauthorized access and patient data loss.

5. Conclusions

In conclusion, the security of ICT systems within SMEs is critically important, especially when addressing human threats. These threats, stemming from a range of human vulnerabilities, are often overlooked in traditional risk management approaches. Regular assessments and tailored risk-treatment measures can help SMEs mitigate the negative impacts of human threats. The Human Risk Management (HRM) methodology proposed in this paper builds upon ISO 27001 methodologies and leverages available tools for assessing technical threats and estimating associated risks. For human element-related threats, HRM employs socio-psychological techniques to evaluate the maturity of ICT users in adopting security practices and the strength of potential adversaries. It develops and estimates profiles of ICT users and adversaries, incorporating these estimates into overall risk evaluations.

From a technical perspective, the HRM methodology highlights the importance of integrating human-centric data into risk assessment tools, enabling a more comprehensive approach to mitigating risks. Managerially, organizations should focus on fostering a strong cybersecurity culture by implementing structured awareness programs and allocating resources to address human vulnerabilities. Educationally, this methodology underscores the value of continuous training initiatives tailored to the specific needs of employees, such as phishing recognition and secure data handling.

However, the HRM methodology is not without limitations. The accuracy of adversary and user profile estimations depends heavily on the quality of available data and the reliability of socio-psychological evaluations. Furthermore, SMEs with limited resources may face challenges in implementing HRM comprehensively. Future research will focus on verifying the HRM methodology by conducting empirical studies in diverse SME sectors, evaluating its effectiveness in improving cybersecurity resilience. Additionally, pilot projects will be designed to assess the practicality and scalability of the proposed model in real-world settings. Refining socio-psychological profiling techniques, automating the integration of human element data into technical risk assessment tools, and exploring sector-specific adaptations of the HRM methodology will also be key directions for further work.

In the use case presented, a healthcare SME implements the HRM methodology by utilizing existing risk assessment tools and estimating the cybersecurity maturity of healthcare participants interacting with the ICT system. Controls in this use case include regular training sessions for medical staff on recognizing phishing attempts and ensuring proper data-handling practices to protect patient information. By enhancing the cybersecurity maturity of employees and fostering a robust cybersecurity culture within the SME, human threats can be significantly reduced, thereby improving overall cybersecurity resilience.

Author Contributions: Conceptualization, K.K. and N.P.; Methodology, K.K. and N.P.; Formal analysis, E.S. and N.P.; Writing—review & editing, K.K., E.S. and N.P.; Funding acquisition, N.P. All authors have read and agreed to the published version of the manuscript.

Funding: This research was funded by the following projects: The 'Collaborative, Multi-modal, and Agile Professional Cybersecurity Training Program for a Skilled Workforce in the European Digital Single Market and Industries' (CyberSecPro) project, which has received funding from the European Union's Digital Europe Programme (DEP) under grant agreement No. 101083594; the 'Human-centered Trustworthiness Optimization in Hybrid Decision Support' (THEMIS 5.0) project, which has received funding from the European Union's Horizon Programme under grant agreement No. 101121042; the 'Advanced Cybersecurity Awareness Ecosystem for SMEs' (NERO) project, which has received funding from the European Union's DEP programme under grant agreement No. 101127411; the 'A Certification approach for dynamic, agile and reusable assessment for composite systems of ICT products, services, and processes' (CUSTODES) which has received funding from the European Union's Horizon Programme under grant agreement No. 101120684; the 'Harmonizing People, Processes, and Technology for Robust Cybersecurity' (CyberSynchrony) project, which has received funding from the European Union's Digital Europe Programme (DEP) under grant agreement No. 101158555; and the 'Fostering Artificial Intelligence Trust for Humans towards the Optimization of Trustworthiness through Large-scale Pilots in Critical Domains' (FAITH) project, which has received funding from the European Union's Horizon Programme under grant agreement No. 101135932.

Data Availability Statement: The original contributions presented in this study are included in the article. Further inquiries can be directed to the corresponding author.

Conflicts of Interest: The views expressed in this paper represent only the views of the authors and not those of the European Commission or the partners in the above-mentioned projects. Finally, all authors were employed by the company trustilio B.V. They declare that the research was conducted in the absence of any commercial or financial relationships that could be construed as a potential conflict of interest.

References

1. *ISO/IEC 27001:2005*; Information Technology—Security Techniques—Information Security Management Systems—Requirements. ISO: Geneva, Switzerland, 2005.
2. ISO/IEC—Global Standards. Available online: https://www.iso.org/home.html (accessed on 5 September 2024).
3. *ISO 31000:2018*; Risk Management—Guidelines. International Organization for Standardization (ISO): Geneva, Switzerland, 2018.
4. NIST Cyber Hygiene Guidelines. Available online: https://www.nist.gov/blogs/taking-measure/stay-safe-and-secure-online-during-cybersecurity-awareness-month-and-all-year (accessed on 5 September 2024).
5. Katsumata, P.; Hemenway, J.; Gavins, W. Cybersecurity risk management. In Proceedings of the Milcom 2010 Military Communications Conference, San Jose, CA, USA, 31 October–3 November 2010; pp. 890–895.
6. Al-Zahrani, A. Assessing and Proposing Countermeasures for Cyber-Security Attacks. *Int. J. Adv. Comput. Sci. Appl. West Yorks.* **2022**, *13*, 885–895. [CrossRef]
7. Kioskli, K.; Polemi, N. Estimating attackers' profiles results in more realistic vulnerability severity scores. In Proceedings of the 13th International Conference on Applied Human factors and Ergonomics (AHFE2022), New York, NY, USA, 24–28 July 2022; Volume 53, pp. 138–150.
8. Kioskli, K.; Fotis, T.; Nifakos, S.; Mouratidis, H. The Importance of conceptualising the human-centric approach in maintaining and promoting cybersecurity-hygiene in healthcare 4.0. *Appl. Sci. Spec. Issue Ehealth Innov. Approaches Appl.* **2023**, *13*, 3410. [CrossRef]
9. Alwaheidi, M.; Islam, S.; Papastergiou, S.; Kioskli, K. Integrating Human Factors into Data-driven Threat Management for Overall Security Enhancement. In *Human Factors in Cybersecurity, Proceedings of the AHFE (2024) International Conference, Nice, France, 24–27 July 2025*; Moallem, A., Ed.; AHFE Open Access; AHFE International: Orlando, FL, USA, 2024; Volume 127. [CrossRef]
10. ENISA Risk Management Toolbox. Available online: https://www.enisa.europa.eu/publications/interoperable-eu-risk-management-toolbox (accessed on 5 September 2024).
11. OWASP Risk Assessment Calculator. Available online: https://owasp-risk-rating.com/ (accessed on 5 September 2024).

12. OWASP Threat Modeling Process. Available online: https://owasp.org/www-community/Threat_Modeling_Process (accessed on 5 September 2024).
13. MISP Project. Available online: https://www.misp-project.org/ (accessed on 5 September 2024).
14. Cyberwatching. The European watch on Cybersecurity & Privacy. Available online: https://cyberrisk.cyberwatching.eu/Pages/Home.aspx (accessed on 5 September 2024).
15. Egelman, S.; Peer, E. *The Security Behaviour Intentions Scale*; Frontiers: Lausanne, Switzerland, 2015.
16. Nobles, C. Understanding the Human Factor of Cyber Security. *IEEE IT Prof.* **2018**, *20*, 7–15. [CrossRef]
17. Fogg, B.J. A behavior model for persuasive design. In Proceedings of the 4th International Conference on Persuasive Technology, Claremont, CA, USA, 26–29 April 2009; pp. 1–7.
18. Kioskli, K.; Polemi, N. A psychosocial approach to cyber threat intelligence. *Int. J. Chaotic Comput.* **2020**, *7*, 159–165. [CrossRef]
19. Williams, H. The impact of collective intelligence on cybersecurity. *Cyber Psychol.* **2020**, *7*, 111–126.
20. Schneier, B. *Liars and Outliers: Enabling the Trust That Society Needs to Thrive*; Wiley: Hoboken, NJ, USA, 2012.
21. West, D.M. *Digital Government: Technology and Public Sector Performance*; Princeton University Press: Princeton, NJ, USA, 2012.
22. Brown, T. *Change by Design: How Design Thinking Transforms Organizations and Inspires Innovation*; HarperBusiness: New York, NY, USA, 2009.
23. Stoneburner, G.; Goguen, A.; Feringa, A. *Risk Management Guide for Information Technology Systems (NIST Special Publication 800-30)*; National Institute of Standards and Technology: Gaithersburg, MD, USA, 2022.
24. Ramaswamy, V.; Ozcan, K. What is co-creation? An interactional creation framework and its implications for value creation. *J. Bus. Res.* **2018**, *84*, 196–205. [CrossRef]
25. ENISA ECSF. Available online: https://www.enisa.europa.eu/topics/education/european-cybersecurity-skills-framework (accessed on 4 September 2024).
26. StaySafeOnline Guidelines. Available online: https://staysafeonline.org/resources/online-safety-basics/ (accessed on 5 September 2024).
27. Smith, J.; Doe, A.; James, S. The efficacy of questionnaires in the assessment of secure behaviors in IT users. *J. Cybersecur. Res.* **2019**, *12*, 45–59.
28. Kioskli, K.; Polemi, N. Measuring psychosocial and behavioural factors improves attack potential estimates. In Proceedings of the 15th International Conference for Internet Technology and Secured Transactions, London, UK, 8–10 December 2020; pp. 216–219.
29. Kioskli, K.; Polemi, N. A socio-technical approach to cyber risk assessment. *Int. J. Electr. Comput. Eng.* **2020**, *14*, 305–309.
30. Mattelmäki, T.; Vaajakallio, K.; Koskinen, I. What happened to empathic design? *Des. Issues* **2014**, *30*, 67–77. [CrossRef]
31. *ISO/IEC 27005:2022*; Information Security, Cybersecurity and Privacy Protection—Guidance on Managing Information Security Risks. International Organization for Standardization (ISO) and International Electrotechnical Commission (IEC): Geneva, Switzerland, 2022.
32. *ISO/IEC 27005:2018*; Information Technology—Security Techniques—Information Security Risk Management. International Organization for Standardization (ISO) and International Electrotechnical Commission (IEC): Geneva, Switzerland, 2018.
33. *ISO/IEC 27000:2018*; Information Technology—Security Techniques—Information Security Management Systems—Overview and Vocabulary. International Organization for Standardization (ISO) and International Electrotechnical Commission (IEC): Geneva, Switzerland, 2018.

MDPI AG
Grosspeteranlage 5
4052 Basel
Switzerland
Tel.: +41 61 683 77 34

Electronics Editorial Office
E-mail: electronics@mdpi.com
www.mdpi.com/journal/electronics

www.ingramcontent.com/pod-product-compliance
Lightning Source LLC
Chambersburg PA
CBHW061555210926
51850CB00009B/2113
* 9 7 8 3 7 2 5 8 7 3 8 0 7 *